Creative
Energies

Integrative Energy Psychotherapy
for Self-Expression and Healing

Dorothea Hover-Kramer, Ed.D., C.N.S., R.N.

W. W. Norton & Compar
New York • London

For information about permission to reproduce selections from this book, write to Permissions, W. W. Norton & Company, Inc., 500 Fifth Avenue, New York, NY 10110

Library of Congress Cataloging-in-Publication Data
Hover-Kramer, Dorothea
   Creative energies : integrative energy psychotherapy for self-expression and healing / Dorothea Hover-Kramer.
      p. cm. — (The Norton energy psychology series)
   Includes bibliographical references and index.
   ISBN 0-393-70384-3
   1. Bioenergetic psychotherapy. 2. Self-realization. 3. Mental healing. I. Title.
II. Series.
RC489.B5 H68 2002
616.89'14—dc21   2001044550

W. W. Norton & Company, Inc., 500 Fifth Avenue, New York, N.Y. 10110
www.wwnorton.com

W. W. Norton & Company Ltd., Castle House, 75/76 Wells Street, London W1T 3QT

1 2 3 4 5 6 7 8 9 0

Contents

I History and Background of Energy-Oriented Healing

II The Human Vibrational Matrix

III Integrative Energy Psychology Interventions
for Emotional Relief

IV Integrative Energy Psychology Interventions
for Accessing Creativity

List of Learning Exercises

Chapter 8 Exercises

Chapter 10 Exercises

Chapter 11 Exercises

Chapter 12 Exercises

Chapter 14 Exercises

List of Figures

Acknowledgments

T he author would like to thank the following clinicians, educators, and administrators for reviewing this book for content accuracy
and for giving generously of their time in providing helpful comments:

David Grudermeyer, Ph.D., first president of the Association for
Comprehensive Energy Psychology (ACEP), director Willingness
Works, and licensed psychologist, San Diego, California

Lynn Joseph, Ph.D., secretary/treasurer of ACEP, Director of Discovery Dynamics, Inc., specializing in business applications, Riverside,
California

Peter Lambrou, Ph.D., coauthor of *Instant Emotional Healing*, licensed
clinical psychologist, La Jolla, California

Phyllis Mabbett, Ph.D., R.N., Administrative Director Scripps Center for Integrative Medicine, La Jolla, California

George Pratt, Ph.D., coauthor of *Instant Emotional Healing*, licensed
clinical psychologist, La Jolla, California

I have profound gratitude to the many whose inventive thinking and
ability to find new pathways came together to create this new orientation within the wider field of psychotherapy and mind/body psychology. These innovators bring their unique perceptions and create a
synergy, a whole picture of energy psychotherapy that is greater than

any individual discipline. Here is a partial listing of these leading-edge creative teachers from whom I have had the privilege of learning: Gloria Aronsen, M.A.; Pati Beaudoin, Ed.D.; Dan Benor, M.D.; Gary Craig, M.A.; Patricia Carrington, Ph.D.; Asha Clinton, Ph.D.; John Diepold, Ph.D.; James Durlacher, D.C.; Donna Eden; Stephanie Eldringhoff, L.M.T.; Tapas Fleming, L.Ac.; Norma Feldman, L.C.S.W.; David Feinstein, Ph.D.; Fred Gallo, Ph.D.; Marjorie Herman, D.M.; Lynn Joseph, Ph.D.; Peter Lambrou, Ph.D.; Willem Lammers, C.T.S.; Phyllis Mabbett, Ph.D., RN; Greg Nicosia, Ph.D.; Larry Nims, Ph.D.; George Pratt, Ph.D.; Lee Pulos, Ph.D.; Sandi Radomski, L.Ac., L.C.S.W.; Karilee Shames, Ph.D., RN; Mary Sise, C.S.W.; Kate Sorensen, M.A.; Judith Swack, Ph.D.; Scott Walker, D.C.; and "Mo" Wheeler, Ph.D.

I would also like to thank Deborah Malmud and her assistant Anne Hellman and the kind staff of W. W. Norton for their assistance.

Foreword

Carl Jung coined the term *synchronicity* for coincident events that are causally and meaningfully related—the proverbial *meant-to-be*. Along with serendipity, synchronicity seems to weave a tapestry through our personal lives and also accounts for many scientific and neoscientific discoveries.[*] This principle has been instrumental also in the advancement of energy psychology. Goodheart reports many such events in the development of applied kinesiology, and Callahan discusses similar phenomena that led to his discoveries. I've also had my share of synchronicity, which led to the publication of *Energy Psychology* and *Energy Diagnostic and Treatment Methods* (Gallo, 1998, 2000). The publication of *Creative Energies* has a similar history.

In 1997, while returning home after presenting at a conference on "power therapies," in the shuttle to the airport I had a conversation with a person who had not attended the conference. I told her about a book that I was writing on psychotherapy that involved, among other things, stimulating acupuncture energy meridian points (Gallo, 1998). She

---

[*]While empirical validation is needed, many of the newer scientific and psychotherapeutic formulations are sometimes denigrated as *pseudoscience*, since the neoscientific paradigm has not been incorporated into our intellectual and scientific culture.

mentioned that she had taken an interest in therapeutic touch, the approach developed by Dolores Krieger, and was attending related courses in hopes of eventually become a therapist. Then she showed me a copy of *Energetic Approaches to Emotional Healing* by Dorothea Hover-Kramer and Karilee Halo Shames (1997), which I leafed through with interest. Then I told my fellow passenger about the work of Barbara Brennan (1993), Valerie Hunt (1995), and others who have explored the therapeutic use of chakras and biofields. After returning home, I bought and perused a copy of *Energetic Approaches to Emotional Healing.* I recall thinking that the approaches described in that book would be a powerful addition to the meridian-based methods that I was studying and applying.

About a year later, I had the opportunity of meeting Dorothea Hover-Kramer at the Energy Psychology Conference in Toronto, Ontario. Dorothea had developed a collegial relationship with David and Rebecca Grudermeyer, who had studied a variety of energy psychotherapy methods. The three developed their own approach to energy psychology and were now launching the Association for Comprehensive Energy Psychology (ACEP) in order to lend greater structure and professional visibility to the field. I related to Dorothea my serendipitous introduction to her work, and we have remained close colleagues ever since.

This book is a worthy addition to the developing literature on energy psychology and energy psychotherapy. Dorothea has charted new territory, as energy psychology labors its way into the mainstream. Here we have scholarly coverage of meridians, chakras, and biofields—the human vibrational matrix. In a similar way that I introduced energy psychology's meridian-based methodology (Gallo, 1998, 2000, 2002; Gallo & Vincenzi, 2000) and its integration with cognitive neurophysics (Furman & Gallo, 2000), Dorothea offers the field the benefits of her search and discovery of an array of energetic means to therapeutic ends. I appreciate her chapter on ethics, since energetic therapies contain many aspects that are radically distinct from traditional approaches (e.g., manual muscle testing). Because of these features and the uncommon theoretical positions found in energy psychology, a new level of informed consent is necessary that is not required of many other therapeutic approaches. She also offers a variety of ways for therapists to impact psychological problems from energetic perspectives.

I anticipate that this work will be embraced by the psychotherapeutic communities and will remain a benchmark for many years to come.

Fred P. Gallo, Ph.D.
Energy Psychology Series Editor

Foreword

Just as peace is not merely the absence of war, high-level wellness is not merely the absence of psychological baggage or physical sickness. High-level wellness is characterized by a state of creative flow, just as peace is characterized by a state of what I refer to as "creative lovingness." Both are as much actions or behaviors as they are states of mind and heart. Achieving high-level psychological and, dare I add, spiritual wellness is increasingly being referred to as the territory of positive psychology. Energy psychotherapy methods appear to be particularly adept at helping people attain their positive psychology goals.

Energy psychology comprises a family of methods for rebalancing what Dr. Dorothea Hover-Kramer aptly refers to as the human vibrational matrix, which in turn contains many interactive human energy systems. The three systems that have received the most attention thus far (the biofield, chakra, and meridian systems) show dramatic promise in their ability to facilitate not only healing but also the high-level wellness that occupies the frontier beyond healing.

This remarkably thorough and professionally responsible book, by one of the pioneers in energy psychology (who intuitively began working with energy when a young child!), takes you on an amazing journey culminating in your ability to embody your own ways of being more fully creative. Being creative is for everyone, not just a select few. For Dorothea, creativity and artistic activity are "about finding a way of being that reflects our innate capacity for appreciating each precious moment." Who among us would not want to enjoy living in such a state?

Creative Energies contains exercises for diagnosing and energetically clearing away baggage that is blocking creative expression. These exercises are followed by energetic strategies for directly nourishing your own forms of creativity. Dorothea carefully provides easy-to-learn methods for diagnosing energetic imbalances and for balancing your energy system and that of your clients. And she offers illustrative examples to stimulate your own creativity in using these methods to better your own life.

I invite you to take this precious journey toward deepening your inner creative connection, through reading—and using—this valuable book.

David Grudermeyer, Ph.D.
First president of Association for
Comprehensive Energy Psychology

Introduction

Inside you is an artist that you do not know.

—Jellaludin Rumi,
13th-century Sufi poet

Creativity, bringing something new into being, appears to be one of our most distinguishing human characteristics. Over a million and a half years ago, our ancestors learned that splitting rocks made tools, and ever since, we have been creating new thoughts, ideas, and resources to bring a sense of satisfaction and enjoyment to our lives. Creativity is the most human of our traits and the foundation of our cultural heritage (Csikszentmihalyi, 1996).

This book explores not only our roles as helping professionals using the resources of an integrative, comprehensive energy psychology but also our ability to see our interactions with clients as an art form. Artistic activity, in this light, is not about producing something of beauty or lasting value for others, but rather about finding a way of being that reflects our innate capacity for appreciating each precious moment—time with our clients, time for reflection and recovery, time for inner development and fulfillment.

We are all born with the natural talent to make the most of each day, to explore fully what it means to be alive. When we connect with these inner resources, the overflow of energy can lead to exploration, playfulness, the desire to make something original, and the deep compassion for others, which is at the heart of the counseling endeavor. This inner connection can be seen in our drive to put things together in new ways, to create images or symbols that bring comfort, to make choices that enhance others' daily lives, and to give our existence meaning.

COUNSELING AS A CREATIVE ENDEAVOR

My personal belief is that counseling is a fine art, a new human art form. Finding the words, suggestions, or images that assist clients to unlock their own blocked inner wisdom requires a high form of creativity. Since the client can go no further than the therapist's personal sense of self-mastery, we as therapists must explore our own inner artist and release blocks to our innate inventiveness in order to engage fully with life. Profound self-understanding and acceptance are required to become one's own life-artist.

Most of our clients learn self-doubt at an early age. Whether from harsh parenting, school settings inured with criticism, or peer pressure, sooner or later many people develop confusion about their innate skills and sensitivities. External judgment and rejection can become so internalized that it may take extensive counseling for individuals to reclaim their inner artist. An effective therapeutic relationship allows clients to recover the confidence that they once knew as children.

Overcoming self-doubt and developing the traits of a successful life-artist are seldom accomplished alone. Most clients need some form of mentoring to access creative living as adults. In its broadest sense, then, counseling allows for such mentoring to occur in the form of life-modeling. Beyond addressing the personal problems that usually bring clients to therapy, the true art of counseling rests in how we communicate our innate wisdom and bring clients to new visions of themselves.

Creative Energies is about discovering paths to personal creativity whether one is an interested seeker or a skilled counselor. In addition, this book explores the varied resources of the new energy-oriented therapies that can help us understand ourselves from an energetic perspective. Thus, we are bringing together two relatively uncharted streams into a new synthesis—the vast domain of human potential and the gifts of a comprehensive energy psychology.

Energy-oriented psychotherapy is grounded in the already well-known mind/body therapies. Since the advent of biofeedback over 30 years ago, the interaction between the psychological and the physical has been studied and researched. This led to the blossoming of therapeutic approaches that assist the body and emotions through work with mental processes such as relaxation techniques, stress management modalities, healing imagery, meditation, and self-expressive therapies through the arts.

More recently, creative healing artists have found that awareness of specific physical movement and activity can impact psychological functioning as well. Based on the premise that the human organism is a finely tuned vibrational matrix of electromagnetic energy flows, the energy therapies give us direct resources for accessing these energy pathways to bring about right/left brain integration and to facilitate processing of trauma. Some examples of energy therapies currently being used are Therapeutic Touch and Healing Touch, which work with the biofield and chakras, meridian-based therapies such as Emotional Freedom Technique (EFT) and Thought Field Therapy (TFT), as well as Comprehensive Energy Psychotherapy (CEP), which integrates all aspects of the human vibrational matrix.

The energy psychotherapies that we will be exploring in this book add significantly to our clinical repertoire. They not only give inventive resources for dealing with complex client issues but also can be readily integrated with other valued therapeutic modalities such as Eye Movement Desensitization and Reprocessing (EMDR), Gestalt therapy, family therapy, behavioral/cognitive therapy, and in-depth psychodynamic work that deals with core issues. Furthermore, they assist in leading clients to new dimensions of self-appreciation and creative, high-level functioning.

PERSONAL JOURNEYS IN CREATIVITY

My personal experience has been a lifelong quest for healing through rediscovering and developing latent abilities. My earliest form of socially acceptable self-expression was through music. It was a safe way to release the anger and grief I felt as a child of Europe's major war and its many losses. Years of piano practice, while other children seemed to be having more fun, brought me to early success as a concert artist and as recipient of a substantial music scholarship. But my training had been one-sided and lacked the joy of inner playfulness; I had learned to memorize and perform from a very narrow range of skills. It only took one year of lonely practicing in order to reach my goal of the first freshman concert and to also realize that there must be more interactive ways of expressing myself. Because I felt more oriented toward people, I entered a nursing program. Somewhere in the third year of a traditional diploma nursing program I rediscovered the gifts of music. Surprising myself, I played the piano by choice, exploring all of Beethoven's sonatas to nourish my hungry soul in the hectic days of an affiliation with a famous children's hospital.

From then on, music has become my friend and support, not the tense taskmaster of the past. I now perform regularly with a wonderful chamber music ensemble, which allows me to feel connected with others and to have a sense of personal satisfaction while practicing daily. The help of many fine mentors and therapists led me to new ways of enjoying a lifetime friendship with music. Curiously though, as I later sought to improvise or compose music, I began hearing poetry instead. Writing down what I heard gave me a new career: making poems and writing books.

As I think of the many misperceptions that surrounded my early musical career, I can only imagine the distortions about creativity that we all share. We may falsely believe that we are not good enough to make anything useful out of our own abilities; we may criticize or reject our humanness and capacity for playfulness; we may doubt our intuition, or inner wisdom, about finding the paths that best fit our individual styles. Worst of all, we may miss the very essence of human inventiveness—that of making choices each day and treasuring each moment in order to enhance our sense of personal satisfaction and life's meaning. These choices can help us to become more fully engaged with life, to become true life-artists and compassionate therapists.

My choices, supported by increasing trust in daily meditation, music, poetry, and intuition, led me to share the gifts I had received from my mentors. After years of nursing (with a specialty in public health) I sought out a doctorate in psychology and later attended workshops given by leading therapists. I also began exploring Therapeutic Touch (Krieger, 1993) and learned how to balance the human energy field in helping my most distressed clients. I later helped to found a large national program in Healing Touch (1996, 2002) through the American Holistic Nurses' Association and began writing about ways that energy concepts—in particular, the biofield and the chakras—might be useful in relieving emotional distress (Hover-Kramer & Shames, 1997).

My ears perked up when I started hearing about energy psychology (Callahan, 2001; Gallo, 1998; Lambrou & Pratt, 2000), which focused primarily on the effectiveness of meridian-based therapies. While I was studying with these new teachers, I began to see interconnections between the energetic approaches I had been using for 20 years and meridian acupoints. Not surprisingly, my therapy practice turned into a daily adventure of finding new combinations that utilized different components of the human energy system.

DEVELOPMENT OF COMPREHENSIVE ENERGY PSYCHOTHERAPY

Combining the various approaches to energy-related therapy into a comprehensive, integrative energy psychology became my next step. It seemed essential that practitioners should choose energetic modalities from the chakras, the biofield, and the meridians. This emphasis led me to two new, engaging friends and colleagues, the psychologists David and Rebecca Grudermeyer. They were similarly investigating the aspects of integrative energy work. Together, over brunch, we conceptualized and became co-founders of the Association for Comprehensive Energy Psychology (ACEP). In three short years, the association has grown by leaps and bounds with many hundred members worldwide. It has also been involved in sponsoring and co-sponsoring numerous national and international conferences.

In retrospect, all the events that brought me to this writing seem very logical and sequential, as if they had been written down somewhere and I just needed to follow the outline. Many fine minds were already exploring similar areas, and I simply needed to connect with them. These counseling artists had the daily persistence, resilience, curiosity, and intuition that brought about formation of the new domain of comprehensive energy psychotherapy. The emergence of this book demonstrates the vast capacity for creativity within many counseling disciplines.

Creative Energies is an honoring of the inventive minds that came together to give us a whole new way of looking at healing endeavors. It is a celebration of the art form of counseling. Beyond addressing treatment for emotional distress in psychologically sound and effective ways, energy therapies permit us to help clients and ourselves to access self-care, self-expression, and personal creativity, all through dynamic new resources.

In the opening section, we look at the history and research background of energy-oriented healing. Next, we consider aspects of the human vibrational matrix and ways of assessing patterns in the meridians, the biofield, and the energy centers. The heart of energetic approaches for emotional healing is addressed in part III with examples, learning exercises, and references. Our model expands to include comprehensive energy psychology interventions for accessing personal creativity in part IV and concludes with consideration of future developments in this dynamic field.

Finally, this book is about ways that each of us—therapists, clients, and persons interested in healing and actualizing our potentials—can

develop the traits that allow our personal talents to touch others effectively. It is about understanding ourselves as energy beings who can
access pathways that maintain and enhance vitality on a daily basis.
Throughout, we will see how the energetic model can transform our
lives from the humdrum to the vital, and can move us from emotional
pain toward confidence and joyfulness, from limited thinking to full
empowerment.

Part I

History and Background of Energy-Oriented Healing

Chapter I

New Resources for Emotional Healing and Enhanced Creativity

We must expand our apertures of consciousness in order to expand the effectiveness of our therapeutic strategies. —Lee Pulos

At the very time when medical technology is advancing to unprecedented heights, the healing archetype is becoming increasingly visible and active. This seeming paradox can best be understood if we look at the inherent nature of healing as a creative, ongoing process that leads to increasing wholeness and harmony within each person. Beyond simply receiving chemical or technological interventions when we are ill, we need a personal touch, a caring advocate, a belief that we can be restored to health, and a sense of hope and purpose in order to improve our sense of well-being.

There are many definitions of healing that encompass these qualities. Webster's *New Universal Unabridged Dictionary* (1996) defines the verb to heal primarily as "to make healthy, whole, or sound," whereas "to mend, get well, or cure" is secondary. The word heal is derived from the Greek stem *holos*, meaning wholeness, while the Old English *haelen* and the German *heilen*, both meaning to heal or make well, imply restoring a sense of balance and harmony that goes beyond merely overcoming an illness.

Some theorists see life as a continuous flow of the essential life force, or *qi* (pronounced chee). In this context, healing implies movement from a disturbed or impeded qi pattern to a more balanced, harmonious one. This newly found balance affects our psychological states as well as our immediate surroundings, families, communities, the world, and the wonders of the universe. Thus, the process of healing is conceptualized as an integral part of a functioning organic whole. Noted nursing theorist Martha Rogers (Rawnsley, 1985) views healing as a movement toward harmony of the human and his/her environment to ever more evolved patterns of integration. Another nursing leader, Janet Quinn (1992) describes healing as finding the right relationship between the individual and the environment. Positive psychologists Seligman and Csikszentmilhalyi (2000) see the development of hope, resilience, endurance, and courage, even in the face of severe distress, as integral to psychological healing. These definitions suggest that healing is not only an internal process toward more effective functioning but also one of harmonious, positive interaction with our living surroundings.

Inherent in the concept of healing is a wider interpretation of our human reality: illness is not only a physical problem but also an indication that there may be imbalance in other aspects of one's life. True well-being is much more than mere homeostasis of the organs. It is a harmonious evolution toward wholeness within physical, emotional, mental, and spiritual aspects of our being. While we are physical beings with material bodies, we are also emotional beings whose feelings can deeply influence the physical; we are mental, idea-generating beings whose thought patterns impact and interact with physical and emotional aspects; and, most significantly, we are spiritual beings having a brief human experience. We are ultimately connected to the Creative Source, something greater beyond our personal selves. Healing, in this light, is a multidimensional process toward ever-increasing levels of wellness in every aspect of our reality and can occur even in the face of an ongoing or chronic, physical problem.

Genuine healing, then, encompasses not only overcoming trauma, an obstacle, or impediment to health but also includes the ability to tap into our vast potentials for creativity and resourcefulness. Every human life, our clients' and our own, is an opportunity to demonstrate and develop human potential as part of the personal healing process.

EVOLUTION TO A HOLISTIC, INTEGRATIVE VIEW

Changing definitions of illness and wellness have led to increased consumer use of nontraditional modalities (Eisenberg et al., 1998). Until recently, physical health was defined as the absence of physical distress or symptoms, while psychological health meant making peace with one's demons by coping with emotional pathology. With the evolution of a more integrative, holistic view, health is seen more and more as ever-increasing levels of well-being, especially in the psychological and spiritual domains. Even aging is no longer seen as the inevitable demise of our physical prowess but rather as an opportunity for learning how our dynamic human systems achieve and maintain high levels of functioning as we become more chronologically gifted. The presence of pain or *dis-ease* is now seen as a feedback signal from the entire human system that allows us to learn more about ourselves. Pain is no longer something to be discarded, ignored, or medicated but rather an opportunity for our learning.

In the current Western model of medical care, the goal is symptom removal or *cure*. The latter is defined (Webster's *New Universal Unabridged Dictionary*, 1996) as "a means of healing and restoring to health; remedy; a means of correcting or relieving anything that is troublesome or detrimental" and is derived from the Latin word *cura*, for "the care of souls." There is little in current, mainstream health care that addresses healing at the level of care for the soul. If the goal of health is merely to be physically symptom free, then the giving of a chemical to remove pain, or surgery to remove a dysfunctional body part, is all that is required. Curing, then, in current usage of the term, is quite different, philosophically speaking, from healing. Curing is seen as an external mechanism for providing physical symptom relief, preferably with complete eradication of the problem. Healing, on the other hand, is a multidimensional, ongoing, lifelong process toward wholeness, balance, and harmony from within. Curing in its current model is severely limited when there is an ongoing physical problem or life-threatening illness. Physicians or caregivers in this model will often say discouragingly, "We have done all we can." Healing, in contrast, is open-ended and allows the health-care practitioner to explore the many possibilities for emotional, mental, and spiritual balancing, even in the face of chronic or terminal physical illness. Healing is essentially hopeful and trusting of the innate self-regulating capacity, at whatever level possible, for the individual. Our many counseling practices have attempted to provide the human touch and personal insights—in other words, the healing—that is lacking in the reductionistic medical treatment model.

This book will focus primarily on energy psychotherapy and the healing interventions that address rebalancing, or repatterning, of the human energies to assist movement to higher levels of functioning and personal creativity. Energy therapy utilizes interventions that incorporate understanding of the human vibrational matrix—the biofield, the meridians with their specific acupoints, and the energy centers. These interventions are natural and have been used, as we shall see, throughout human history. They promote a balancing of energetic resources within the whole person, allowing new perspective, harmony, and right relationship to emerge.

The movement toward healing in the client always comes from within but is facilitated by the intention and centering of the healer. We will explore the theoretical basis of these concepts and their application in the chapters to come. For now, let us consider an example showing how energy-oriented counseling facilitated psychological healing in a family facing one of the most complex life tasks—the challenge of dealing positively and creatively with dying, death, and its aftermath.

ASHLEY AND HER FATHER: A STORY OF HEALING WHILE DYING

"Ashley," a very attractive young businesswoman, came to see me because she wanted to learn how to save her father. All her life she had experienced a sense of magic when her hands touched someone in need. Now that her father had been diagnosed with a severe form of cancer, she wanted to help him "beat the odds" of his 1-year prognosis and keep him alive.

The father held a strong bond with his daughter but unfortunately spent most of his adult life as a high-functioning alcoholic. Some inner clock told him to stop drinking and reorganize his life 2 weeks before he noticed chest and lung congestion. The joy of his newfound sobriety early in January was dimmed when he was given a dreaded diagnosis of advanced lung cancer. Ashley could not believe that her father had made a remarkable recovery from his addiction just to die from another disease.

Both father and daughter set their goals to live each moment together as fully as possible, although each had family and careers in different cities. When Ashley came for therapy in May, her father had already received all the usual medical treatments, consisting of "aggressive" chemotherapy and extensive radiation. Although the cancer had receded, he had pain with every breath. Ashley was determined to help him with energy-oriented practices.

I began by teaching her centering exercises, such as the Brush Down, Central Alignment, Chakra Rotation, Belly Button Correction, and Crossover Correction that are described in later chapters of this book. I felt it was important to teach Ashley self-management resources while she was facing the emotional challenges of her father's illness. I encouraged her to use these centering practices before meeting with her father, or during her attempts to help him, so that her own energy could remain balanced. Most important, Ashley learned the art of trusting in a higher wisdom through the energy exercises.

No one could actually predict the outcome of this illness. Although the medical prognosis was grim, there was always the possibility of spontaneous healing, or remission. Research on the act of praying has demonstrated that nondirectional prayers are most powerful. Thus, it was important to pray for the father's highest good, rather than for the specific outcome of a long life that Ashley wanted. She agreed that prayer and meditation in addition to centering practices would become a part of her daily life.

I began teaching Ashley how to enlarge her understanding of healing and its multidimensional nature at the very first session. She understood that emotional and spiritual healing can sometimes assist the physical body in repairing itself. Sometimes, the body may be too damaged for full repair, but resolution of life issues, fears, and conflicts can become arenas for needed psychological and spiritual healing. After our first few sessions, we both asked for the father's healing at all possible levels. It would turn out to be a fortuitous choice.

Ashley wanted her father to obtain complementary therapies once he had exhausted the available medical treatments. With steel-edged determination she set about to change his staid views about health care, personally taking him to a variety of available resources. While he scoffed at first, he felt a little better after receiving acupuncture, learned to use imagery from a psychologist in his city, and began taking herbs and nutritional supplements. Ashley "unruffled, or cleared" his biofield to relieve pain each weekend she visited. She also added gentle holding of his meridian acupoints that I had taught her because the usual tapping was too intense a stimulus for him.

Despite all these maneuvers, however, the father's health continued to decline. Both agreed to try the best-known alternative method—a 3-week restoration of the immune system at a Mexican clinic. The attending physician there was kind and warm-hearted, a welcome alternative to the hard clinical dictates of the oncologists who said basically, "You will be gone in a year no matter what you do." The physician in Mexico said, "There is always room for hope—each system heals in its own unique way; we honor your innate healing capacities."

Ashley was elated after the trip. But intuition, corroborated by muscle checking as an access to her intuitive knowing, indicated that the father's physical life might indeed be very short. I encouraged Ashley to make a list of all the things she wanted to tell her father. I also asked her to find out his final wishes, just to be prepared.

Ashley's spiritual life and sense of connection with her father grew steadily. They agreed that he would always be connected to her spiritually and that he would be at her right shoulder whenever they were apart. During the respite after the Mexico trip, Ashley found out that her father wanted to die at home surrounded by his family, his ashes scattered over the sea. She also learned that he had intense fears of pain, of feeling helpless, of being out of control, and that these fears grew with every physical symptom.

Early in September, I taught Ashley how to help her father to use imagery along with clearing of the biofield to help him calm down. My preparations were timely: he was admitted to intensive care with severe atrial fibrillation the very next day.

His physical body did not respond to any medications or treatments, and he was not expected to survive the night. Ashley was determined to get her father home to live, and die, as he wished. Step by step, she overlapped the images of their last walk on the beach with the repeated smoothing or clearing of his biofield. Then she sent her caring intention into his heart center. Over the next few hours, a seeming miracle occurred. The man who had spent most of his life being overwhelmed by his emotions and drugging himself to escape their impact, faced his panic. He literally calmed himself. The heart rate dropped from 170 to a reasonable 90. He continued to improve and was discharged to hospice care at home. The hospital staff was amazed at the shift in his condition, for which they could give no known medical explanation.

At home, Ashley continued to teach her father how to manage his sense of panic, especially when breathing was difficult. She also continued to center and calm herself with the balancing exercises I had taught her and was continuously amazed at how strong she felt. Three days later, the father was greatly improved, sitting up and eating, talking with many family members who had assembled in the morning. Ashley and her brother helped him to sit up later, each one holding his hand. The three of them prayed together as they had done so often. They celebrated a moment of indescribable peace and joy.

Then, abruptly, he breathed deeply, smiled, and was gone.

In less than nine months, a large, seemingly healthy 52-year-old man died of lung cancer. It could be seen as a defeat for all the traditional and nontraditional methods that had been tried. For me, a therapist oriented to the mysteries of multidimensional healing, it was a confirmation that important work can be accomplished during every moment of life. My respect for the beautiful willingness Ashley showed in learning from this difficult time continues to reverberate and to enhance my clinical knowledge of what is possible.

When I next saw Ashley a few weeks later, she was poised and confident, preparing for a family gathering to scatter the ashes. She describes her experience in this way: "It has been at once the most awful and most awesome experience of my life. When I decided to do all I could for my father, I had no idea how painful, gut-wrenching and exhilarating it would be. I cry often because I miss him. I cry for my future children that won't know his face or breath like my brother and I did. I cry when my relatives cry, of course. Otherwise, I have a sense of deep peace. Everything that I could imagine doing, I was able to do. I learned to trust higher wisdom. I learned about healing. Best of all, I learned that I am always connected to my father's love. Right now, you know, there's a warm spot by my right shoulder."

CLINICAL REFLECTIONS

As clinicians review this story, they will recognize that ongoing work needed to be done during the grieving process. A significant loss is continuous even if all our efforts during the loved one's life were successful.

Together, Ashley and I dealt with unexpected issues that emerged during the grief work. One was an eating addiction, a mechanism Ashley had used during earlier crises for self-soothing. But the sudden weight gain and craving for gallons of ice cream three months after her loss was an unwelcome surprise. We were able to treat it with specific meridian-based interventions, including the tapping of acupoints that will be described later. Another unexpected (but frequently encountered) symptom of grief was sleep disturbance exacerbated by her intense fear of further loss, including the death of her partner or her pets. Again, we were able to use the interventions described in succeeding chapters to relieve the fears and restore restful sleep.

I continued to see Ashley for a year to support her healing and insights, her "good grief" as we came to call it. She not only felt her father's presence but began to draw pictures from their times together. Even more remarkable were spontaneous water colors depicting her father surrounded by his angels—lovely, etheric images of the life beyond this one by someone who had hardly ever touched a brush before. It was as if the reality of the grieving process opened doors to unexpressed aspects of Ashley's personality. She literally moved beyond her pain to a new dimension of creativity and personality integration.

I am exceedingly grateful that the resources of energy psychology—working with Ashley's biofield, chakras, and meridian acupoints—were available to me while her father was dying and during the succeeding grief work. Traditional talk therapy might have eased her emotional pain in a cognitive way and helped to anticipate the death, but with this work, Ashley had ongoing resources for self-care as well as for sharing with her loved ones. Indirectly, the father seemed also to have benefited from my work with Ashley. As Ashley matured through her learning, the whole family also grew, both in wisdom and sense of interconnection. Ashley was able to be a loving, centered presence for healing during the challenging time of the dying process, the time of the death, and its ever-expanding aftermath.

In the succeeding chapters, we will explore the remarkable resources of energy psychotherapies that may greatly enlarge and enhance our therapeutic repertoire. We will also consider the practical aspects for clients. And we will consider specific recommendations for energy-based interventions that will not only assist in overcoming emotional distress but also facilitate full healing in order to access creative potentials.

Chapter 2

A Brief History of Energy-Related Healing

It is only with the heart that one can see rightly; what is essential is invisible to the eye.　　　　　　　　　　　　—Antoine de Saint-Exupery

The term "energy healing" refers to a family of approaches that work with the human energy system. As already suggested, healing is the lifelong evolution toward wholeness in all dimensions of our being. "Energy" refers to the vital life force, beyond the breath and heartbeat, the very essence that differentiates the living from the nonliving. The integration of this animating life force with healing endeavors is as old as human consciousness.

For tens of thousands of years and cross-culturally, humans have assisted each other by rebalancing disturbances in the flow of life energy. These disruptions of animating life force could manifest either as physical or psychological distress. The person who experienced depleted or disturbed energy was assisted by men and women with skill and positive intent to help. This external resource, designated as healers or shamans in the community, insured that their own energy was balanced by dedicating their lives to personal inner work with daily centering practices. Their work was to activate temporarily their clients' inner life force until their self-healing resources could resume functioning.

Although we do not use energy-linked language in modern psychotherapy, there is indeed a sense in which much more than words is communicated when we lend our presence to someone in need. Something of the intent and clarity of an effective therapist reaches the client, although we may not recall any of the specific words that were said. It is as if we share our essential human essence with our clients through our own vitality and intuition.

What is this quality that communicates beyond our words? And how can we utilize energy concepts to enhance our clinical effectiveness? We will be exploring these arenas throughout this volume. But first, let us take a short journey into the history of energy concepts to give us a context for our investigation.

ENERGY-RELATED TERMS

In classical Greece, Hippocrates described energy as a force of flow from healers' hands. Pythagoras, in the Greece of 500 B.C, referred to vital energy as a luminous body that could produce cures. Paracelsus discussed the interaction of vital life force and matter, calling it *illiaster* (Brennan, 1993). Throughout human history, a variety of terms have been used by many cultures to name the animating force, or energy, that resides in each living organism and differentiates the living from the nonliving.

Table 2.1 gives some of the most commonly known names for the vital life force.

Here we can see the great variety of names describing human energies. For clarity, we will use the terms *life force* and qi, predominantly when referring to the essential human energy. The term *prana* will be used when referring to energetic concepts from the Eastern Indian philosophical stream.

BELIEFS ABOUT ILLNESS AND HEALING

Inherent in all of the energy-healing modalities is assessment of the vital life force flow via intuitive means. Interventions, then, relieve blockage or disturbances in the flow of energy, or qi, and to allow balancing of the system. The underlying metaphor is that disturbance in the flow or energy of one's vitality can affect physical, emotional, or spiritual well-being. Distortions in the qi can occur through stagnation, depletion, congestion, or blockage of energy flow either to specific organs or in the entire person. Restoration to harmony and balance that activates the innate capacity for self-healing requires a temporary external source, such as a healer, who stimulates points or areas that affect the various flows in order to repattern and rebalance the disturbed area. Ultimately,

Table 2.1
SOME TERMS FOR HUMAN ENERGY

Energy Name	Cultural Source
Apu	Incan heritage, Peru
Ankh	Ancient Egypt
Arunquiltha	Australian Aborigine
Bioenergy	USA/England/Russia
Biomagnetism	USA/England
Gana	South America
Huaca	Peru/Bolivia
Ki	Japan
Life force, vital life force	General usage
Mana	Polynesia
Orenda	Iroquois Native Americans
Pneuma	Ancient Greece
Prana	India
Qi (pronounced "chee")	China
Subtle energy	USA/Europe
Ton	Dakota Native Americans
Walkan	Lakota Native Americans

the client's own capacities are activated and the individual moves to a higher level of self-understanding.

In ancient African beliefs, sickness or injury was understood as a process in which the individual was out of alignment with the animal spirits, ancestral dead, or deities (Katz, Biesler, & St. Denis, 1997). The community of healers worked through dance to move energy vigorously through the patient's body in order to enhance his consciousness, to help him to understand his problems, and to keep him from being carried off prematurely into death.

In shamanism, the medicine man or woman traveled among the worlds—the deeper realms, the present reality, and the higher planes—to bring information to the community. This included retrieving soul parts, negotiating healing for the sick, and petitioning nature to assist the tribe (Villodo, 2000). Much power was attributed to healers who knew the invisible spiritual world and interpreted environmental events, animal movement, and illness.

In the East, ancient practices worked with qi. *T'ai Qi* and *Qi Gong* are two practices known in the West to help move the vital life force toward health maintenance and healing (Harpur, 1994). Acupuncture, an increasingly well-known health-promoting modality, is believed to stimulate the movement of qi along energy pathways, known as meridians. This increased motility balances the energy flow of blocked or stagnant areas to restore physical and emotional health.

Another Eastern practice, known for 5,000 years, is the Ayurvedic tradition within yoga (Rose & Keegan, 2000). Here, activation of the human energy vortices is used to maintain balance in the individual's basic constitution for ongoing self-healing. Nutrition specific to the individual's body type as well as movement exercises further enhance the health-promoting qualities of the many forms of yoga.

In the Judeo-Christian tradition, Jesus provided many healings that drove out demonic forces and offered messages of hope. Forty-one incidents of Jesus's healing activity are recorded in the New Testament, and half involved light touching, even of "untouchable" lepers (Smith, 2000). Christian healers are reported to have continued these compassionate acts even after the powerful church establishment of the Middle Ages forbade them to engage in such activities.

As unusual as these energy concepts may seem to the modern, rational, scientific mind, they are deeply rooted in worldwide human experience. Energy-based healing is now resurfacing as part of holistic, integrative medical models and the broad category of alternative or complementary therapies that include mind/body psychology and energy psychotherapy. This is a fascinating development, coming at a time when Western medicine has become so highly technological that patient welfare is almost considered to be secondary. It appears that we must humanize our "high-tech" culture by returning to ways of communicating our deep human essence through "high-touch" approaches included in energy therapy.

TWO MAIN PHILOSOPHIES ABOUT HUMAN ENERGIES

Two main philosophical streams, from China and from India, are converging with Western thinking to bring about this new synthesis. In Chinese tradition, the meridians, as pathways carrying qi to the entire body and mind, have been identified and utilized in healing work for at least 5,000 years. In Indian heritage, the human *aura*, or *biofield* surrounding the body, was seen to support the inner flows of *prana* and its energy vortices, known as *chakras*. The Indian traditions, elucidated and practiced in yoga, are recorded over 5,000 years as well (Goswami, 1999). Because the meridians, the biofield, and the chakras are slightly different components of the overall energetic matrix, which appears to have other more subtle components as well, we will be using the term *human vibrational matrix* to describe the interacting aspects that form the human energy system. As these understandings of human energies converge with the efforts of helping professionals, we have rich and creative new approaches to counseling and psychotherapy.

Documentation of the Meridians

A recent find allowed the world community to learn about the actual day-to-day life of a shepherd in the Italian Alps 5,200 years ago (PBS TV documentary, February, 2000). Because his body and skin were unusually well preserved in a glacier, we even know what Iceman Oetzi had for dinner before he was frozen in time. We know that he carried medicinal herbs, including an antibiotic fungus, along with a special tinder box giving him numerous ways to start a fire. The clearly etched tattoo markings along his spine, right knee, and foot, however, were a puzzle. Further investigation showed that Oetzi suffered from osteoarthritis in these areas, but the tattoos made no sense until a practitioner of acupuncture examined the markings. The tatoos were, in fact, lines tracing the specific meridians and acupoints, the electromagnetic pathways for the flow of qi, which could assist in relieving pain and facilitating healing. Stimulation of acupoints by tattooing, heating, tapping, or insertion of needles continues to this day as the practice of acupuncture, or acupressure, and is one of many recognized energy-healing modalities.

The significance of the Iceman discovery predates the known practice of acupuncture in Europe by several thousand years. The earliest written evidence of energetic healing in the East is in the *Huang Ti Ching Su Wen* from 2,500 to 5,000 years ago (Veth, 1949).

Acupuncture, while known in the West, became popularized when

James Reston, President Nixon's press secretary on his historic trip to China in 1972, chose acupuncture as anesthesia for an emergency appendectomy. Western medical practitioners were incredulous at the pain-free operation and the speed of Reston's recovery.

Nonetheless, it was not until 1997 that the National Institutes of Health issued a position statement validating the use of acupuncture (NIH, 1997). In the meantime, a number of creative therapists were exploring the relevance of working with acupoints along the 14 major meridians to effect relief from emotional distress. This pioneering work over the last 20 years laid the foundation for the discipline we now know as energy psychology (Callahan, 2001; Gallo, 1998, 2000). While energy psychology became best known as a number of meridian-based interventions, a more comprehensive approach, integrating other aspects of the human vibrational matrix, is emerging.

Historical Evidence of Biofields and Chakras

Other energy-healing modalities are evidenced through cave drawings and a vast number of depictions from ancient cultures. Notable among these is rock art from the mountains of South Africa, several thousand years old, that shows healing dances with energy configurations (Ouzman & Loubser, 2000). In cave drawings from France, estimated to be from 15,000 to 25,000 years old, hands were depicted in healing gestures, and healing with consciousness-directed flow from the hands was recorded in early scriptures of all faiths (Harper, 1994). Furthermore, pictures of healing from the Egyptian Third Dynasty demonstrate energetic conceptualization (Pavek, 1993). In addition, this author (1993) saw numerous reliefs depicting the *ka*, the energetic envelope surrounding the physical body, and gestures of energy movement for healing on a trip to Egypt while accompanied by an interpreter of hieroglyphs.

Perhaps one of the oldest visual references to the chakras, the human energy centers, is the famous 5,000-year-old Kon-tiki statue located in the Tihuanaku temple complex in Bolivia. The 12-foot-tall statue, believed to be more ancient even than the surrounding temples, holds the right hand over the heart center, and the left, over the solar plexus in a gesture of empowerment and strength (Merejildo, 1997; Hover-Kramer, 2001).

As already noted, the traditions of yoga offer vast intuitive references for understanding the chakras and their effects on human well-being, as well as information about essential energy flows. These flows include the central vessel for *pranic* flow, the *sushumna*, and the two intersecting, spiraling flows of *ida* and *pingala* that form the energy vortices within the body and interact with the "sheath," or aura, which extends beyond the body (Goswami, 1999, p. 166). Interestingly, Goswami's extensive investigation of ancient texts also names 14 energy flows through the body, which seem to be akin to the 14 major meridians defined in Eastern medicine.

In 1970, nursing professor Dolores Krieger and her friend, the medical intuitive Dora Kunz, developed a direct healing intervention based on pranic concepts of the chakras and the biofield. They called it Therapeutic Touch (1993) describing it as a modern application of many ancient healing practices. Since that time, Therapeutic Touch has almost become a household word, having reached the lives of millions—nurses, physicians, and health caregivers, and their patients worldwide. This one form of healing literally opened the door to the development of many other forms of energy-related healing. We now have a rich variety of resources for restoring and rebalancing human energies, including Healing Touch, Pranic Healing, Energy Medicine, SHEN, Reiki, as well as the schools of many healers such as Barbara Brennan (1988, 1993) and Rosalyn Bruyere (1989).

From this brief historical perspective, we find that knowledge about the human vibrational matrix and its different components was derived by intuitive means. Remarkably, most of it, despite some fanciful descriptions, was quite accurate. We now have scientific instrumentation to support the existence of the energy system, and we can document results of energy-healing interventions as we shall see in the next chapter. However, we do not know the actual mechanisms by which energetic interventions work—the best we can provide are beginning theoretical models and metaphors. Nonetheless, the fact that energetic modalities have been so well-known over millennia—and are now resurfacing in the practices of creative therapists and health-care practitioners—suggests that there is a basic truth that exceeds current cognitive understanding. The work of energy psychology is an invitation to creative, open-minded inquiry, which holds promise and hope for our clients, joy and adventure to us as helping professionals.

Chapter 3

Research Supporting Biofield, Chakra, and Meridian Interventions for Counseling

We will never understand the scientific basis of everything. We must be open to approaches that work even when we don't understand how or why they work. —Ralph Snyderman (2000)

W hat is the value of working with different aspects of the human vibrational matrix to facilitate emotional healing? What are the clinical and research outcomes known about this work in psychotherapy? And, finally, what is the relationship of these concepts to the new, emerging field of comprehensive energy psychology?

We need to remember that while psychotherapeutic treatment with acupoints and related meridians is a relatively recent development (Gallo, 1998, 2000), concepts of working with the human biofield and energy centers have been known and utilized in mainstream health care for over 30 years (Krieger, 1979; Quinn, 1984). Although most of the emphasis so far has been on physical healing, the effects of chakra and biofield interventions for relieving psychological distress have been described, documented, and researched to some extent.

Broadly speaking, all energy-healing approaches work with aspects of the human vibrational matrix in a variety of forms. In this chapter, we will explore the research related to energy healing, the family of modalities that redirect and balance blocked or impeded flows of qi in order to enhance physical, emotional, and spiritual well-being. In particular, we will look at outcomes related to therapeutic work with the three most prominent aspects of the human energy system—the biofield, the chakras, and the meridians.

RESEARCH RELATED TO BIOFIELD/CHAKRA INTERVENTIONS

Since the beginnings of Therapeutic Touch in 1970, research to support the clinical practice of rebalancing hospitalized patients' depleted or disturbed biofields has been ongoing. Several hundred documentations, dissertations, and research papers published in peer-reviewed professional journals exist. Findings continue to be compiled in the annals of the Nurse Healers–Professional Associates, the professional Therapeutic Touch organization (NH–PA, Inc., 2001). Similarly, the Healing Touch community, which offers over 600 workshops to health-care professionals a year, has compiled and maintained a compendium of ongoing research projects over the last six years (Healing Touch International, 2001). So pervasive is the research literature that "energy-field disturbance" has been designated as an official nursing diagnosis since 1996 (North American Nursing Diagnosis Association [NANDA]). This diagnosis, determined through hand assessments and intuitive perceptions of practitioners, serves as the basis for implementing energy-healing interventions, such as Therapeutic Touch, in major hospitals and clinics.

The outcomes of over 200 research studies of energy healing with human subjects (compiled in Benor, 2001) were surprisingly similar. The effects of decreased anxiety and pain were always noted along with an increase in relaxation and overall sense of well-being. Put another way, it appeared that the parasympathetic component of the autonomic nervous system was somehow activated by energy-healing methods. More often than not, statistical significance (to the $>.05$ confidence level or lower) of these outcomes was achieved. Even when significance was not statistically established, clients reported changes in their sense of self-efficacy and hope.

The research projects generally have a pre/post intervention design, with populations randomized into control and experimental groups in medical settings. Research in the early years of Therapeutic Touch interventions showed increased hemoglobin levels in treatment groups (reported in Krieger, 1990, 1993), while more recent projects report increased immune system responses (Olson, Sneed, & La Via, 1997; Quinn & Strelkauskas, 1993), relief of pre- and post-procedural anxiety (Heidt, 1981), overall pain relief (Peck, 1997), relief of pain and anxiety in burn patients (Turner, Clark, Gauthier, & Williams, 1998), and of accelerated wound healing (Wirth, 1990)—to name just a few of the most stellar projects. All projects demonstrate that the effects of energy interventions are in the direction of increased well-being as evidenced in patients' decreased pain and anxiety. Responses vary according to the needs of the individual and may be immediate or may develop over several days. The rate of responsiveness may also depend on the extent of dysfunction or imbalance of the flow of qi in the biofield and chakras. For example, a hot, inflamed area of the body often becomes cooler after treatment, while a cold, depleted area, as that evidenced in long-term pain, becomes gradually warmer or more vibrant. Similarly, an agitated, distressed person becomes calmer, while someone who is fatigued or depressed usually reports feeling more awake and focused.

For counselors, several studies are particularly relevant. The calming effects of simple clearing and balancing of the biofield via Therapeutic Touch on institutionalized, confused elderly persons were documented in several settings (Simington & Lang, 1993). Olson and Sneed (1995) further substantiated relief of anxiety as a major outcome of Therapeutic Touch, while Gagne and Toyne (1994) were able to establish that Therapeutic Touch was as effective in reducing anxiety among institutionalized patients as more traditional relaxation and stress management therapies. Pioneering in an adolescent psychiatric care unit, nurse clinical specialist Pamela Hughes and her associates showed that energy-healing interventions, via five Therapeutic Touch sessions, helped severely acting-out teens who reported feeling more self-controlled and were able to establish internal locus of control (Hughes et al., 1997). In addition, a study of depression in breast cancer patients showed improved affect, as measured on the Beck depression scale, and sense of vitality, via client self-report, with a course of three Healing Touch sessions (Moreland, 1997).

For psychotherapists, the use of noninvasive methods that do not require physical touching but allow empathic communication between the biofields of healer and client is a superb complement to traditional counseling skills. My personal experiences in helping clients balance their biofields and related chakras have involved teaching clients how to practice self-care as well as offering psychoenergetic interventions to those who are unable to focus and center. (Client-informed consent is, of course, established before any psychoenergetic interventions begin and will be discussed further in chapter 9.)

Because most biofield therapies start with the practitioner's centered, intentional state of consciousness, methods to bring about systemic psychoenergetic balancing are a natural starting place. Thus, therapist energy hygiene, using the biofield and chakra methods described in chapters 5 and 6, is crucial to maximizing our therapeutic effectiveness as well as our personal well-being.

Teaching clients methods for treating pervasive energetic disturbance is exceedingly helpful in almost all counseling settings, even when other energetic interventions might not be appropriate (selection of clients for energetic treatment is discussed further in the ethics chapter 9). Relaxation and increased ability to concentrate are often the first effects when clients learn systemic focusing through balancing of the biofield. This means that our clients are more available for in-depth work and for resolving specific issues after they center themselves.

EFFECTS OF INTENTION

Since direct physical contact is not needed for the relief experienced by clients receiving energy healing, a number of researchers are exploring the effects of healing over distance, in which healer intentionality is the main ingredient. One hypothesis put forth by internist Larry Dossey (1993) is that nonlocal interconnections exist between persons, especially when the strong emotion of human caring exists. He documents numerous studies of the positive change brought about by intentional focusing that emanates from a caring person toward someone in need. Prayer and meditation are two forms of such human intention that do not require physical contacting and are not limited by distance between the participants.

Another physician, Bruce Greyson (1996), conducted a study using a randomized, double-blind, longitudinal design with adult patients suffering from major depression. In addition to receiving standard treatments for depression, the experimental group received daily distant healing for 6 weeks by volunteers trained in LeShan's (1976) meditation techniques. Although the outcomes were not statistically significant (as measured on the Hamilton Rating Scale for Depression, Brief Psychiatric Rating Scale, Global Assessment of Function, and visual analog scale for depression before and after the intervention), the subjects reported a number of important affective changes. One was an increased sense of well-being similar to that reported by the subjects receiving Therapeutic Touch. Another was a statistically significant correlation of the treatment group in receptivity and responsiveness toward other therapy sessions they received during the 6-week period of the distant, or nonlocal, healing. We might conclude, then, that intentional efforts from positively connected, caring individuals accelerated severely depressed clients' responsiveness to other interventions, such as medication and psychotherapy.

EXPERIENTIAL OUTCOMES OF MERIDIAN
INTERVENTIONS

For the past 20 years, psychologist Roger Callahan has investigated work with the meridians and related acupoints that brings about relief from severe emotional distress such as phobias, anxiety states, panic attacks, post-traumatic stress disorder (PTSD), and love pain. His operating model is that these distresses cause "perturbations" in a client's thought field and can be cured through stimulation of specific acupoints on selected meridian pathways which activate the body's intrinsic healing mechanisms (Callahan, 2001). He has held much of his teaching as proprietary until recently, and true replicable research, acceptable for publication in peer-reviewed professional journals, has not been carried out. Instead, Callahan reports his "extensive evidence supporting the effectiveness of Thought Field Therapy (TFT)," his brainchild (Callahan, 2001, pp. 41–68). He cites, for example, 23 radio shows on which he treated 68 patients with phobias and achieved a 97% success rate as measured through client self-report; a follow-up study with one of his trainees showed similar results (2001, p. 46). In addition, Callahan mentions studies by Bray and Folkes (2001, p. 47) in helping immigrants with PTSD, and by Graham (2001, p. 48) in which 177 subjects were treated with diagnostically elicited algorithms, or specific treatment patterns, to achieve a 94% success rate. In 1995, Figley and Carbonell at Florida State University compared TFT and three other current therapies for PTSD and found TFT algorithms to give the most effective results (Figley & Carbonnell, 1995).

Fortunately, the lack of published research evidence concerning treatment of emotional distress with meridian acupoint stimulation is being remedied through a number of more academically oriented energy psychology practitioners who are also leading mental health professionals. In addition, the newly formed Association for Comprehensive Energy Psychology (ACEP) has a strong research direction under the leadership of Patricia Carrington (2001), and continuous research updates are given at each annual international energy psychology conference (1999, 2000, 2001).

One valuable study currently submitted for publication examines changes in brain activity using the generic algorithm developed by Craig and Fowlie (1995), called Emotional Freedom Technique (EFT). Full-brain electroencephalograms were obtained from clients traumatized by an automobile accident prior to and 3 months following EFT treatment of their driving phobia (Swingle, Pulos, & Swingle, 2001). The results showed that successfully treated clients had statistically significant "larger increases in brainwave amplitudes in the occipital region (an indicator of mental quiescence), greater frontal lobe balance (an indicator of positive mood state), and increased amplitude over the sensory motor cortex (an indicator of body quiescence)" (Pulos, 2002).

Another research project currently submitted for publication is by Wells (2001) to evaluate the effectiveness of EFT in enhancing peak performance among Olympic athletes in Australia. In addition, preliminary work to understand correlations between brain functioning (as measured by the magnetoencephalogram) before and after brief TFT interventions, is being developed by psychologists Lambrou and Pratt (2001). Their most recent findings show that stimulation of a specific acupoint (GB 37) produces a demonstrable increase in alpha brain waves, the frequency of a meditative state of mind. Studies of brain activity to measure effectiveness of specific therapeutic interventions seem especially appropriate, since a number of researchers are demonstrating the brainwave effects of dysfunctional emotional patterns, like social phobia (Davidson, Marshall, Tomarken, & Henriquest, 2000). At the International Forum of New Science, Lambrou and Pratt, along with researchers Chevalier and Nicosia (1999), have also presented evidence concerning the effectiveness of meridian psychotherapy methods for rapid emotional relief.

Furthermore, Baker and Siegel (2001) report striking effects of EFT treatment on subjects who had intense fear of rats, spiders, and waterbugs, which support the dramatic results claimed by innovators such as Craig and Callahan. In Baker and Siegel's study, before and after treatment changes were measured behaviorally by how close a subject could walk toward the feared object. Reactivity was further measured by three different self-report measures of fear and anxiety. Although these are preliminary findings, they point to the direction of predictable treatment outcomes with meridian-based interventions—decreased anxiety, increased personal efficacy, and calming states of mind.

NEED FOR ONGOING QUANTITATIVE AND QUALITATIVE RESEARCH

It is quite evident from this discussion that much more needs to be done to study clients' affective outcomes with energetic interventions, especially in considering the meridian therapies. While thousands of clinicians can attest to remarkable and rapid relief of emotional distress in their clients, we do not yet have the research base to validate these methods as a standard psychotherapeutic approach. At best, we can say the energetic approaches seem to offer additional resources for therapists and clients who are open to the use of an innovative or novel modality. All new therapies are inevitably met with skepticism; they are used when clinicians begin searching for new solutions to complex cases, and gradually become accepted only when the therapies show repeatedly demonstrable outcomes. In the meantime, it behooves all of us in the field of energy psychotherapy to move with care, clinical skill, and the highest ethical considerations when suggesting one or several energy modalities to clients.

Unfortunately, the "gold standard" of randomized, doubleblind controlled, quantitative studies does not lend itself well to evaluation of psychotherapeutic healing endeavors, which have a profound number of extraneous variables. Quantitative design is woefully inadequate for capturing the nuances of the healing experience from either the recipient's or the practitioner's perspective. Practitioner consciousness, intent, centering, and other subtle qualities of the healing interaction are by definition excluded in quantitative research.

In addition, experimenter biases may be even more evident when we attempt to measure an energetic, creative intervention between the interactive biofields of counselors and their clients. Larry Dossey analyzes the bias this way: "It appears that the double-blind studies can sometimes be steered in directions that correspond to the thoughts and attitudes of the experimenters. This might shed light on why skeptical experimenters appear unable to replicate the findings of believers, and why 'true believers' seem more able to produce positive results. The validity of decades of experimental findings in medical research would need to be reevaluated if it is proved that the mind can 'shove the data around' " (1993, p. 195). As we shall see in the next chapter, there is growing evidence of Heisenberg's uncertainty principle—that as soon as something is studied, it changes in structure; the human mind can, in certain ways, influence matter.

One way around observer bias and quantitative design limitations is to embrace the healing experience in ways that transcend counting and statistical analysis. There has been an important shift in research methodology, at least in the social sciences, toward the collection of *qualitative* as well as *quantitative* data about human experience. While quantitative studies are an inquiry into a human problem based on testing a theory composed of variables that are measured with numbers and analyzed with statistical procedures, qualitative studies are an inquiry into a human situation that is conducted in natural settings to capture the informant's lived experience (Creswell, 1994). Qualitative data, thus, yields information gathered by interview about the personal meaning of human experience through conversation, visual expression, music, art, poetry, journaling, and reflective dialogue. In Healing Touch research, for example, qualitative data is an accepted approach for reporting efficacy of various energy-healing techniques and an overall healing session (Geddes, 2002).

With this in mind, we might say that more of *both* quantitative and qualitative data are needed to establish the validity of meridian, chakra, and biofield interventions for relief of emotional distress. However, the current reports from clinicians and single-study projects are extremely encouraging for the future direction of integrative energy psychotherapy as a viable approach in therapeutic endeavors.

Chapter 4

The Scientific Basis for Energy-Oriented Psychotherapy

I sing the body electric.
—Walt Whitman

To date, research and clinical experience show us *what* is known in the field of energy-oriented therapies: there are psychologically positive effects through approaches that work with clients' biofields, chakras, and/or meridians. While clients report significant relief from severe emotional distress such as panic attacks, anxiety disorders, phobias, mood disturbance, and traumatic stress reactions, there also seem to be cumulative effects because of energy interventions—clients relate differently to their history and begin to see their lives from new perspectives. So far, we do not have the empirical base to understand fully the actual mechanisms, the *how*, of these therapeutic outcomes. But we can use metaphors, or models, to address our curiosity and to begin forming a conceptual framework. As the body of knowledge and research grows, we will be able to develop more well-defined theories to support the use of energy-oriented approaches in psychotherapy.

One thing is clear so far—vital life energy and its flows are a natural component of human awareness and our operating mind/body dynamic. To give us ideas of how these energies effect psychological change, we will consider recent scientific developments, known information about mind/body interactions, current understandings in physics, and emerging studies of consciousness and intentionality.

RECENT DEVELOPMENTS

Science as a whole is moving toward a more fluid understanding of nature and the cosmos. What was once seen as separate in the reductionistic models of the past is now seen as interactive and interrelated. From the macrocosm to the microcosm, the universe around us seems to function more and more as a unified whole rather than as separate entities and systems. Linear models of direct causation, as posited in Newton's laws of thermodynamics, are rapidly being replaced by Einstein's relativity theory and the dynamics of quantum mechanics put forth by leading theorists such as Planck, Heisenberg, Bohm, Bell, and Pribram (Herbert, 1985). Matter, energy, and human thought or consciousness are profoundly interconnected in the conceptualizations of leading physicist William Tiller (1997).

The term "subtle energy" was first used by famed physicist Albert Einstein to describe the minute, ongoing interrelationships between subatomic particles. In his quest for a unified field theory, he proposed that an ongoing interaction exists between matter and energy: Energy, the driving force that we observe in the known universe, is related to matter and a proposed constant, which Einstein presumed to be the speed of light (his famous formula is $E=mc^2$). Translated into human terms, it appears that our vital life force, qi or prana, is the very stuff of the universe. This energy continuously interacts with matter, as exemplified in the physical body with its many interactive components. In addition, our thoughts, intentional awareness, and sensitivity to our highest, creative potentials profoundly influence both energy and matter (Tiller, 1997).

The actual presence of subtle energies in relation to the human organism is being explored by a number of scientists and is empirically supported now that more sophisticated instrumentation is available. For example, in the early 1960s, orthopedic surgeon Robert Becker began to explore the miniscule electrical circuitry of the human body to understand nonunion problems in complex bone fractures (1985). He identified numerous but slight direct currents of electricity that flow throughout the body; these currents reverse electrical polarity at the site of an injury. Becker discovered that this "current of injury" (Becker, 1990, pp. 36–39) was supported with a small amount of electrical stimulation, bone healing accelerated. Over the next 30 years, he mapped out a human energetic system that appears to parallel the human nervous system, is electromagnetic in nature, and functions to inform all parts of the human organism (Becker, 1990, p. 80). He proposed the presence of dual information systems—the physical aspects of the human nervous system (brain cells, nerves, neural plexi, and ganglions) and the subtle energy system consisting of numerous electrical circuits or meridians, energy centers, and an electromagnetic field. He believed that this dual system was an example of natural *redundancy*: if one or more aspects of either system do not function fully, other aspects can take over and allow information to continue flowing to vital tissues and organs. For example, if a person has suffered a severe stroke with total hemiplegia, he or she can still think, digest food, produce endorphins, and, over time, recover many functions by using alternate aspects of either the neurological or energetic system.

In a different vein, Hiroshi Motoyama, physicist and yoga master from Japan, demonstrated the reality of human electronic circuitry by using sophisticated instrumentation (Motoyama, 1997). His most recent work to assist in early medical diagnoses includes refinement of the Apparatus for Meridian Identification (AMI), a computer that analyzes meridian-flow patterns via electrodes placed on acupoints at the sides of fingers and toes. Electronic signals from these acupoints identify imbalances in each of the meridians and their related organs. The signals also help to identify distortions of qi flow in the major energy centers. Imbalance in the human energetic system, including the biofield and the chakras, is further being studied in the copper-shielded room at Motoyama's center in California (personal communications, Dr. Gaetan Chevalier, California Institute of Human Sciences, Encinitas, California, 2001). This environment prevents any external sources, stray photon emissions, or electronic artifacts from interfering with the measuring of subtle energies in selected subjects. Thus sophisticated current scientific instrumentation is beginning to demonstrate the three major elements of the human vibrational matrix in a tangible manner via computer-generated imagery.

Scientific evidence helps us to understand the physical presence of the subtle energy matrix, which seems to function as a complex electromagnetic information processing system. Although we have no direct proof yet, we can *infer* that the direct current in the meridians carries information throughout the body to facilitate intercellular communication. We can also say that the biofield *acts like* an electromagetic field and that the chakras *resemble* energy transformation stations, functioning similar to electrical transformers, capacitors, and semiconductors (Freeman, 1990, pp. 164–165). To take the biocomputer metaphor further, theorist Victoria Slater (personal communication, May, 2001) proposes that "our bodies act like the hardware of a computer and our hemoglobin and clay-based cells may act as our electromagnetic core. Chakras act like the software, the biofield stores the data, and the meridians act as if they carry data and provide the electrical power to control the system."

As a whole, this threefold subtle energy system is continuously inter-acting within itself and with physiological informational systems such as blood circulation, lymph flows, chemical messengers, and neural path-ways. We might correctly say that these interactions are vibrational in nature. In fact, medical practice is quickly becoming more energy ori-ented, while scientific advances move forward at an ever-increasing pace as described in physician Richard Gerber's groundbreaking book, *Vibra-tional Medicine*, now in its third edition (2001). Take for instance, the energetic principles that underlie use of the well-known magnetic reso-nance imaging (MRI) device. Briefly stated, the magnetic properties of protons (hydrogen atoms in water within the cells) of the organ tissue under study are stimulated with a strong magnetic field; a second stim-ulus via a radio-frequency beam is applied, and energy is released from the stimulated protons in the radio-frequency range and sensed by detectors of the scanner; the structure of the selected organ tissue is then mathematically analyzed while computers interpret the electronic data and generate a diagnostic image (Gerber, 2001, pp. 104–106).

Vibratory patterns are evidenced everywhere in the human body and have become the basis of many other current medical diagnostic tools (Oschman, 2000). Properties of an organism can be measured *elec-trically* with the electrocardiogram and electroencephalogram; they can be measured *magnetically* with the magnetocardiogram and magnetoen-cephalogram; they can be measured *acoustically* and treated with lithotrypsy (devices that use sound waves to break up stone formations in the body); and the body can be evaluated by measuring *temperature* dif-ferentials by using photometry, thermographic imagery, and infrared imaging.

It is helpful and accurate, then, to think of each human being as a vast network of vibrational interrelationships supported by the complex, subtle energy circuitry suggested—indeed, a vibrational matrix. Because this information is so new in the world of health care, we do not yet have working theories to explain the psychological outcomes that clin-ical experience and research are demonstrating. But we can come up with several additional metaphors derived from the known scientific bases of inquiry into mind/body interactions, current physics, and human consciousness, all of which helps us to understand subtle energy networks.

MIND/BODY INTERACTIONS

The interrelation of mental and emotional states to body physiology is well-known in counseling disciplines through recent advances in understanding stress responses. The American Psychological Association defines health psychology, or mind/body psychology, as an identified discipline that has its own national division for information exchange. Research in psychoneuroimmunology, the interactive study of psychology, neurology, and immune responses is expanding on an almost daily basis. Pert's (1997) research, for instance, demonstrates the direct effect of mental states or imagery on the production of chemical messengers, called endorphins, their interaction with neuroreceptors, and their impact on immune function. To paraphrase the title of Pert's book, we can literally speak of molecules of emotion that influence physiological functioning as much as known chemical influences do. The best-known current examples of mind/body therapies are stress management (Selye, 1978), training to activate the relaxation response (Benson, 1996; Stefano, Frichiore, Slinglsey, & Benson, 2001), various self-management practices such as meditation (Murphy & Donovan, 1997), the use of interactive guided imagery (Achterberg, Dossey, & Kolkmeier, 1994; Rossman, 1987), enhancing self-esteem through imagery (Joseph & Greenberg, 2001), and work to facilitate client self-expression (Cornell, 1994; Fox, 1995).

We now know that stimulation of defined aspects of the body can assist psychological functioning as well. For example, the simple work of bilateral hemispheric stimulation via visual, acoustic, or kinesthetic means helps to bring about normal processing the trauma, which releases "looping" behavior, that is, repeatedly reliving the trauma via flashbacks and nightmares. Although the exact mechanisms of this form of therapy, called Eye Movement Desensitization and Reprocessing (EMDR), are not fully understood (Shapiro, 1995), there is increasing neurological evidence that actual changes in brain wave patterns and brain processing occur that permit relief from looping (van der Kolk, McFarlane, & Weisaeth, 1996). Because of the client outcome research over the past 14 years, EMDR is now an accepted new modality for treating post-traumatic stress disorder (PTSD) and is continuing to bring remarkable results to clients in need (Phillips, 2000).

One possible model for energetic modalities that stimulate meridian acupoints, balance chakras, or smooth the biofield is that these actions also interrupt established looping patterns in the emotional neurological circuitry, just as the presumed mechanisms for EMDR do. Perhaps the very act of having clients touch their bodies in a purposeful way allows *psyche* and *soma* to integrate in new ways and changes, for example, the energetic signature of depression. As clients' cellular mechanisms remember their own harmony and rhythm toward self-healing, psychological rebalancing is supported as well.

Recently, some of the best-documented and most extensive examples of mind/body harmony come from the Institute of Heart Math (2001). The Institute uses heart-rate variability (HRV) as a measure of autonomic nervous system function; heart rate varies per minute based on contrasting aspects of the autonomic nervous system—the sympathetic (excitatory mechanisms) and parasympathetic (calming mechanisms). HRV demonstrates immune-enhancing effects of positive emotional states and the long-term immune-suppressive effects of negative emotions. More specifically, extensive research trials show that this variability is very high when clients experience frustration, decreases with caring and appreciation, and becomes near zero when subjects move to internal coherence or a centered state of mind (Slater, 2000, p. 145). "This work," writes physicist Tiller, "tends to suggest that the heart is the 'mainframe' of the body and that humans function best and most effectively when all the biological oscillators of the body take their lead from the heart" (1997, p. 227). The heart sends out the strongest electrical signal of any organ in the body, and when it is in balance, all body organs resonate to its frequency. In addition, the heart, energetically speaking, is the seat of human connectiveness, acceptance, and forgiveness. We can surmise the importance of establishing heart-centered balance for healing work (discussed in chapter 6).

HRV research shows us that when clients learn to be more caring toward themselves through energetic approaches, they begin to bring significant changes to their whole body/mind system. Human caring, a benevolent heart vibration, results in profound electrophysiological changes (McCraty, Atkinson, & Tiller, 1993). In addition, it is possible that as we develop our therapeutic counseling skills, we also develop ever-expanding sets of caring structures in our neural and subtle energy networks. As we consciously choose to center and focus, we develop internal coherence that allows discrete shifts from random thoughts and feelings toward maximum mental coherence.

Through awareness of these mind/body mechanisms we come to the importance of thought and consciousness in healing endeavors. Behind all the possible mechanisms in psychoenergetic work is the operator— the minds of the client and therapist that effect thousands of complex interactive processes to access new possibilities. Let us turn now to studies of consciousness and the power of human intention.

CURRENT UNDERSTANDINGS IN PHYSICS

The advent of quantum mechanics in the middle of the 20th century marked the development of concepts in physics that superceded Ein-

stein's theories and demonstrated a world of remarkable interconnect-
edness (Freeman, 1990; Lindley, 1996). Bell's theorem (Bell, 1964) irrev-
ocably demonstrated the interrelationship of subatomic particles to each
other over distance and time, while recent experiments confirm instan-
taneous communication between previously entangled photons over
vast distances (Watson, 1997).

In this strange new understanding of the world, mind is much more
than the cells of the brain. Beyond the cells, brain, and individual human
being, there seems to be a larger, nonlocal frequency that permits
instant communication and alignment to a higher vibration that for now
exceeds our capacities for comprehension (Dossey, 1989). Tiller suggests that our present model of a four- dimensional world is simply too
limiting to encompass all observed phenomena. He proposes a ten-
dimensional universe that allows for a much wider perspective and from
which solutions, in harmony with natural principles, are simple to derive
(1997, pp. 41–92). Such a model would encompass events we currently
deem to be nonlinear inconsistencies or paranormal phenomena, such as
the dual nature of light as both wave and particle and the change in
quantum particles as soon as human consciousness enters the picture.
The possibility, for instance, that a minute change in electron structure
can influence a whole system to change and access new probabilities is
borne out by quantum theory. We experience these kinds of shifts in
everyday events when we have sudden emotional insight or breakthrough ideas. On a more global scale, we are learning that minute
changes in ocean currents and temperature can affect global climates for
decades (Zachos, Pagani, Sloan, Thomas, & Billups, 2001).

Another way of understanding the principles of nature is to look at
the organizing energy blueprints (called L fields, or life fields) that seem
to precede actual physical life and appear to be connected to a larger
unifying principle. Over 50 years ago, Yale anatomist Burr (1972) per-
formed extensive experiments with these life fields and determined that
the information for cellular formation exists as an electrical field prior to
molecular development. In a similar vein, biologist Sheldrake speaks of
shape-generating patterns that carry genetic messages and information
from one generation to the next (Sheldrake, 1981, 1988). These morphogenetic fields, as he calls them, suggest that human beings, as well
as other forms of life, are oscillating energy fields that have intrinsic harmonious rhythms and patterns of balance. Any disturbance in this harmony—for example, when we have an anxious thought—creates a
disequilibrium, perturbation, or disruption in the overall balance of the
field. But when a strong harmonizing rhythm is applied to this vibrational field—for example, when we stimulate acupoints—the disturbed

portion will entrain back to coherence and orderliness. Thus, when we give energetic interventions—stimulating acupoints, balancing the qi of the chakras, or clearing the biofield—we may be creating repatterning that allows the morphogenetic field to return to its highest vibration and unifying principle.

STUDIES OF HUMAN CONSCIOUSNESS

Physicists, physical scientists, and social scientists all seem to be arriving at the same conclusion—that everything is influenced by human consciousness, defined psychologically as the total impressions, thoughts, and feelings of an individual. We are learning that directed, focused human intention to help someone in need is a powerful force for psychological change. If clients are able to incorporate their intention via focused choice and balanced energies, the likelihood of positive outcomes undoubtedly increases.

In addition, new studies are demonstrating that consciousness may influence matter directly. Physicists Goswami and associates (Goswami, Reed, & Goswami, 1995) propose that consciousness is the formative principle for the generation of matter; consciousness is a unifying, nonlocal form of mind that seems to generate the information-bearing field. Psychologist David Chamberlain (1998) has worked for 30 years to establish that the minds of pre-born and newborn babies have much more knowledge and understanding than could have been learned by the newly formed neurological structures during the gestation period alone. Another psychologist, Paul Pearsall (1998) extensively researched the extraordinary experiences of transplant patients who were able to "remember" details from their donor's life. The possibility of such transcendent consciousness requires willingness to go beyond our usual modes of understanding, certainly beyond our present four-dimensional model of the universe.

But it does not take great stretches of our imaginations to comprehend the influence of focused attention on something as technically neutral as a random number generator (RNG). Building on research begun by Princeton professor Roger Nelson, Dean Radin and his associates (1996, 1998) were able to identify influences that make the RNG less random. The RNG machine generates chance events just like an electronic coin flipper does and therefore has an average of zero order, i.e., its results are totally random, with a 50/50 chance of producing "0" or "1" over many trials permitting meta-analysis of millions of events. At the time of nationally televised events such as the opening ceremonies of the Olympic Games, computations on the RNG showed that randomness decreased and that there was a statistically significant increase in orderliness toward generating "1's." Radin and his researchers conclude that the more focused the attention of large numbers of people, the more random events move toward increasing order; the focused attention of millions of people influences a device as neutral as the RNG. In other words, as the mind moves, so seemingly does matter.

The pervasive influence of mind over distances is further supported by studies dealing with the effects of prayer (Dossey, 1993) and the imagery studies of Braud and Schlitz (1989) in which subjects focused on centering and a sense of union with their Higher Power. In the latter, numerous experiments demonstrated that focused intention with visualization from 20 meters away could influence electrodermal activity, blood pressure, tension headaches, and sympathetic nervous system activation. If human consciousness is this pervasive, Tiller (1997, p. 285) warns that current research designs with the presence of sizeable control groups may, in fact, dilute experimental effects, particularly those measuring subtle energies.

Intentionality is a special kind of human consciousness. Gough and Shacklett (1993, p. 198) describe intention as focused choice that engenders four physiological consequences—"intensity of feelings, heart-felt motivation, lowered heart-rate variability, and brain hemisphere synchronization." As practitioners of energy therapies, we will therefore do well for ourselves and our clients by clearly identifying our intentions. The ability to maintain centered intention distinguishes experts from novices, and "intention may add to the effect of an energetic healing treatment by increasing the intensity of heart-felt caring, the sense of peace due to decreased heart-rate variability, and increased brain wave synchronicity between client and healer" (Slater, 2000, p. 146).

Numerous studies on established energy healers reveal that these individuals hold unique brain wave properties: Fahrion and associates (1992) showed that healing practitioners produce high-amplitude alpha (slow) brain waves, while Wilson (1993) demonstrated that energy-healing practitioners shift low-frequency, high-amplitude brain wave patterns to their temporal brain lobes which are associated with more intuitive, analog thinking. Stravena (2000) studied Krieger and numerous Therapeutic Touch practitioners to prove that they produced synchronous slow brain wave patterns, and the experiences of centered therapists and clients produced the most consistent therapeutic effects, such as relaxation and pain relief (Zimmerman, 1990).

Psychoenergetic therapies operate as a form of mind/body modality that is facilitated through the therapist's coherent focus, knowledge, and

skill. The practitioner's intention helps clients to release vibrational disturbances and to establish new patterns in alignment with their highest
good.

To date, we know that the true mechanisms of energetic interventions
for emotional healing cannot be delineated by empirical science alone.
There is an incredible flexibility within the human biocomputer that
permits willing clients to change the electronic data laid down many
years ago while experiencing trauma. Furthermore, clients are able to
restructure their old, repeated patterns into new insights based on the
fresh information gathered in a counseling session. Thus we may define
psychoenergetic healing as the creative act of reorganizing the past to
understand the present and to attract an effective future.

Part II

The Human
Vibrational Matrix

Chapter 5

The Human Biofield

The concept of "field" provides a means of perceiving people and their respective environments as irreducible wholes. —Martha Rogers (1970)

ANGELINA'S STORY

In the early 1980s, while consulting for a hospice in the Southeast, I met a fascinating middle-aged woman named Angelina. She was a Mexican clinical social worker who had grown up in the ghettos of New York City. After a few sessions we established strong rapport.

Unexpectedly, a medical crisis of acute renal failure changed her life. She was given a diagnosis of end-stage renal dysfunction, which meant no possible recovery of kidney function; death would ensue from systemic uremia within a few days unless renal dialysis was instituted or Angelina received a kidney transplant. Since there were no available donors for a transplant, Angelina chose dialysis, which meant that for three days a week she would be hooked up to a kidney center machine that cleansed and exchanged her blood over a four-hour period. I supported her through this difficult transition time by making hospital visits, praying, and maintaining a sense of hopefulness for the future despite the exceedingly grim diagnosis.

After the acute stages, Angelina resumed her counseling appointments with me, coming in right after one of her dialysis treatments. It took only a quick, intuitive look to discern that there had been a massive shift in Angelina's whole energy dynamic since our previous meeting. There seemed to be jagged, irregular edges around her head; she reported feeling "scattered, fragmented, and disconnected." She could barely speak. Clearly, cognitive therapy could not touch such pervasive systemic disruption. We later agreed there were psychological, physiological, and energetic components to this disturbance—and called it a *psychoenergetic imbalance*. At the moment, however, we both asked for guidance in finding what would be most helpful. I remembered material I had read about Therapeutic Touch, the work used in nursing to rebalance the human energy field. While Angelina relaxed in a recliner, I moved my hands a few inches over her body, from head to toe several times, to smooth the jagged edges I could feel around her body. Later, I learned that this process was akin to Krieger's "clearing or unruffling" (Krieger, 1993) and Mentgen's "magnetic full-body unruffle" (Hover-Kramer, 1996).

At the time, I only paid attention to the outcome. In less than 5 minutes, my client breathed several deep sighs and relaxed; her blood pressure stabilized, her pulse became regular. She sat up, smiled, and said, "I feel oriented and together." A deep and constructive therapy session followed.

My curiosity ignited by this unusual event, I read all the available literature on dialysis and its possible effects on the mind and body. Studies were beginning to report the profound effects of kidney dialysis on the human psyche, as well as physical after-effects such as erratic blood pressure and irregular heartbeats. I also devoured books and studies about Therapeutic Touch and later helped to found the Healing Touch program through the support of the American Holistic Nurses' Association. But for now, Angelina and I had learned valuable lessons about her treatment—the need for active emotional support that included frequent energetic rebalancing to treat massive psychoenergetic disturbances triggered by dialysis procedures.

REALITY OF PSYCHOENERGETIC IMBALANCE

With this direct introduction to the reality of psychoenergetic distress, I began to notice that many of my clients also had disturbances in the flow of vital life force, which impacted their sense of inner harmony and balance. It was as if some almost visible blockage impeded the possibility of symmetry in the area immediately surrounding the body. This imbalance in what we now term the biofield was easiest to sense in clients with known physical illness such as cancer or immune deficiency syndrome. Often, the affected part of the body would appear darker or less vibrant to me. Clients with other long-term physical illness had similar patterns: fullness around the head while the rest of the body felt flat or depleted. It was as if an expansion of mental and intuitive capacities was compensating for the diminished vitality in the rest of the body.

I also began to notice distorted areas, or blockage, in the fields of those clients suffering from acute emotional distress. Undoubtedly, most therapists have noticed a sense of heaviness in depressed clients, as if they were carrying some tremendous load. This intuitive perception may be an accurate reflection of the actual effects of depression on the biofield. Similarly, we may notice excess energy in clients who are agitated or anxious. The flow of qi may be erratic, scattered, or come in spurts, much like the pattern of pressured speech or tangential thought that we observe in such clients.

Over the past 20 years, my perceptions as a therapist have been enhanced by allowing an intuitive sense about a client's energy configuration to come to me at the beginning of each session. I notice the differences as compared with previous sessions—how a client greets me, how he/she moves, the body language, and the expressions of thought. Sometimes, an image or word comes to me. At other times, I will use a quick hand scan, as detailed later, to give me feedback about patterns in the client's biofield.

Usually, I ask clients to tell me about their energy levels as a form of self-report. Although energy concepts are still new to Western scientific language, few clients have difficulty describing their energy states. Comments such as "I'm depleted (of energy); I'm dragging; I'm fragmented; I need my batteries need to be charged; I feel scattered, or pulled, or pushed; and I'm falling apart" are so common in our vernacular that we may not think of them as a communication about internal energy states. These statements of self-report can allow us to "see" the overall condition of the client, especially if we make an image of the statements. Naturally, energetic perceptions are not intended to replace the solid diagnostic efforts reflected in the *DSM-IV*, but these perceptions add another level of understanding to our clients' dilemmas and needs. In addition, assessment of a client's energetic condition permits us to make specific interventions that help to reestablish balance.

For example, if I sense a diminished flow of energy in a client's field, I might encourage movement or specific interventions to activate the flow of qi. If a client is agitated or anxious, a number of interventions are effective in calming the ruffled, disturbed energy. Such interventions at the beginning of each session may actually help the client to be more sensitive to the therapeutic relationship and to the learning of new insights. Once the client's biofield is balanced, increased resources, such as clear cognitions and insights, are more available for addressing specific issues.

THE HUMAN BIOFIELD

We begin our discussion with the biofield in light of the practices of TherapeuticTouch and its first cousin, Healing Touch, two of the best-known energy-healing therapies. Over the past 100 years, the idea of a field, to describe invisible, nonmaterial, influencing emanations from one object to another has become common in scientific terminology. For example, the electromagnetic "envelope" generated by a dynamo is called its electromagnetic field. Increasing evidence from quantum mechanics holds that all bodies—from atoms, to insects, animals, humans, even the great earth—have their own fields, regardless of size (Capra, 1977, p. 196). These fields are continuously interacting with each other—take, for example, the well-established fact that some human emotional states vary with the seasons, the sun's magnetic storms, and lunar cycles. Recent research also confirms what was predicted in quantum mechanics, that photons can demonstrate instant communication with each other over great distances (Watson, 1997). As we are continually influenced by each other's interactive fields and those of our environment at very subtle levels, phenomena of telepathy and remote viewing become more understandable.

Michael Faraday, the 19th-century British physicist, saw with intuitive perception the lines of force surrounding magnets. He called them "force fields" and used this perception to describe the action of electrons traveling along a current (Dossey, 2000, p. 109). Faraday also sensed that the entire universe is made up of these force fields, and he perceived light as a form of electromagnetic radiation long before science could prove the nature of light as both wave and particle.

The animal kingdom makes good use of the reality of fields in a variety of ways. Sharks and rays, for instance, have electroreceptors that help them find future meals (all living organisms emit electromagnetic vibrations). These fields can be detected over more than a mile away in murky oceans by gifted predators. Bees and migratory birds seem to have slightly different mechanisms for reaching their far-flung destinations. Using the magnetite in their brain cells they are able to sense the direction of their goal, which emits a form of magnetic vibration that establishes its relationship to earth's magnetic north pole (Levy, 1999).

It appears, then, that the energy field is a fundamental unit of all matter that is especially prominent in living systems. It is not so much that we *have* an energy field but rather that we *are* a complex vibrational matrix of subtle energies. The physical body is the most visible and dense form of our electromagnetic energy, while the biofield is more diffuse and far-reaching.

THERAPEUTIC TOUCH

Work with interactive fields has been developed in nursing to assist in relieving anxiety and pain in hospital settings. In 1970, long before scientific documentation of the interconnections of human beings with their social and natural environments was available, prominent nursing theorist Martha Rogers published her concepts of the human energy field in the *Science of Unitary Man*. She described her ideas, based on extensive study of quantum mechanics and physics, as follows:

> An energy field identifies the conceptual boundaries of man. This field is electrical in nature, is in a continual state of flux, and varies continuously in its intensity, density, and extent. . . . The human field is postulated to have its boundary continuous with the boundary of the environment. The environment is, itself, an energy field electrical in nature. The interaction between the human field and the environmental field takes place across the conceptual boundaries of these two fields which together are co-extensive with the universe. (Rogers, 1970, p. 90)

Thus we have an early formulation of the irreducible nature of the human being as an energy field that is interactive with other biofields. This became the conceptual foundation for the use of noninvasive, energetic interventions to assist someone in whom the field was impaired, blocked, or depleted. Dolores Krieger, co-founder with Dora Kunz of Therapeutic Touch, was one of Rogers's students at New York University. Together they posited that the nurse/patient relationship is an interaction between two human biofields—the field of the nurse and that of the patient. As teachings around this metaphor advanced, Krieger found that the practitioner who was centered, focused, and intentional was more effective in assisting distressed patients presumed to have a blocked or impaired flow of energy in their biofields. After centering themselves, caregivers learned to assess the biofield for irregularities with their hands. Based on these observations, caregivers could "clear" a congested area of the patient's biofield and bring enhanced balance by holding their stilled hands over imbalanced areas. They called the work Therapeutic Touch, which is basically a four-phase process to correct imbalance in the biofield. The four phases, briefly, are *centering* of the practitioner, *assessment* of the client's field, *unruffling* or *clearing* the disturbed energy pattern in the client's field, and *modulating energy* by holding focus over the affected area or the entire field until a sense of balance and harmony is restored.

So new were the ideas of interacting energy-fields 30 years ago that early practitioners called themselves "Krieger's Krazies" as a way of bonding with each other in the face of massive public skepticism. However, no one could argue with the outcomes of this seemingly strange procedure. Generally, deep relaxation, pain relief, increased sense of well-being, and increased immune function have been established as the outcomes of Therapeutic Touch interventions. Since that time, both Therapeutic Touch and Healing Touch have become nationally and internationally recognized, reaching hundreds of thousands of caregivers and their clients. In many modern hospitals, energy-healing protocols are accepted nursing procedures while energy-field disturbance is an identified nursing diagnosis (North American Nursing Diagnosis Association, 1996). Today, many consumers of health care request energy healing before and after surgery or other medical procedures to find relief from anxiety, reduce pain, and relax more fully. Medication and surgery, the established bastions of modern medicine, are complemented with energetic interventions to bring about the multidimensional healing that therapists and consumers of health care have come to value.

DESCRIPTIONS OF THE BIOFIELD

The human biofield is a subtle form of electromagnetic emanation that extends beyond the physical body. Much like earth's magnetosphere or energy field, the biofield was presumed to exist long before scientific measurements could ascertain its existence. Just recently, spacecraft technology using photon and neutral atom imaging and radio-sounding techniques provided global shots of earth's magnetosphere (Burch et al., 2001). Undoubtedly, we will also develop sophisticated means to "see" the human biomagnetic field and its different frequency bands in more detail. At this time, feedback from the SQUID (superconducting quantum interference device) has established that the human subtle energy field exists and that it appears to vary with the health of the individual. James Oschman, a psychologist and researcher, corroborates this: "From the research done over the last few decades, we can definitely conclude that living organisms have biomagnetic fields around them; that these fields change from moment to moment in relation to events taking place inside the body; and that these fields give a clearer representation of what is going on in the body than the classical electrical diagnostic tools such as the electrocardiogram and the electroencephalogram" (Oschman, 1998, p. 122).

To elaborate further, depleted or diminished areas in the biofield suggest possible physical dysfunction, while a very strong, symmetrical emanation appears indicative of health and high-level functioning. Figure 5.1 is a representation of the biofield with its layers and energy vortices, intuited from the work of major healing artists throughout history.

According to energy-healing practitioners, the biofield varies with the physical and psychological health of the individual. A highly functioning, focused, and intentional healer may have smooth, strong emanations

Figure 5.1
HUMAN BIOFIELD AND INTUITED LAYERS

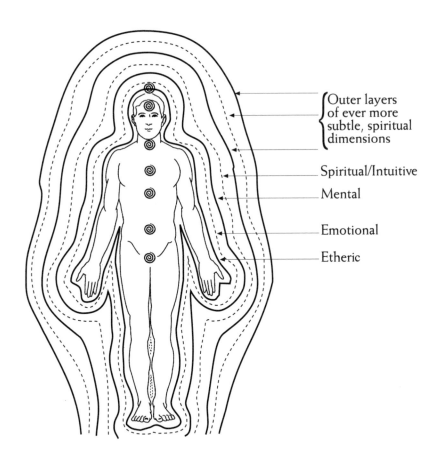

{ Outer layers of ever more subtle, spiritual dimensions

Spiritual/Intuitive

Mental

Emotional

Etheric

that extend 5 to 15 feet beyond the physical body, whereas an ill or emotionally stressed individual may have a wispy or fragmented field that may be much harder to detect. The biofield also seems to protect the physical body. A full, intact biofield seems to allow tension or even trauma to "bounce off" with minimal damage, whereas a person with a disturbed or diminished field seems to suffer frequent accidents and psychological injury. This may explain why a relatively simple injury may have disastrous effects on one individual but a major accident may leave another relatively unharmed. Physically and psychically, we are better off when we have balanced, intact biofields with their associated sense of inner harmony and peace. Put another way, when we are psychoenergetically balanced, we are much more resilient to life's many stressors.

The biofield is intimately connected to the multidimensional nature of healing as well. For example, the experience of only a fender-bender or slight accident can leave us shaken and feeling disconnected, even though there is no detectable physical damage. This suggests that some form or rebalancing is required to bring the emotional, mental, and spiritual dimensions back into realignment even after minor trauma. We can well imagine, then, that major physical trauma and/or emotional injury might require more extensive attention to relieve psychoenergetic disturbances. Many of our clients have experienced surgical interventions that left them feeling depleted for weeks, although the skin wound mended quickly. If we think of healing as a multidimensional process involving the whole person, we can understand the need for rebalancing the entire vibrational matrix, an idea that has been missing from the technological emphasis of most medical practice.

One of the most devastating impacts on the human biofield seems to be the loss of hope, causing spiritual depletion in the outer layers. This depletion may gradually affect other dimensions, which may lead to the formation of limiting beliefs, or negative emotions, and finally to the development of physical symptoms. Although scientific evidence is not yet conclusive, it is believed that a significant loss of hope, 18 to 36 months prior, may be involved in the onset of cancer symptoms in adults (Simonton, Matthews-Simonton, & Creighton, 1981). Early interventions, such as psychotherapy and psychoenergetic balancing, can therefore be significant in preventing life-threatening illnesses linked to despair, grief, or constricting emotions.

CLINICAL APPLICATIONS

No lasting clinical outcomes, cognitive or psychoenergetic, can occur if the client's biofield is in a state of disarray. This is true for the therapist as well, because we communicate our state of consciousness in treatment settings via our subtle energies, whether we are aware of these energies or not. Clients cannot learn or integrate new information if their biofield is distorted or if they are receiving confusing messages from the therapist. We might liken pervasive biofield imbalance to having a fine car in which one is unable to start the engine, or to having a machine that is not plugged into its power source. Many clients who have long-term biofield disturbances report a lifetime of dissatisfaction, depression, difficulty following directions, perceptual distortions, and, often, a history of seeing many therapists. Short-term psychoenergetic disturbance, as the one described in Angelina's case, is usually situational, related to acute trauma. Both conditions respond to centering interventions, such as the ones listed here and in chapter 10. The only difference is that one or two centering practices may be sufficient for the acute situation, whereas long-term imbalance may require frequent repetition over many weeks before the client is truly ready for other forms of therapy. Addressing specific issues before clients are able to establish and maintain psychoenergetic balance is the primary cause of treatment failure from an energy psychotherapy perspective.

For the practitioner, centering or focusing is taught in most energy- healing practices, especially in Therapeutic Touch and Healing Touch classes. Since the biofield of the therapist is interactive with the client's, the integrity of the therapist's field is crucial in assisting the client's energy to move to a higher vibrational pattern. Therapist energy hygiene is therefore an essential part of our preparation, and some of the processes described here have value for personal centering.

The following biofield exercises are written so that you can use them in teaching clients. These exercises can, of course, be used alone or in combination with other practices that have the intent of balancing the biofield and increasing readiness for treatment. Clinician discretion and skill is required in considering appropriate clients for these interventions and in maintaining good rapport.

Exercise 1. Centering

You might begin the treatment phase of a client session with the following: "This is one of the many centering practices that allows a sense of inner focus to develop. Each time you repeat this exercise you may notice changes in your breathing or your level of attention."

   1. *"While sitting comfortably, release the breath fully with a sigh, or as if you're blowing out a candle. Do this 2 to 3 times more while imaging stress and ten-*

sion flowing out through your hands and feet. The in-breath will naturally be deeper as your proceed."

2. "Allow yourself to image a peaceful place in nature, seeing, hearing, feeling, even smelling it. Feel the peacefulness filling your body with light and warmth. Continue to release for now any tension or emotional distress with the breath."

3. "After several minutes, notice how you feel, and share any images or ideas that came to you."

Exercise 2. Brush Down

1. "While thinking of a recent stressful event, set your intent to release its effects. While sitting or standing, allow yourself to take a deep breath and let it go, fully releasing pressure and tension to the earth. Again, breathe and let any remaining tension flow out through your hands and feet. "

2. "Bring your hands above your head on the next in-breath and breathe out fully while gently brushing downward head to toe. Allow a sigh or groan to help release the tension fully as the hands touch the floor. "

3. "Continue releasing with the out-breath, brushing from under each arm, the upper and lower back, and the groin area."

4. "Notice how you feel after 3 to 5 minutes of this exercise."

Exercise 3. The Central Alignment

"Here is another centering practice that allows a sense of personal integration to develop and can be used frequently throughout the working day."

1. "Standing or sitting comfortably, visualize a vibrant line of energy that flows through the center of your body in relation to your head and spine. See the connection from the base of the spine and through the feet to the very core of the earth."

2. "Place your hands on the gravitational center of the body, which is an inch or so below the navel. You will always move in balanced ways when your focus is on this hara area, which is a yoga point for physical focusing. Visualize the connection between the hara and the earth's core."

3. "Let your awareness shift as you move one hand to the upper mid-chest while keeping the other hand on the hara. The upper mid-chest is considered the 'soul seat,' the area where we begin to experience our sense of personal purpose and meaning. Allow the connection between the two hands to strengthen while breathing fully. Continue to feel the grounding to the earth."

4. "While keeping one hand on the hara, move the other hand from the mid-chest to the crown of the head. Then stretch this hand upward to your favorite celestial star. Sense the alignment between all parts of your unique energy line—the hara, the soul seat, your star, and the connection to the earth."

5. "Allow a sense of color or sound to assist your image of this central line.

Some people 'see' vibrant images of the spiral double helix, the structural arrangement of DNA, as they do this exercise."

6. "Gently return to full awareness, letting your hands drop, noting changes is your body and mind. Practice walking around the room with your sense of this central alignment. Notice your feelings as you imagine walking like this while dealing with a difficult situation at work or at home."

Chapter 6

The Chakras and Their Psychological Meaning

If one is to explore the world of inner experiences, his thoughts, his emotions and learn about himself, he must have some framework in which to do this. . . . The framework provided by understanding the centers of consciousness (chakras) gives him a place to do this. It provides the student with a structured inner space in which he can play.

—Rama, Ballentine, and Ajaya (1981)

The word chakra means "wheel" or "vortex" in Sanskrit, suggesting a whirling center of human energy, or qi. There are seven major energy vortices that form an essential component of the human vibrational matrix; in addition, there are minor energy vortices at each joint in the human body. Because the seven major chakras have a direct relationship to the physical body, they are the easiest for clients to sense. These seven energy centers are located along the midline and human spine, from the base of the tailbone to the area above the top of the head (see Figure 6.1). And they are known in some form in all human cultures, perhaps because they have roots in many native healing traditions long before written communication developed.

Chakras relate directly to the human *soma* (body) and *psyche* (soul). They can readily be sensed in some way by even the most concrete thinkers, the 60% of the population Aron (1997) calls "insensitive." Thus the chakras give access to somatic and psychological awareness in persons who might otherwise reject the reality of personal intuition and inner awareness.

Figure 6.1
HUMAN BIOFIELD AND ENERGY CENTERS

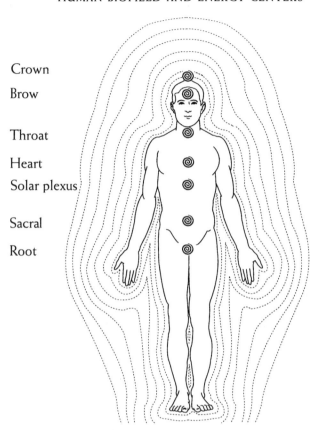

Crown

Brow

Throat

Heart

Solar plexus

Sacral

Root

The physical, emotional, mental, and spiritual aspects of optimally functioning chakras are described in many current works (Dale, 1998; Hover-Kramer, 1996, 2002; Judith, 1996; Motoyama, 1995) and have been extensively explored in classical texts as well (Goswami, 1999; Leadbeater, 1927). Each author brings unique perceptions and interpretations; no two texts describe the chakras in exactly the same way, confirming how individual differences and perceptions differ. The discussion here is based on my extensive reading and many years of counseling, which included work with the chakras. While these understandings are by no means exhaustive, they capture the flavor, dynamic, and psychological functions of the energy centers.

Impaired, blocked, or diminished chakra functions have profound effects on all dimensions of our well-being. Understanding this has direct implications for client assessment and application of the healing interventions that we will be discussing. Sometimes, one or more chakras may have excessive qi, resulting from overcompensation for lesser vitality in another area. We will be discussing the implications of diminished or excessive qi in relation to each chakra as well.

The chakras seem to act like energy transfer stations. That is, they allow the inflow of qi from the energy in the universe to enter the human organism. They allow this qi to be dispersed throughout the individual's system, and they permit release, or outflow, of excessive, unneeded, or blocked energy. Because attention to the chakras is meaningful for physical as well as psychological healing, including the chakras in comprehensive energy psychotherapy is becoming more widely recognized (Grudermeyer, Grudermeyer, & Hover-Kramer, 2000; Hover-Kramer & Shames, 1997; Luthke & Stein-Luthke, 2001).

In my experience, nearly all clients can sense disturbance related to a specific chakra, since each chakra has well-known somatic links to parts of the body. For instance, fear of public speaking is most typically felt as "a knot or a sinking feeling" in the body's solar plexus area which corresponds to the third chakra. This center relates to one's sense of personal power and assertiveness. In another example, significant loss of money or a life-sustaining relationship affects the physical body near the base of the spine; persons describe this feeling as "the bottom dropping out." The first, or root, chakra is the center that relates to our sense of personal survival and safety and is hence most affected by experiences of personal insecurity.

Many clients experience the physical component of an affect-generating issue, whether they have knowledge of the chakras or not. Psychotherapeutic work with the chakras is, therefore, a powerful resource for increased somatic and psychological awareness. The chakras also facilitate the release of emotional distress and can assist in restoring a sense of harmony, as we will explore further on.

Table 6.1 gives an overview of the seven major human energy centers, the physical areas of the body most influenced by each vortex, the related glands of the endocrine network, and the psychological dynamic that influences the emotions, thought patterns, and spiritual sensitivity. Because each of these energy stations has a different vibrational signature, different colors and sound frequencies are emitted by each chakra as well. These different electromagnetic frequencies have been extensively studied by Valerie Hunt of UCLA, who compared the intuitive perceptions of a clairvoyant with the actual output measured by electronic spectography while subjects consciously focused attention on selected chakras (Hunt, 1995). In addition, there appears to be a cumu-

Table 6.1 OVERVIEW OF THE CHAKRAS AND THEIR ASSOCIATED PHYSICAL AND PSYCHOLOGICAL ATTRIBUTES

Location	Physical Area of Influence	Endocrinal Interface	Major Psychological Functions
Root (base of spine)	Feet, legs, hips, perineum	Adrenal glands	Experiencing survival and safety needs, as well as sense of vitality, joy
Sacral (below navel, at sacrum)	Lower abdomen, pelvis, large intestines	Reproductive organs	Feeling, letting emotions act as sensors, choosing, sexuality
Solar plexus (upper abdomen)	Pancreas, spleen, liver, stomach, and small intestines	Insulin production from pancreatic cells	Ego identity, sense of power, control, self-esteem
Heart (mid-chest)	Circulation and lymph flows	Thymus gland	Caring, compassion, forgiveness
Throat	Neck, voice, throat	Thyroid gland	Self-expression, creativity, humor, singing, writing
Brow (middle of forehead)	Face, eyes, ears, limbic system	Pituitary gland	Seeing clearly, insight, intuition, clairvoyance
Crown (top of head)	Brain, biological rhythms	Pineal gland	Sense of spiritual connectedness, transpersonal awareness

lative, supportive effect throughout the human energy system when focus shifts from the most simple frequency at the base of the spine to the ever-more subtle energies and higher vibrational patterns of the upper chakras.

PSYCHOLOGICAL DEVELOPMENT AND THE CENTERS OF CONSCIOUSNESS

Because the chakras seem to integrate all of our dimensions, physical as well as psychological and spiritual, they are often called "centers of consciousness" (Rama et al., 1981). From a developmental point of view, the chakras and their psychological functions correspond to our developmental life tasks. For instance, the identified life tasks and stages described by Erik Erikson (1970) begin with security issues of trust versus mistrust and end with adult later-life choices between generativity and stagnation, integrity and despair. The well-known hierarchy of needs of Abraham Maslow (1961), and his later work in understanding transcendence and spiritual oneness (Maslow, 1971), also parallel the psychological and spiritual aspects of the chakras. It is as if sages of the ancient yoga traditions knew something about distinctive stages of human psychological development.

It is relevant to define the chakras as centers of consciousness in light of their psychological functioning. The fact that each energy center also has association with important body organs, intersections of major blood vessels, nerve plexi, and endocrine glands gives us additional resources to help our clients in holistic, integrative ways. The easiest way to conceptualize the chakras is to image them associated with the area of the body to which they are in closest proximity. Let us look at each of the major chakras in more detail now.

The Root Center: Safety, Survival, and the Will to Live

The root chakra, located at the base of the spine, relates to the hips, legs, feet, and eliminative functions of the bladder and lower colon. It is connected to our most intrinsic survival mechanisms through the adrenal endocrine glands that both trigger our fight/flight response to stress (Selye, 1978) and release adrenaline for an extra surge of energy in times of peril. In this way, the root center is connected to our basic sense of vitality and aliveness. Nowhere is the mind/body connection more evident than in this survival mechanism. Unfortunately, modern life with its daily challenges of commuter traffic and interpersonal conflicts may trigger so many adrenaline surges that the adrenals can become exhausted. Repeated distress can cause the adrenals to produce the more harmful cortisol, affect the immune system, and bring on psychological effects like discouragement, depression, and decreased will to live (Kemeny, 2001).

Perceived or presumed dangers will trigger the adrenals' fight/flight response as much as an actual *in vivo* threat to life or limb. Each time we even imagine a dangerous situation, the sympathetic nervous system goes into high gear, repeating stress responses until they become a generalized adaptation. These adaptations may result in high blood pressure, called essential hypertension, decreased immune function, and such systemic illnesses as chronic fatigue immune deficiency syndrome (CFIDS, 1998), autoimmune diseases, and severe environmental allergies.

The fact that real or imagined stress has a large psychological component gives us opportunity to influence physiological mechanisms through mind/body energy-based interventions. The root chakra, for example, regulates the inflow of qi into our bodies as well as enhancing the inflow of vital life force to the entire vibrational matrix. Exercises like the Chakra Rotation, given later in this chapter, vitalize the entire system and may help to overcome early forms of energy depletion noted as heaviness or temporary fatigue. The longer a condition of depletion exists, of course, the more persistent the client may need to be in using these interventions to "jump start" the sloggy system.

In its optimum levels of functioning, the root chakra makes possible a steady inflow of energy that allows us to experience the full enjoyment of being alive. When this is coupled with realistic and appropriate trust, a sense of security pervades even in the face of life crises, and the person has confidence that the universe is basically friendly.

For many of our clients, this basic sense of security and safety is impaired due to life trauma or ongoing stress. Clients may speak of feeling "drained, exhausted, tired all the time," or "just barely hanging on." Some of our clients may be unsure about even wanting to live; they are filled with fear and self-doubt, without inner joy or enthusiasm. Others may overcompensate for life's insecurities by focusing excessively on material gains and greediness.

"Jack" was a client who seemed to be "in limbo," unwilling to commit to life. He sought medical help for a number of vague symptoms that could not be diagnosed. Out of sheer frustration, he turned to counseling. Jack had poor interpersonal relationships and no sense of life goals or purpose. Although he functioned as a high-level computer programmer, he characterized himself as simply going through the motions of being normal. Inside, he was awash in despair, which was reflected in his gray, vague, and tenuous affect. When asked about his will to live, he gave a blank stare and admitted never wanting to be alive. Since childhood, he had felt his birth was accidental and would be corrected sooner or later by some life-terminating disaster.

Obviously, there are many therapeutic approaches we might consider with such a client. From an energetic viewpoint, attention to the depleted root chakra with the Chakra Rotation exercise would help to start the dynamic flow of qi. Affirmations to support his ability to feel the body and enjoy his energy could follow full exploration of his feelings to release sadness and grief underlying the despair. As the flow of vitality increases through the root chakra, other energy centers become activated, a process known as the opening of the *kundalini* energy flow in yoga tradition (Kieffer, 1988). As the client becomes more engaged in life, he might develop interests that nourish him more than just to his computer job, perhaps owning a pet, engaging in a hobby, or connecting with nature. There is literally no limit to the creative options that therapist and client can explore once there is a healthy reconnection with the basic sense of security, trust, and aliveness.

The Sacral Center: Awareness of Feelings and Choices

The second energy vortex, located below the navel and at the sacral area of the back, is empowered by an open root center. Each chakra builds upon and is supported by the preceding lower center. The ability to feel emotions and make beneficial choices, two of the major psychological aspects of the sacral, requires the root center's connection with basic survival and a sense of confidence that one's life has meaning and purpose.

Since the sacral relates to the lower abdominal zone and the location of the reproductive organs, we conclude that it is associated with sexuality and the many choices that constructive relationships require. In addition, physical aspects of the lower abdominal area include assimilation of body foods and fluids, and the release of waste. In a similar vein, the emotional aspects of the sacral chakra are associated with recognizing feelings, integrating desirable emotions, releasing the negative, and choosing what is most desirable. The related developmental tasks have to do with autonomy to overcome self-doubt and to establish healthy attachments.

Needless to say, many clients have distortions, either depletion or excess of qi in this area. The lower abdominal part of the body is often guarded or protected, as seen in stooped body posture or in the presence of excess weight. From a therapeutic perspective, disturbance of this center can be seen in persons who have poor attachments, become co-dependent, have difficulty expressing their feelings, or use addictive substances to numb what they feel. On the one hand, we may see a person who has difficulty with intimate relationships and withdraws as a way of avoiding possible pain while, on the other hand, we may see a person who chooses compulsive means of feeling closer to others. Chemical dependency can include addictive use of drugs, alcohol, nicotine, caffeine, sugar, and even chocolate. And there can be behavioral addictions, such as sexual excesses, hysteria, and loyalty to others far beyond the reach of logical reason.

"Tracy," a very attractive psychology student, reported distress over arguments with her professors. As the counseling sessions proceeded, however, it became evident that she was constantly soothing her emotions with a variety of sexual partners. It was not until one man stole her possessions and emails to insure his absolute control over her that she realized her sexual adventures were becoming self-destructive. Her constant need for sexual reassurance had its roots in poor attachments with self-centered parents who themselves made poor choices, indulged in sexual promiscuity, and were involved in shady financial dealings.

Work with the sacral center first involved permission for Tracy to connect more deeply with her feelings. This resulted in intense expression of emotions around past events, as well as increased awareness of current sensitivities. When Tracy placed her hands over the sacral center, a flood of memories of abuse and neglect emerged spontaneously. Reconnecting with forgotten or repressed material brought relief, or catharsis, and required a number of sessions. Gradually, Tracy was able to see the depth of her sexual addiction and the need to make more life-supporting choices. The court process of applying for a restraining order to set boundaries with the controlling man was a valuable lesson. Through the lengthy legal proceedings, she was able to connect with a women's group that addressed sexual addiction and codependency issues. Gradually, she was able to rebuild a sense of healthy boundaries and self-esteem, listening to her feelings in the lower "gut" while thinking clearly about her future goals.

Some clients simply release intense distortions from the sacral area without specific cognitive detail. This is especially true if the repressed material is linked with childhood events from a precognitive stage of development or is related to "unspeakable" events such as abuse or sexual invasion. From this, we can note the relevance of energy methods for therapy with issues that are too deep-seated for purely cognitive approaches.

The Solar Plexus Center:
Assertiveness, Control, and Power

When security and issues of feelings are addressed, clients can move into the sense of personal power that is associated with the solar plexus chakra. This area constitutes a major intersection of blood vessels, nerve

ganglia, and essential body organs. It is, therefore, a place of great vul-
nerability; in boxing it is known as the "knock-out" point. In the energy
system, the solar plexus is the focal point of ego identity, clear thinking, decision-making, effective assertiveness, and problem solving.
Effective communication with others and ability to complete one's goals
are hallmarks of this center. Developmental tasks relate to industry, ability to get things done, and self-identity as opposed to role confusion.

Distortions in energy patterning of this chakra can again result in
diminished or excessive flow of qi to the area. High achievers and controlling, driven people show excessive qi in this chakra, while passive,
timid, or unassertive personalities are more likely to have energy defi-
ciencies. Very passive people often explode when situations become too
unbearable, which may result in the passive-aggressive behaviors that
often bring people into clinical treatment.

A successful businessman named "Tom" excelled in his career by
being compulsive and detail-oriented. At home, he was a virtual tyrant,
bossing and intimidating his children and telling his wife how to run "a
tight ship." Although the family looked prosperous, seeds of discontent
grew in unhealthy family interactions and finally resulted in acting-out
behavior from the teenagers.

The treatment plan for Tom's family was not limited to setting
boundaries with the teenagers; it called for assisting the family to devise
new ways of establishing and maintaining respectful relationships. From
an energy-oriented concept, Tom needed to learn to use his power, emanating from the third chakra, with wisdom. This meant reconnecting
with his root center issues to face fears of loss and basic insecurities. It
also required him to express feelings and needs, second chakra issues,
with the sensitivity that they deserved. Having accomplished these
developmental tasks, he learned to tread more lightly, balanced his over-
controlling style, and gradually began to enjoy his family more fully.

The lower three energy centers are linked with three essential psychological functions—our basic sense of security and vitality, the willingness to sense and connect with our emotions, and the ability to
communicate who we are effectively. Perhaps 90% of my clients have
some association with dysfunction in one or more of the lower three
centers. We will be exploring specific treatment issues and relevant
energetic approaches further, but first, a brief journey into the psychological meaning of the upper, more subtle energy centers.

The Heart Center: Unconditional Caring and Forgiveness

Heart-centered consciousness means unconditional caring and forgiveness toward others as well as oneself. This stands in strong contrast to

possessive, security-seeking, or sentimental forms of what is popularly called "love." It is fascinating to consider various forms of attachment disorders in light of the developmental issues of the lower three centers. For example, most popular love songs are actually about lower chakra issues such as abandonment, rejection, poor timing, blame of others, unwillingness to accept personal responsibility, disappointment due to lack of insight, and belief that there is only one person who can make us happy.

When the energy of the heart center is open and flowing, we find that our capacity for accepting others expands. Even though we may see another's faults, we no longer hold onto grudges and can forgive readily. More important, we learn to accept ourselves, including our shadow aspects and obvious failings. Burdens literally lighten as we open our hearts energetically. Being able to step back from over-involvement and to see things with a sense of humor become possible as we activate this chakra.

The heart center is pivotal, located halfway between the basic life tasks of the lower three centers and the more subtle energies of the three upper centers. Conscious alignment with the heart-centered vibration of caring and the strong electromagnetic emanations of the physical heart (as discussed in chapter 4) gives coherence to human intention and brings the multidimensional body to harmony. Heart-centered consciousness is, thus, the optimal state for anyone wishing to help others.

For many people, the heart center never had an opportunity to develop because the issues of the lower centers drained the energetic flow needed to support higher-level development. This would be true for people who make lukewarm commitments, lack emotional self-understanding, or have low self-esteem. We appropriately speak of such a person as being "half-hearted." True caring for others can only emerge out of the fullness of an open heart center that is supported by a solid foundation.

The developmental tasks associated with the heart chakra are, thus, healthy self-respect and intimacy as opposed to isolation. Distortions of the heart center are often linked to the will to do good without having the adequate psychological preparation needed. Although many philosophies and disciplines teach the need to serve others, few teach the basic requirements of self-nurturing that are needed to reach out to others with caring, patience, forgiveness, and a sense of humor.

For example, "Jim" a young-adult client, recalled being beaten by the teaching nuns in his parish for keeping allowance money in his pocket. In the name of their religious order, they ridiculed him in front of his class for treasuring his hard-earned coins. In spite of having chosen a caregiving profession, the teachers apparently had limited self-esteem: there was no energy with which to give to others or to appreciate a young boy's achievements.

The optimal energy of the heart chakra is to give and receive warmth and caring in a continuous pattern of inflow and outflow of qi. Much like the breath, this flow is steady and life-giving. Ideally, this open-hearted style is one we would wish for our clients' well-being; it is also one we might incorporate into our therapeutic style.

The Throat Center: Creativity and Self-Expression

The outflow of creative self-expression comes from the deepening sense of self-esteem when the lower chakras are activated. Almost any activity has the potential for innovation and play—making a place of beauty in one's home, writing a letter or poem, singing a song, sharing an idea. One of the easiest ways for many of us to move into higher levels of awareness is to connect with nature by looking at a picture, touching the earth, listening to a birdsong, or feeling the sun on our skin.

When the flow of qi is impaired in the throat chakra, we notice various forms of holding back. In clients we might see hesitant speech, unwillingness to share inner thoughts, lack of permission to speak out or to be heard. Self-absorption and stagnation are characteristic of adults who were told as children to be quiet or polite. The inner critic, in the form of internalized parental injunctions, limits spontanaeity, playfulness, and creativity.

The release of these blockages, once the kundalini flow is activated, may result in an outpouring of ideas and various forms of self-expression. It is essential that budding attempts at such generativity be free from criticism. Therefore, beginning development of creativity often requires safety and freedom from negative self-talk, which we can provide in counseling settings.

The Brow Center: Seeing with Intuition and Compassion

The development of intuition is related to the brow chakra; this mid-brow area has been referred to as the "third eye" since ancient times. As we accomplish the developmental tasks of the lower centers, our capacity for insight and empathy for others emerges. Intuition is simply the ability to feel into someone else's situation and to access the capacity of self-reflection. This sensitivity is something that most of us have learned over time as therapists, and something that may be very difficult for our clients while they are struggling with life problems. As intuitive capacity develops, we may be able to hear, see, or sense events in someone's life as if we were watching a movie sequence.

Constriction of qi in the brow area is present when we make excessive judgments of self or others and cannot comprehend someone's dilemmas with compassion. This lack of insight can seriously inhibit the development of deep, satisfying relationships and personal enjoyment. A feeling of existential despair may pervade and limit our sense of inner integrity and wholeness.

Another serious distortion of this center occurs when individuals want to be intuitive without taking on the learning tasks of the lower centers. The wish for transcendence and quick intuitive perception has led to many ill-fated explorations with drugs or the seeking out of quick fix approaches. The result, unfortunately, can be the energetic equivalent of running a 220-volt current through wiring that only has 110-volt capacity. In other words, the individual may literally burn out energy sensitivities through impatience, with the possibility of suffering lifelong physical and emotional damage as a result.

From this discussion we see that intuition is a gift that can and does develop naturally as we mature. However, there are no shortcuts or spiritual bypasses. Superficial attempts to adopt someone else's path to intuition, like relying on psychic readings or following a guru, usually are not effective in the long run. The path to compassion and intuitional clarity—*clairvoyance* (clear seeing), *clairaudience* (clear hearing, listening with the third ear), and *clairsentience* (clear feeling, or intuitive sensing)—has to develop in unique ways within each person.

The Crown Center: Connecting to the Transpersonal

The open and flowing crown center connects us to dimensions that are beyond our personal selves. The transpersonal realm may involve a sense of a personal connection to a higher power or simply a sense of being in harmony with the world of nature. Expression of this dimension is highly individualistic because each person has distinctive ways of understanding spirituality. There is a sense of joy and peacefulness when we are able to sense the crown center after having accomplished other developmental tasks. There may be momentary glimpses of unity with higher will for our lives, a sense of a mystical experience, or a sense of knowing at the deepest level.

In many traditions of yoga, the crown center is perceived to have one to five additional subtle energy chakras above it (Goswami, 1999, p. 256), each pointing to different stages of spiritual development. Achieving *sahasrara*, unity or oneness with the divine qualities, is understood as the highest possible level of human development. This state of consciousness is imaged as an umbrella that protects the lower aspects and as a beautiful lotus blossom with a thousand petals.

More recently, Maslow began to write about transpersonal consciousness—what he called the final stage of human development—during the last two years of his life after a near-fatal heart attack (Cleary & Shapiro, 1995). He spoke of a state of consciousness that has no particular emotion other than the joyous contemplation of being. In contrast to his earlier work with "peak experiences" and emotional development toward self-actualization, Maslow called this state the "high plateau"; it is akin to what we call crown-centered consciousness here. As described by a major Maslow biographer, "The high plateau always has a noetic and cognitive element. . . . It is far more volitional than the peak experience; for example, a mother who sits quietly gazing at her baby playing on the floor beside her" (Hoffman, 1988, p. 340).

Technically, there are no distortions in the crown center since we are always connected to our source of vitality. However, we can easily limit our beliefs about our infinite potentials and resources. It is as if we forget our true selves by choosing to focus on some present distress rather than on our full capacities. We may obsess about clouds on a rainy day instead of remembering the eternal presence of the sun beyond them. Consciously reconnecting with all of our energy centers maintains a vitalizing flow of energy from the root through to the crown chakras.

INTERRELATIONSHIP OF THE CHAKRAS AND THE BIOFIELD

Some theorists, notably Barbara Brennan (1988, 1993), propose an interrelationship between the chakras and the different dimensions, or layers, of the biofield. Thus, focus on the root center, at the base of the spine, also gives access to the etheric, or vital, layer of the biofield, the one closest to the physical body. Professionals who wish to assist clients suffering from physical distress should focus their efforts mostly in this domain to help strengthen the energy grid. Shifting focus to the sacral center, below the navel, and at the sacrum on the back allows the helper to assist clients in clearing strong emotional responses or in balancing depleted areas in the emotional layer. To work with the mental aspects of the biofield, the therapist should direct intent to the solar plexus area, the center associated with power, identity, effective communication, and clear thinking. The domains of spiritual awareness and the ever -more subtle transpersonal ones will open up once we bring our focus to the heart center and its transformative qualities of forgiveness and acceptance.

Figure 6.2 depicts a simplified, schematic image of this interconnection between the chakras and the biofield. An interactive dynamic exists between these two aspects of the human vibrational matrix that allows biofield processes to influence each of the chakras and permits more specific balancing to generalize throughout the different dimensions of the biofield.

Exercise 1. The Chakra Rotation

This is one example of many ways in which clients can experience their own centers of consciousness and bring movement into the multi-dimensional body. It is ideal for a morning ritual or for revitalizing during the day.

1. *"While standing comfortably, allow yourself to center and feel grounded to the earth. Begin by spreading your hands on your thighs, bending your*

Figure 6.2
INTERRELATIONSHIP OF BIOFIELD LAYERS

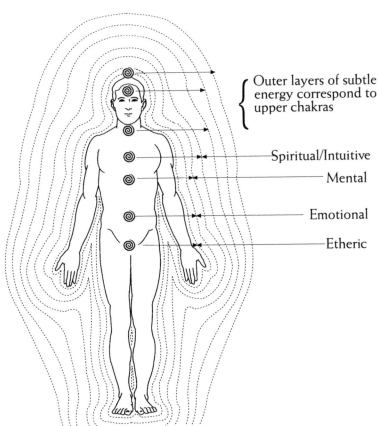

Outer layers of subtle energy correspond to upper chakras

Spiritual/Intuitive

Mental

Emotional

Etheric

knees, sensing the connection to the earth through the outflow of qi from your hands and feet."

2. "Sense the inflow of your life force from nature and the sun into your heart center. Your hands may be held facing each other over the heart center as you focus with a sense of gratitude and thanksgiving. Remember that there are strong energy vortices in the palms of the hands and soles of the feet."

3. "Bring the energy of gratitude from the heart center to the root chakra area at the base of the spine while affirming your joy of being alive in the physical body. If desired, add vigorous rotations to the right with your hips as you would if you were spinning a hula hoop."

4. "Now, allow qi to flow from your hands to the sacral center, front and back. Affirm your ability to select and choose the nutrients, people, and situations that are right for you. Rotate your body while focusing your attention on the sacral area."

5. "Bring your awareness and your hands to the solar plexus with its strengths for taking charge and communicating effectively. Add a slight rotation of your body while feeling your own power."

6. "Let qi now flow freely from your hands to the heart center, enjoying a sense of acceptance and forgiveness. Imagine reaching out to your loved ones and then bringing in their caring with large arm movements."

7. "Bring the hands over the throat center, front and back, while sensing support from the universe for your creativity. Allow your voice to make a sound, finding the tone that is most pleasing to you. Try all five vowels with this tone; play with various sounds; make up rhymes or simple poems."

8. "Allow the hands to rest above the brow area, both front and back, affirming your ability to develop higher sense perception and to see with insight and compassion."

9. "Bring the hands to the crown while feeling the inflow of qi from the universe. Sense the connection with infinite peace, love, and wisdom for your life, and its special gifts and sense of purpose."

10. "Let your whole being continue to resonate with a sense of peace and enhanced alertness, feeling the joy of being alive throughout your energy system. Notice changes in your body and mind before going on to your next task."

Chapter 7

The Meridians and Related Acupoints

Regardless of the pressures, stresses, and new circumstances that tend to overwhelm your meridian system, if you can keep the energy highways open, minimize the traffic jams, maintain the import and export systems, remove stagnant energy, and bring in a fresh energy supply, you will be healthier.   —Donna Eden (1998)

The meridians are a major component of the human energy system and permit flow of the vital life force throughout our multidimensional body. The three major components that we have identified in this volume—the biofield, the chakras, and the meridians—are the best-known aspects of the human vibrational matrix. There are other components, such as the basic grid, seasonal flows, and radiant circuits (Eden, 2001), and undoubtedly more awaiting future discovery. But now we will pursue our understanding of the most basic three and their resources for healing and creativity.

To use a crude metaphor, the biofield is like the glow we see at night around a large metropolis; the chakras resemble the districts or sections of the metropolis that integrate with the whole city and its communication systems; the meridians are the streets, streams, and highways that allow local transportation of energy. Furthermore, the streetlike meridians have traffic lights, or intersections, known as acupoints, which serve to boost or augment the smooth flow of information to all parts of the metropolis.

SCIENTIFIC EVIDENCE OF THE MERIDIANS

In more scientific language, the meridians, which are located in proximity to the skin and course deep into tissues, are a specialized network of energy transportation that brings rapid communication into the entire organism. Robert Becker (1990), the noted orthopedic surgeon and researcher, considers that the whole human energy system functions in parallel with the neurological system. While the neurological system has identifiable cells and structures, the human vibrational matrix appears to be predominantly electromagnetic in nature and can be demonstrated through more refined measurements of subtle energies (see chapter 4).

The first aspect of the vibrational matrix to be scientifically confirmed was the meridian structure. Hiroshi Motoyama, yoga adept and researcher from Japan, established the reality of the meridians in 1981. He found that meridians exist in the dermal layer of skin tissue and have a direction of qi flow that can be detected electrically. When qi is moving in different directions than it should (the equivalent of traveling the wrong direction on a one-way street), it is slowed down; reverse flows have a lower amount of qi and may precede physical impairment, whereas properly directed qi flows more rapidly and is associated with health (Motoyama 1981, p. 73; 1986). His research led to the development of a computerized system for analyzing the meridians. The apparatus for meridian identification, the AMI, is currently under evaluation in San Diego area hospitals and at the California Institute for Human Science in Encinitas, California, as a resource for early diagnosis of physical dysfunction (Motoyama, 1999). The model teaches that if a meridian is demonstrated via the AMI to be low in qi, the organs most influenced by the meridian may suffer depletion of qi and cause biochemical changes that become precursors of illness.

By using infrared technology, Chinese researchers have confirmed the presence of meridians through the use of infrared technology (Li, 1996; Wang, Hu, & Wu, 1993; Zhang, Fu, Wang, Wei, & Wang, 1996) while a German research institute has confirmed quantifiable effects of acupuncture on the human brain, such as cerebral oxygenation (Litscher & Wang, 2000). Furthermore, the research of Z. H. Cho and his associates (1998) confirmed that selected points on the foot, that are linked with the vision meridian, actually stimulate the occipital/visual cortex of the brain. Although this effect has been presumed in Chinese meridian theory, Cho's studies with functional magnetic resonance imaging (MRI) were the first to prove that such an interrelationship actually exists, and he published the results in one of the nation's most prestigious scientific journal. Despite this growing evidence, it is still difficult for most of us to grasp the complex intercellular relationships of the communicating meridians.

We assume a similar dynamic for emotional aspects as well, since Eastern medicine does not distinguish between physical and psychological issues as we do in our Western style of reductionistic thinking. Treatment of meridians in which the flow of qi is stagnant, depleted, or reversed is presumed to heal and rebalance the entire human organism. Eastern medicine assigns a profound intelligence to see these energy pathways: stimulation of a meridian releases and redistributes the bottlenecks of energy flow that cause all forms of dysfunction, e.g., unclear thinking, negative emotions, and physical distress (Kaptchuk, 1983). We can infer, then, that by treating early meridian disruptions in counseling settings we might prevent later onset of illness or more severe psychological dysfunction.

MERIDIANS IN RELATION TO EMOTIONS

There are 14 major meridian pathways that have been identified in both Chinese traditions of the last 3–5,000 millennia and in current meridian research. It is presumed that these pathways are actually so interrelated as to form one continuous meridian highway, but for practical purposes we will use the subdivisions that are customary in acupuncture nomenclature (Kaptchuk, 1983). Figure 7.1 schematically shows the approximate locations of the 14 major meridians in relation to the physical body.

The two central meridians provide the most basic flow patterns and establish balance within the energy system. In Eastern tradition, the *central vessel,* or *conception vessel,* flows from the pubic bone to the lower lip and palate under the tongue, while the *governing vessel* flows from the upper palate and under the nose, up the head, and down to the base of the spine. Thus, a continuous flow of qi can be established simply by moving the tongue from the upper palate to the lower palate below the tongue, a process that is integrated in many practices such as Qi Gong.

The other 12 meridians are named in relation to specific organs, such as the stomach or spleen through which they course in their complex meandering through the physical body. Again, we must remember that the energetic flows are not limited to the physical body alone but also have profound implications for emotional well-being. Well-known author Fred Gallo (2000, p. 13) writes: "There appears to be an interface between meridians and emotions, such that various positive emotions are evident when the meridians are balanced (e.g., love, joy, cheer,

Figure 7.1
SCHEMATIC DRAWING OF THE 14 MERIDIANS FROM
VARIOUS PERSPECTIVES

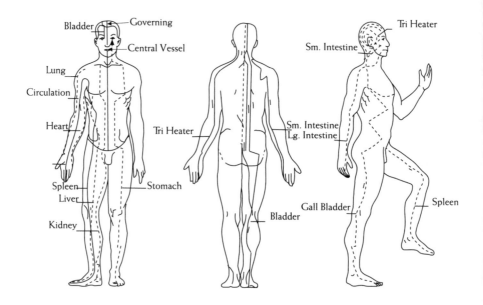

forgiveness, tranquility) and various negative emotions predominate when the meridians are disrupted (e.g., hate, sadness, unhappiness, anger, disgust)." Although some authors (Diamond, 1985; Durlacher, 1994; Teeguarden, 1996; Whisenant, 1994) correlate specific emotions with specific meridians, there is enough difference of opinion to suggest that this approach is too limiting to be optimally useful. Whisenant goes further to correlate each meridian with specific psychological functions and mythological figures (1994). What is important from a clinical perspective is to assess the client's pattern in relation to meridian flows, to understand the psychological impact of the pattern, and to reestablish balance where there is disturbance in the form of either too much or too little flow of qi.

It may, however, be helpful to think of analogies to organ function in considering the emotional meaning of specific meridians. For example, as we tap on one specific point related to the kidneys, we may be able to clear out not only chemical toxins but also harmful emotional debris since the kidneys serve the function of purification. Alternately, working with the spleen meridian, which is part of the body's nurturing immune responses, seems to have positive impact on the immune function, the lymph glands, and one's overall sense of well-being. Since the small intestines serve to select the nutrients that are nourishing to the body and to delete those that are unnecessary for waste release, stimulating one of the points for the small intestine meridian seems helpful in releasing compulsions from the emotional body.

TREATMENT POINTS FOR EFFECTING EMOTIONAL RELIEF

As you have already surmised, treatment of meridians is effected through the many acupoints that have been identified along each meridian. These points seem to serve as energy relay stations along the meridians. They function as tiny electrical energy boosters and show a slight difference in electrical resistance from the rest of the meridian pathway (Becker, 1990, p. 47). Each meridian has multiple acupoints; over 365 acupoints are identified in classical Chinese medicine, while modern innovations have increased that number to over 2,000 (Kaptchuk, 1983, p. 80). The acupoints serve different functions—some stimulate or tonify the meridians; some serve as sedation or calming points; others, like the triple warmer (also known as the tri-heater, triple heater, and triple stimulator), seem to communicate with the whole systemic network (Eden, 2001). There is some indication that each acupoint has unique vibrations or energetic frequencies as well as neurologic specificity, depending on its location along the meridian (Gallo, 2000, p. 6). For our purposes, we will focus on one major acupoint from each meridian as a resource for establishing harmony in emotions, behavior, and thinking.

In the Easterm traditions, acupoints have been stimulated by inserting fine needles into the flesh—known as acupuncture—or by burning of herbs over an acupoint, known as moxibustion. More recent applications of acupuncture concepts include stimulation of acupoints with lasers (Radomski, 2001). Manual pressure to an acupoint is used in *shiatsu*, a modern Japanese application of meridian theory, and acupressure, a Western adaptation (Teeguarden, 1996). For psychotherapy purposes, the client is taught to use light percussive movements, like tapping on an acupoint. Although it is helpful to learn alternate acupoints for each meridian, one point on each meridian is usually sufficient to bring about significant relief from emotional distress. The most common acupoints for psychological assessment and treatment are shown in Table 7.1. and described in Figure 7.2.

Work with the acupoints, and their related meridians, empowers profound change in emotions and thoughts. It is the central ingredient of

Table 7.1 BASIC MERIDIAN TREATMENT POINTS FOR PSYCHOTHERAPEUTIC INTERVENTIONS

Number in Figure 7.2	Western Acupoint Name and Abbreviation	Treatment Point Location and Instruction	Eastern Medicine Name of Meridian
1	Eyebrow = eb	Tap in corner where eyebrow meets the nose	Bladder
2	Outer eye = oe	Tap in the soft spot at the temple between the eye and the hairline	Gall bladder
3	Under eye = ue	Tap on the middle of lower eye orbit bone, below the pupil	Stomach
4	Under nose = un	Tap on middle of upper lip between the ridges of the lip	Governing vessel
5	Under lip = ul	Tap under lip in middle where chin begins protruding	Central vessel
6	Under collarbone= uc	Tap indentation under collarbone at each side of suprasternal notch	Kidney
7	Under armpit = ua	Tap on side of body about 3 inches below armpit, parallel with nipple	Spleen
8	Ribcage = r	Slap lightly with open palms on ribcage below breasts	Liver
9	Thumbnail = t	Tap on medial aspect of thumbnail bed	Lung
10	Index fingernail = if	Tap on medial aspect of index fingernail bed	Large intestines
11	Middle fingernail = mf	Tap on medial aspect of middle fingernail bed	Circulation/ sex
12	Little fingernail = lf	Tap on medial aspect of little fingernail bed	Heart
13	Side of hand = sh	Tap on side of hand at the end ofthe life line crease, or at "karate chop" point	Small intestines

Table 7.1 continued			
Number in Figure 7.2	Western Acupoint Name and Abbreviation	Treatment Point Location and Instruction	Eastern Medicine Name of Meridian
14	Valley /gamut spot = v or g	Tap in valley between ring and little finger knuckles	Tri-heater, triple warmer, or thyroid
NLR	Neuro lymphatic reflex point = nlr	Firmly rub in clockwise motion on indentation at heart side of chest, approximately halfway between nipple and collarbone	Not a meridian; treatment point for self-affirmation

Figure 7.2
FOURTEEN MERIDIAN ACUPOINTS USED FOR
PSYCHOTHERAPEUTIC TREATMENT

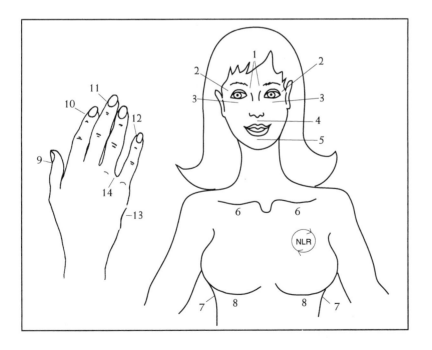

what is currently called energy psychology. Enhancing this work with the rich heritage of the biofield and chakra philosophies creates a comprehensive, integrative psychotherapy that is especially powerful in addressing issues where no one method by itself may be sufficient.

MERIDIAN-ORIENTED EXERCISES

Our discussion on the meridians has been brief: the reader may wish to refer to more in-depth discussions available from leaders in the field, such as Gallo (1998, 2000), Eden (1998), and Lambrou and Pratt (2000). Utilizing the concepts presented in this chapter, we can suggest the following exercises to clients as a means of relieving emotional distress or mental confusion.

Exercise 1. The Zip Up

This exercise traces the pathway of one of the two most central of the meridians, known as the central or conception (idea-generating) vessel. It is possible to trace each meridian on its circuitous route as one way of bringing more qi into the system.

You might present this simplest form of meridian tracing to a client in the following manner: "This exercise permits you to reintegrate quickly your sense of focus when you have become distracted or are tired from a long day of work."

1. *"While standing or sitting comfortably, cup the palms of your hands together over the public bone and set your intent on energizing yourself. Take a deep breath and release it fully. Then, while inhaling, bring the hands slowly up along the midline until you come to the lower lip. Let the hands drop and simultaneously release the breath fully."*

2. *"Repeat this procedure several more times until you feel a surge of confidence and self-esteem within yourself. You are now ready to move on to your next task."*

3. *"Repeat the whole process as often as needed to give yourself an energetic boost."*

Exercise 2. The Crossover Correction

This exercise, adapted from Educational Kinesiology (Dennison & Dennison, 1982), includes a yoga posture, permits integration of the right and left hemispheres of the brain, the two central meridians, and the breath. It crosses as many central flow pathways as possible. In my practice, I have found it extremely helpful in treating tiredness, confusion, anxiety, and energetic imbalance—in short, symptoms that most of our clients have. You may share it with your clients in the following manner:

1. *"Take a deep breath and release fully. Cross the left ankle over the right and make sure your body is comfortable while you are sitting, lying down, or standing."*
2. *"Bring your hands in front of you with the backs of the hands facing each other and the thumbs pointing down. Cross the right hand over the left and then bring both together toward you while inverting the clasped hands so the thumbs face away from you."*
3. *"Breathe easily while you let the tongue touch the roof of the mouth as you inhale. As you exhale, let the tongue drop down to the floor of the mouth."*
4. *"Hold this posture for several minutes until you feel a sense of inner calm and peace. Release any tension with each out-breath, and let the in-breath increase a sense of calming. If you wish, add the sense of a healing or warming color."*
5. *"Notice any changes in your body and mind after doing this exercise."*

Exercise 3. Treating Energetic Disturbance with Affirmations

One of the most global energetic disturbances that we see in counseling practice is that of low self-esteem. This can be treated quite readily with an affirmation, a self-affirming positive statement, while gently rubbing the neurolymphatic reflex (nlr) point shown in Figure 7.2.

John Diamond (1985) is credited with the extensive use of affirmations in psychotherapy, while Callahan, who collaborated with Diamond briefly, is credited with the idea of using the "nlr point" to enhance the effect of an affirmation (1985). There are numerous neurolymphatic reflex points that can be utilized to treat lymphatic congestion and to energize the physical body (Eden, 1998, pp. 79–85), but this point is the only one that is usually taught in energy therapy.

An easy way to locate the "nlr" spot is to suggest to clients that it is located on the left side of the upper chest, about where they would touch themselves to say the American pledge to the flag. After you ask the client to rub the "pledge" spot gently toward the left shoulder (in a clockwise direction), suggest that he/she repeat the following affirmation three times:

"I deeply and profoundly accept myself with all my faults, problems, and limitations."

Other words can, of course, be used, but it is important to make sure the intent is clear: deep self-acceptance that exceeds all the current problems, issues, and distractions. Some clients prefer a more positively worded affirmation, such as the following:

"I deeply and profoundly accept myself with all by gifts, talents, and ability to love." (Repeated three times).

These affirmations help to establish a sense of hope and positive direction as well as a sense of self-acceptance that empowers receptivity to other energy-oriented treatments. Involving the neurolymphatic reflex point seems to anchor the statement and its meaning into a felt part of the body. It also creates a calming effect as evidenced from clients' self-reports.

Exercise 4. The Generic Tapping Sequence

It is possible to elicit a small number of acupoints for treatment of specific problems, and we will explore those methods in subsequent chapters. For the present, it is helpful to learn a generic sequence that simply treats all 14 of the acupoints related to the 14 major meridians given in Figure 7.2.

It is most important to ask the client to attune to the issue or problem he/she has identified. While a more usual response is to suppress or ignore problems, this technique requires specific remembering of the situation that is causing the distress and rating the distress on a scale of 0 to 10. The subjective units of distress (SUD) scale is frequently used in many settings, but it may be helpful to remind clients that a rating of 10 means the situation is considered extremely life-threatening, while a 1or less means such minimal distress that treatment might not be needed.

After you have obtained the client's distress level in relation to a specific problem, ask the client to keep attuning to the selected issue. You might introduce the generic tapping sequence in the following manner:

1. *"Please think of your issue while you tap each point 10 to 15 times on your body. This may help to reduce the intensity of the emotion in relation to the problem. I will be tapping on my acupoints along with you, because this work helps me as well. We have generally found that using both hands in an alternating fashion is the most effective."*

2. *"While thinking of your issue, please tap at the eyebrow points . . . now the outer eye . . . next, under the eye . . . next, under the nose . . . under the lip . . . next, at the collarbone, just below the junction with the sternum. Now please tap under the armpits. Still thinking about your issue, slap the lower ribcage with the open hands. Next, tap the inner aspect of the thumbnail (you can use the index finger of the other hand to do this, or bend one hand so that you are tapping both medial aspects of the thumbnail area). Next, please tap the inner aspect of the index finger . . . then the inner aspect of the middle finger . . . next, the inner aspect of the little finger. Still thinking of your issue, please tap the side of the hand, the "karate chop" point. Finally, please tap the "valley" spot between the last two knuckles using two fingers of the other hand."*

3. *"Take a deep breath, and release it fully. Now think about your issue and let me know if there is any change in your distress level."*

Often, even with this simple generic tapping sequence, there may be significant reduction in the client's distress level, indicating that this method could be used further until the client gets to 0 and is able to look creatively at other options. If there is no change, or the distress worsens, then a number of other approaches, including work with the chakras and biofield, might be used to assist the client. These methods will be explored more fully as we proceed, but it is advisable not to continue using a method that is not helping the client, because frustration and diminished rapport can result.

CLINICAL CONSIDERATIONS IN COMPREHENSIVE ENERGY PSYCHOTHERAPY

The emerging field of comprehensive, or integrative energy psychology (resources are listed in the Appendix) combines work with the biofield, the merdians, and the chakras to bring relief from psychological distress. Many clients, of course, will be unfamiliar with energy psychology altogether. Skill in rapport-building and sensitivity to the appropriateness of any interventions are essential. It is useful to have as many treatment approaches as possible, since no single method works for every client. Some clients negatively regard energy concepts in general and are therefore not receptive to any of the interventions. It is important always to respect the client's right to informed consent and choice; ethical concerns will be considered more fully in chapter 9.

With skeptical clients, I find introducing relaxation or stress management imagery helpful, both in balancing the biofield and making clients' thinking more amenable to other energy treatment options. When clients experience the therapist's caring and respect for their choices, they may gradually become more receptive.

Since the chakras often give clients a felt sense of their emotional distress, discussing the physical sensation of the distress offers a good starting place for those who are out of touch with their physical and emotional bodies. Awareness of early somatic signals of distress and the affected chakra can give such clients a tremendous boost in self-perception and self-efficacy.

In my experience, very anxious clients do not respond well to the tapping of acupoints; initially it may be too jarring to their psychoenergetic systems. Calmer, more soothing interventions, such as holding the hands over an affected chakra, may offer more direct relief. Anxiety-ridden persons may need to learn interventions that balance the biofield and are applied on a daily, even hourly, basis.

Severely disturbed clients suffering from mood disorders may have too much disruption in the flow of their qi or too many unconsciously held beliefs to be able to respond appropriately to treatment of pervasive energetic disturbance and to address specific issues. Intensive work, over many sessions, may be required to establish a sense of stability in the biofield, over many sessions along with appropriate medication. With time, the combination of centering interventions and medication can help to restore a sense of psychoenergetic balance and enable such clients to benefit from more complex interventions such as the Chakra Rotation or the Generic Tapping Sequence.

Viewing our therapeutic interactions with clients as communication between two biofields gives us an opportunity to honor the unique qualities of each person as an energy being and to recognize that rapport is an energy communication. The energy psychologies seem to facilitate the alignment of both therapist and client to their higher resources and to stretch our human potential to its greatest creativity and personal good.

Chapter 8

Assessment of Patterns in the Human Vibrational Matrix

All of our systems are regulated not only by known energy and material factors but also by invisible organizing fields. . . . The configuration of illness shows in the human energy field long before it precipitates into the body." —Barbara Ann Brennan

Now that we have established some of the parameters of the energy system, we are ready to consider ways of assessing disturbances or imbalance in the patterns of qi. These disturbances can be noted in the overall configuration of the biofield, the balance of each of the chakras, and the flow of qi in the meridians.

Over 30 years ago, Martha Rogers, the theorist behind the practice of Therapeutic Touch, spoke of patterns of interactive energy in the human field and environment (1970). She knew that recognizing a pattern, such as depletion of energy in a patient's field, would allow practitioners to determine the need for an energy-healing intervention. Later, the idea of unbalanced or blocked patterns of qi in the biofield became codified into the nursing diagnosis as energy-field disturbance (NANDA, 1996). In current practice, this nursing diagnosis gives the practitioner a context from which to institute Therapeutic Touch or other energy-related techniques. After making an energetic assessment of the patient, the caregiver can select the most appropriate energetic technique, implement it, evaluate the effects, and document the whole process from diagnosis to outcome in the patient's progress notes.

In a similar vein, therapists using meridian-based therapies establish an energetic diagnosis derived from client self-report as well as by checking a client's muscle strength relative to congruent or incongruent self-statements. This energy diagnosis then becomes the basis for selecting an intervention, implementing a procedure, and re-assessing for change in the client's emotional or mental aspects.

A number of resources for assessment are available to the energy-oriented counselor. These include the therapist's skilled intuition, client self-report, assessment with the therapist's or client's hands, pendulum dowsing, and clinical kinesiology, also known as muscle testing, or muscle checking. We will consider each of these tools in turn and then demonstrate how we might help ourselves to "see" or sense patterns in the biofield, the chakras, and the meridians.

THERAPIST INTUITION

Often, skilled therapists have a felt sense of the client's energy state well before verbal interactions begin. This first impression can give valuable information about the client's internal state and help to formulate the direction of therapy. With practice, the development of intuition adds another dimension to counselor perceptions. I have found that jotting down my very first impression, no matter how strange or bizarre, is the best teacher because it allows me to check and recheck my initial input with each subsequent client session. If I do not write down my intuitive first impression, it is usually lost in the barrage of information that clients share.

Recently, "Jackie" was referred through a local employee assistance program. I knew nothing else about her. As she walked through the door of my office, two guesses immediately came to me: one was "walking wounded," the other was "dazed." As she told her story, I noted that she was indeed dazed, in shock from a date rape at knifepoint a week earlier. The intuitive energetic assessment I made helped me to work carefully and gently with her, using only positive affirmations with the neurolymphatic reflex point, the pledge spot described in the previous chapter. This was enough to help Jackie to regain some self-esteem and for us to establish sufficient rapport for her to make a police report. As therapy progressed over several weeks, she became a willing participant in other energy modalities and was able to release the intense emotional distress of the incident.

CLIENT SELF-REPORT

The client's self-perception may also be useful. Jackie, for example, reported "feeling stuck, sometimes just staring ahead," forgetting why she had stopped or where she was—in a sense, she gave an operational definition of my perception of "dazed." When client self-report and therapist intuition match, we might infer that early rapport formation has occurred. In such cases, treatment planning and direction are clear from the outset.

Many clients, however, are disconnected from their feelings and have no way of describing their inner states. Educated guesswork and dialoging is needed to arrive at a therapeutic starting place. Some clients distort or misrepresent themselves. In this case, therapist intuition and client self-report might not match at all. In my experience, approaching such a situation as an opportunity for mutual learning is helpful.

"John," a computer programmer whom I saw in 2001, reported breaking up with his girlfriend as his presenting problem. But, rather than sorting out the issues, John was already engaged in a computer search for another partner and wanted my help in wording his advertisement. "In too much hurry" was my intuitive perception. I shared it with him, since he was not very forthcoming about his feelings. He looked at me with wide eyes and confessed that he never stayed with anything very long. As a vignette, he told me he had built a large backyard pool, only to fill it in with dirt because he tired of maintaining it—he sighed that he never allowed himself to enjoy his accomplishments. As we explored this theme together, it turned out that he had a fairly severe learning disorder with attention deficit components. His whole life had been filled with compensations such as doing things quickly and shifting direction often. In addition to teaching John centering and focusing techniques, I was able to make a referral for neurofeedback therapy to teach him ways of bringing his brain wave patterns to greater harmony and integration (Amen, 2001).

Client self-report is also effected by use of a scale to determine subjective units of distress (SUD) that allows the client to rate the emotional distress on a scale from 0 to 10. Because such a scale is highly subjective, the SUD self-report may also give distortions. However, the SUD level is imminently useful in assessing client progress. A drop of two or more points in the client's self-perception, when a technique such as the Generic Tapping Sequence is used, lets the therapist know that acupoint tapping is a helpful method for the client. If the SUD level does not change at all, or increases, we can surmise that perhaps another approach would be more effective. A number of inner processes may be going on to cause either no change or an increase in the client's subjective self-evaluation. Some of these are as follows:

- The client does not want to make a change—for example, holding onto a secondary gain (a client with a diagnosed mood disorder may wish to keep it for disability insurance purposes).

- The client is energetically too imbalanced to be able to respond to the meridian-based intervention.
- There may be an interfering, unconsciously held belief.
- Another even more disturbing problem has become activated.
- Focusing on the problem has led to increased emotional aware-ness and a level of intensity of which the client was not fully cognizant.

As we can see, client self-report of SUD level is a quick measure that gives us feedback about the client's inner condition. Attention to self-report is a valuable ally in ferreting out client needs and in selecting appropriate interventions.

THE HAND SCAN

Another means of self-report is to have clients scan their own biofield or chakra areas for imbalanced or depleted energy. All that is required of clients is a willingness to learn from their own psychoenergetic system.

Exercise 1. Scanning the Body Map

Many clients enjoy sharing their intuitive perceptions. This exercise uses imagery to access a map of the body and the biofield around it. The client's perceptions may be very helpful in finding needs that have been outside of his/her awareness and in leading to increased insight.

1. *"While seated, center yourself with a breath or a peaceful image and set your intention to scan intuitively for areas of congestion, blockage, or depletion."*
2. *"Imagine that you have a map of your body before you. Scanning head to toe, notice areas that you 'see' or sense as pink and lively, and those that seem gray or sluggish. "*
3. *"Without any judgment or evaluation, please just report what you notice and feel."*

Exercise 2. The Hand Scan

This exercise is similar to the previous one except that here the client actually uses the hands to do the sensing of differences in various areas around the body.

1. *"While standing, scan the biofield with your hands, moving them 2 to 5 inches away from the body. "*
2. *"Start above the crown of the head and slowly move the hands downward over the head and shoulder area, the chest and abdomen, the lower abdomen and pelvis, the thighs and knees, the lower legs and feet."*

3. *"Allow yourself to notice differences—where does it seem warmer or cooler, dense and sticky, or more open and flowing?"*
4. *"Write down or note on your map of the body where the sensations in your hands seem to be different. Do not let any evaluations or judgment get in the way; simply put down your first sensory perceptions."*

On completion of this simple Hand Scan, ask the client if these perceptions have any personal meaning. Even if there is no immediate recognition of relevance, repeated scanning usually leads to some awareness which points to disturbance at a specific location in the psychoenergetic system.

Exercise 3. Therapist Hand Scan

Some clients have too much disturbance in their own perceptions to be able to do the Hand Scan effectively. This may be true especially if systemic psychoenergetic disturbance is present, as in Angelina's case cited in chapter 5. Client rapport and permission are, of course, required if the therapist wishes to assess the client's energy patterns actively.

Instructions here are written for the counselor who decides to assess the client's energy state after client permission has been granted:

1. *"Begin, as always, by centering yourself and setting your clear intent to assist the client to whatever outcome is for the client's highest good."*
2. *"Start 2 to 5 inches above the crown of the client's head and slowly move your hands downward over the client's head and shoulder area, the chest and abdomen, the lower abdomen and pelvis, the thighs and knees, the lower legs and feet."*
3. *"Allow yourself to notice differences—where does the energy seem cooler or warmer, congested or tingly, sticky or more open and flowing?"*
4. *"Scan the back and each of the sides of the client's field and continue noting areas of difference, symmetry, or asymmetry."*

Write down or note on your map of the client's body where the sensations in your hands seem to be different. Do not let evaluation or judgment get in the way; simply put down your first sensory perceptions and then check with the client whether this has any personal meaning.

ASSESSMENT WITH SIMPLE TOOLS

One of the most time-honored means of intuitive perception is that of using an object, such as a pendulum for dowsing, to assess energy intensity (Tiller, 1997). Often, skilled, sensitive persons are employed to find water or other materials in the earth's energy field. Therapists can use a pendulum to assess the state of clients' chakra and biofield energies.

A pendulum is simply any object that swings freely while attached to a string or small chain. Practitioners can hold the pendulum string over the palm of one hand and ask themselves questions to which they seek intuitive answers. Usually, a strong swing from the pendulum in circles means yes while a more sluggish response, back and forth movement, or no movement at all is indicative of a negative response. Milton Erickson's extensive studies of ideomotor movements (Bandler & Grinder, 1975), the tiny, imperceptible movements stemming from the unconscious mind that are used in hypnotherapy, help us to understand how the pendulum may amplify the intuitive knowing of the person using the pendulum. The interrelationship between matter and consciousness, advanced in the new quantum mechanics, gives us means for comprehending how a highly sensitive person may be able to sense the various energy intensities emanating from the earth and the human body.

Although many people are skeptical of this method, it is actively used to assess chakra energy flow in many energy-healing practices. Since the chakras are spinning energy vortices, they can be easily identified and assessed with a pendulum. I remember teaching with a simple pendulum, a paperclip on a string, in a Healing Touch class that included several physicians. They shook their heads about this method. I explained that while the Hand Scan of the biofield and chakras was certainly effective, some people prefer working with something they can see, and for them the pendulum may be helpful. Surprisingly, one physician called me the next day. He excitedly reported that men had come to dig a well for him at his desert home in the eastern foothills of San Diego. The men prepared to dig and pulled out their best tool for determining the location of the well and the depth at which they could find water— their tool was a pendulum in the hands of a dowser. "Now I've seen everything!" he exclaimed.

Use of the pendulum, as well as other intuitive means, requires a willingness to learn from one's unconscious, to set aside any self-criticism, and to practice the method repeatedly. This is suggestive of the psychological openness that is optimal for understanding one of the most central assessment resources used in energy psychology—the use of muscle testing or clinical kinesiology.

CLINICAL KINESIOLOGY

Muscle testing has a brief but interesting history as reported in Gallo's first book, which named the field of energy psychology (1998). Although physical therapists have tested specific muscles for their empirical strength as part of treatment (Kendall & Kendall, 1949), it was not until 1960s that chiropractor George Goodheart decided that a single indicator muscle could be used to give information about the condition of specific organs and systems in the physical body. While acupuncture and work with the meridians became more accepted, Goodheart also began using an indicator muscle to diagnose which meridians were out of balance and needed strengthening (Horowitz, 2001). Beardall (1995) developed these ideas more fully, calling muscle testing *clinical kinesiology*. The mind/body psychologist Whisenant (1994) named muscle testing *psychological kinesiology*, while the trademarked name for muscle testing, Applied Kinesiology (AK), has become an accepted assessment tool in chiropractic practice.

It took the talents of psychologist Roger Callahan to apply concepts of meridian theory to the treatment of emotional issues and to use muscle testing to determine which meridians were involved in severe emotional trauma, phobias, and other psychological disturbances (1996, 2001). Over the past 20 years, Callahan's many students have expanded his original ideas to include the wide variety of energy psychology methods that are now available. However, checking the strength of an indicator muscle to determine what is congruent for the client has remained basically unchanged as the primary assessment tool of energy psychology.

Muscle testing is presumed to give information about the client's interior state, specifically by showing muscle strength if a statement is congruent to the client, and weakness for an incongruent statement. As such, it is a "low -tech" lie detector, a subjective tool that requires clients' willingness to find out their inner states and a sense of neutrality on the part of the tester. It was not until 1999 that an adventurous researcher named Daniel Monti and his associates (1999) published findings with a large sample of subjects that confirmed assumptions about the procedure: a cognitive statement perceived to be true by the testee will show 17% more muscle force and hold strong 59% longer than an untrue statement. This was shown by computerized dynamometer and myographical measurements of the indicator muscle.

The term "muscle testing" implies some kind of challenge or test, and old instructions still in use are for the client to "resist" the pressure exerted by the practitioner. The term clinical kinesiology (CK) can also be used, and "energy kinesiology" was coined by Eden (1998). Personally, I prefer to use the words "muscle checking." They imply a more congenial attitude of "let's learn from your system while I check your indicator muscle." Instructions to the client are simply to "meet my pressure," which we both calibrate together at the outset of the muscle checking exercise.

Exercise 4. Basic Muscle Checking

This exercise begins calibrating the amount of pressure you would use with a client so that information flow from the client can come easily without exertion. Selection of the indicator muscle is done with the client's consent; while the deltoid muscle of the upper arm is usual in classroom settings, I find that a circle made with the client's thumb and index finger allows for much less strain in therapy settings. I simply use light pressure to pull apart the client's thumb and index finger to check the muscles' strength. Other muscles can be used as well. Usually two opposing statements are made by the therapist and repeated by the client to ascertain the system's strong or weak responses. After each statement is made, the practitioner exerts light pressure to test muscle strength and to learn from the response.

After obtaining client permission and selecting an indicator muscle, instruct the standing or sitting client as follows:

1. *"I am going to use this much pressure to test the muscle we have selected." (Demonstrate using about 2 to 3 pounds of pressure.)*
2. *"Please think of something that you like very much; let me know when you have it in your awareness." (Client nods or gives assent when attuned.)*
3. *"I will now use the same pressure as before. Please meet my pressure." (Muscle should test strong.)*
4. *"Now, please think of something that you do not like, and let me know when you are attuned to it." (Client gives signal when attuned.)*
5. *"I will use the same amount of pressure; please meet my pressure." (Muscle should test weak.) If there is no apparent difference in the responses, you may need to recalibrate. If there is a difference that both the client and you can distinguish, you are ready to proceed with a simple test for psychoenergetic disturbance such as paired true/false statements.*
6. *"Please state your name as in 'my name is ————.' "(Muscle should test strong.)*
7. *"Please state fictitious name as in 'my name is Howdy Doody.' "(Muscle should test weak.)*
8. *Another way to test for psychoenergetic disturbance might be to have the client say, "My psychoenergetic system is optimally balanced at this time." (Muscle should test strong.) Alternately, "My psychoenergetic system is not optimally balanced at this time." (Muscle should test weak.)*

With the resource of muscle checking, both therapist and client have access to information beyond cognitive information. This information comes from the client's intuitive knowing or from deeper parts of the unconscious. With this simple, client-centered technique, the therapeutic alliance is strengthened, and logical energy-treatment sequences can be elicited.

VISUALIZING PSYCHOENERGETIC PATTERNS

The various assessment tools described allow us to find the patterns of disturbance in the whole psychoenergetic system and to determine which interventions are needed. Before we discuss treatment considerations, I offer the following visual means of tracking assessments to aid the more visually oriented practitioner.

Patterns in the Biofield

Assessment of the biofield is the easiest way to note systemic or pervasive psychoenergetic disturbance. As noted in chapter 5, this level of disturbance must be addressed first if other more specific treatments are to be effective.

The Hand Scan as described above, done either by clients or therapists, can detect such disturbance by noting differences in the overall biofield configuration. The field should be symmetrical with an even flow of warmth or vibrancy extending beyond the entire body, from head to toe. If this is not the case, we might surmise that there is disturbance in the biofield. Other assessment resources such as client self-report, therapist intuition, and testing of the indicator muscle would be helpful as well, but the Hand Scan specifies the location of asymmetry in the field directly and gives us important clues for treatment.

Figure 8.1 shows the biofield of a client who presented with overly lively affect. "Hank" was a very engaging, successful artist who reported some concern about a diagnosis of HIV that was made 4 years ago. His presenting problem was a recent loss of a relationship and subsequent loneliness. Biofield assessment showed depletion of qi in the entire lower body; Hank was literally living "in his head" as a compensation. The right and left sides were asymmetrical as well, and when questioned, Hank admitted that he had numbness and pain on the more depleted right side. Because of Hank's very outgoing style and willingness to problem-solve, the reality of his pervasive psychoenergetic disturbance might have been missed without the Hand Scan and the learning that it offered.

Patterns in the Chakras

More specific information can be obtained by helping clients to assess the flow of qi in their chakras. Client willingness to learn from their own body and mind is important; while some clients love learning about

Figure 8.1
BIOFIELD PATTERN OF ARTIST WITH HIV

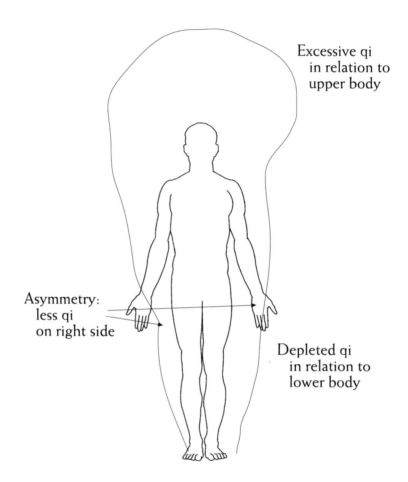

Excessive qi
in relation to
upper body

Asymmetry:
less qi
on right side

Depleted qi
in relation to
lower body

their energy centers, others do not want too much detail but find relating to the felt sense in the body helpful.

Exercise 5. Assessment of the Chakras

Explain to the client that trusting oneself involves learning from the body and its related energy centers. This helps to set the intention for mutual learning.

1. *"While sitting or standing, please think of an event that upset you recently and notice where you first felt it in your body."*
2. *"Please hold your hands over the part of the body that was first impacted by this event and allow yourself to remember it as fully as possible."*

3. *"Notice the feelings and sensations that come to you. Note other areas of the body that resonate with the issues raised by the event as well."*

Usually, we would not stop at this point because the accessed material can lead directly to a meaningful therapy session. Any time clients connect with felt sensations, we have accessed valuable therapeutic material.

As Hank did the exercise, he became aware of how much he wished to deny and forget about his illness. He felt this most specifically over the solar plexus, the power and control area of the chakra system. As he tried to describe how important it was for him to be normal, he noticed a strong headache, as if he had strained an upper chakra to the point of physical distress.

Figure 8.2 shows Hank's chakra system recorded by the therapist as Hank assessed his chakras.

Figure 8.2
CHAKRA PATTERN OF CLIENT DENYING HIV INFECTION

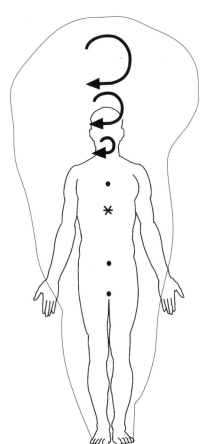

Chakra Assessment

Crown: excessive qi

Brow: excessive qi, headache symptom

Throat: moderate qi

Heart: low qi

Solar plexus: low qi, discomfort symptoms, wanting to deny, control

Sacral: low qi

Root: low qi

Patterns in the Meridians

Usually, patterns in the meridians are too subtle for us to sense because we are talking about 14 meridians and hundreds of acupoints. Muscle checking is definitely our best assessment resource for the specificity that is needed to determine which meridians and related acupoints need to be treated.

Our model holds that specific life issues or trauma weaken the psychoenergetic structure at some level. In order of severity, we need to determine if the trauma has impacted the whole biofield system, has created possible blockages in the chakras, or has weakened an aspect of the meridian system. We can elicit this with muscle checking by use of contrasting statements as given in Exercise 4.

In Hank's case, after systemic imbalance and chakra blockages were cleared with techniques described in the next section, we were able to target his "anxiety about HIV infection" as a treatment issue. He rated his anxiety as a 5, while muscle checking showed it to be an 8, which seemed indicative of Hank's tendency to minimize his distress. Using muscle checking of each acupoint, we were able to elicit which of the 14 meridians were most affected by the anxiety; in other words, which acupoints needed to be strengthened so that he could be more energetically balanced. The pattern we found is illustrated in Figure 8.3—the bladder,

Figure 8.3
MERIDIAN ACUPOINTS ELICITED BY MUSCLE CHECKING
TO TREAT CLIENT'S ANXIETY

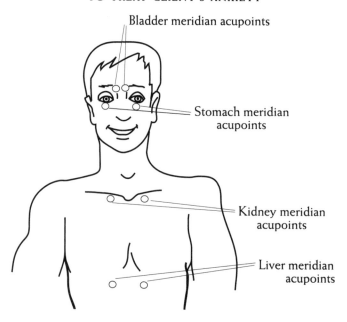

stomach, kidney, and liver meridians needed to be strengthened by energy tapping to bring the anxiety to less stressful levels.

After Hank tapped these treatment points while attuning to his anxiety, his anxiety dropped to a 3, as we determined both by both self-report and muscle checking. Although he was not yet at SUD level of 0, which did not happen until a subsequent session, he was already able to think more constructively about his disease. He began facing what had been "unthinkable" to him just half an hour earlier. He decided to get a good medical checkup and to consider some form of chemotherapy if his T-cell count proved to be low.

Visualizing the patterns in the biofield, the chakras, and the meridians gave me as the therapist ready reference points to focus on the major energy-related issues in Hank's life. As Hank came to know himself better from an intuitive point of view, his sense of vitality became stronger and his loneliness diminished. It was as if connecting with his energy gave him a whole new relationship with himself, one that later became reflected in community art projects and the ability to help others with HIV.

Part III

Integrative Energy Psychology Interventions for Emotional Relief

Chapter 9

Ethical Considerations for Integrated Energy Psychotherapy

Ethical behavior is reverence for life demonstrated by right relationship to another.
—Kylea Taylor (1995)

Far beyond any written laws, it is our ethical principles that guide us as therapists to seek the best technologies and life-enhancing outcomes for our clients. Our facilitation skills involve knowing how to help clients chart a course in the unknown territory of the inner psyche, without imposing our own biases or limitations. In introducing innovative energy-related therapies, this mandate becomes even more evident because we are exploring new treatments that do not have the benefit of years of empirical practice or large accumulations of supportive research. Thus, before we consider specific treatment applications, a review of ethical considerations for using innovative therapies and energy concepts as a whole is necessary.

The energy-healing relationship is a unique interchange in which the therapist's inner values become translated into sensitivity, presence, and responsiveness. Internal congruence from the therapist requires grounded personal integrity and a firm knowledge base. External congruence means choosing a definable code of ethics, adhering to identified standards of care, and being clear about our personal values and goals.

While each discipline in the social sciences developed, codes of practice and ethics emerged to guide its practitioners. For example, psychology (1992), music therapy (1994), holotropic breathwork (1994), and family counseling (1991) all have defined codes of ethics and standards of care that are continuously evolving and changing as the work in each field becomes more defined and specific. Similarly, the emerging field of energy psychotherapy has its own living codes and standards, which were developed through the Association for Comprehensive Energy Psychology (2001; presented in Appendices C and D). These concepts were further defined into a working document entitled *Ethics at the Leading Edge* by those attending the third annual conference (May, 2001). One of the distinguishing features of this new ethic is its emphasis on the multidimensional nature of helping clients, their families, and communities to understand healing from a holistic, integrative framework. Right relationship in energy healing also includes the therapist's self-awareness and personal energy hygiene, since both clients and therapists may have increased sensitivity to each other in energy-based communications. Awareness of subtle energies takes us beyond usual ethical considerations such as mutual goal setting, confidentiality, truth-telling, injunctions against sexual misconduct, nonharming, agreements about fees, etc.

In addition to all these usual ethical concerns there are a number of other readily visible issues. To name a few, these concerns include informed consent for an innovative modality, selection of appropriate clients, clarity about scope of practice, careful setting of intention, sensitivity about appropriate use of intuitive material, and assistance in integration of learning. We will discuss these concerns in the light of their implications for practice and for achieving the competencies required to develop effective energy psychotherapy skills.

IMPLICATIONS FOR PRACTICE

Informed Consent

Of the numerous implications for the practice of innovative, experimental modalities such as the energy psychotherapies, appropriate attention to informed consent is the most basic. Such permission means being sure that the client knows all the possible benefits and risks associated with this new approach.

In relation to energy-healing methods with the biofield, the chakras, and the meridians, the benefits to clients appear to be many: symptom relief, centered and focused attention, increased personal awareness, a sense of personal empowerment, communication beyond words, and possible accessing of unconscious material. Each benefit may also hold an inherent risk. For example, increased self-awareness may heighten the intensity of felt emotions or lead the client to reconsider life decisions. The risks of changing affective intensity and lifestyle can only be correctly assessed by the client. It is important for this reason that we correctly assesses client readiness and have a careful sense of timing. Discussing therapeutic goals at the outset of treatment also permits frequent reevaluation in light of emerging material as therapy progresses.

There are no known instances of therapeutic harm or energy -healing overdose from appropriately trained and skilled practitioners; nor have there been any legal cases involving practitioners in over 30 years of Therapeutic Touch practice. The assessment resources described in the previous chapter ideally allow the therapist to maintain close connection with the client's internal state at all times. The ethic of caring and the rapport between the interactive fields of clients and therapists requires continuous monitoring and careful vigilance.

A sample informed consent form is given in Appendix B. The items on the form can lead to further discussion in helping our clients to consider using the complementary modality of integrated, or comprehensive, energy psychotherapy.

Selection of Clients

Some clients are not appropriate for energy psychotherapy, and it is axiomatic that no one approach is effective with everyone. With our clinical acumen, we need to select the most effective intervention for a variety of needs—the creativity of therapy requires much flexibility and resourcefulness. It is not advisable to use innovative modalities with persons who are suspicious, have thought disorders, suffer from severe dissociative identity disorder, or have not developed a sense of trust with the counselor. Clients with poor ego boundaries, or whose hold on reality is very fragile, may also be poor candidates because they may have difficulty accepting a modality that is outside their usual understanding of reality. However, I have found that very stressed, tired, or overwhelmed clients respond well to the simple self-care exercises of the energy therapies.

Ideal clients for energetic psychotherapy are those who have an active interest in learning from their own inner states and those who express curiosity about energy work. As we have illustrated in several case examples, energetic interventions facilitate rapid relief from emotional distress and deep-seated issues, without the need for long-term therapies. With such rapid accessing of emotional issues, nonjudgmental support from the therapist is essential during a session. Because clients may discover deeper insights and connections after attending a session, clients must know that contact with the therapist is available. It is crucial to respect the clients' pace, following their cues at every step. Muscle checking and intuitive perception, uniquely taught in energy-healing therapies, are the client-centered resources that permit us to pace ourselves with the client's inner readiness and unconscious wishes.

Defining the Scope of Practice

Since we know that energetic approaches are effective for a wide variety of issues, it is important to define our scope of practice. This means differentiating clearly the issues within our expertise and those that require referral. For example, we may find that a client remains energetically imbalanced, giving undifferentiated responses to muscle checking, and suffers from distress that cannot be alleviated with the usual interventions for systemic psychoenergetic disturbance. Neurological dysfunction may be present and require medical referral. Alternately, clients may be impacted by environmental toxins or suffer from internal allergies (Radomski, 2001), have some form of somatic impairment (Prudden, 1986), or experience misalignment of the cranial bones (Upledger, 1997)—these are all outside the scope of most counseling practices. Unless you have extensive expertise in treating such issues, it is best to refer such clients to recognized practitioners that treat environmental sensitivities, allergies, somatic disorders, or cranio-sacral alignment.

On the other end of our treatment continuum, we may have clients whose life situation is too distressing for our personal abilities. Countertransference issues appear to develop more rapidly in energy psychology than in traditional therapies because therapist intuition is much more engaged. In addition, counselor and client fields are consciously understood to be in interaction with each other.

Realistic self-inventory on the therapist's part is needed to avoid possibly damaging interrelationships. I recently asked Anna, a practicing energy psychotherapist, to identify her strengths and weaknesses with various client groups. After thinking for a few moments, she stated, "I prefer to refer very demanding people, clients whose expectations exceed what I feel I can contribute, very young children, and bossy elderly women that remind me of my stepmother. On the other hand, I do well with deep grief, such dilemmas as trauma, rape, and abuse, and with clients who have complex, long-term issues. I delight in working with the curious and those who love to learn." Such self-knowledge becomes the key to the important task of selecting clients whose issues and dilemmas are well within the range of our skills and expertise.

Development of a Personal Code of Ethics

Beyond knowing ourselves and valuing what we know, we need to establish our very personal code of ethics and values in order to define our special connection with energy modalities. Hopefully, this personal code refines and exceeds not only the professional guidelines that encompass our licenses to practice but also the ACEP codes given in the Appendix.

Because awareness of energy psychology has been in the public domain for only about a decade, practitioners are mandated to ascribe to the highest personal ethics. Each interaction with a client, a professional group, or the public will create a trail—one that will either continue to attract persons to the learning that is possible within this new rubric, or one that will turn people away. Readers of this book and colleagues on the leading edge of energy psychology will be the messengers who shape the future of this practice.

Clear intention to assist clients in achieving their highest good is a foundation stone of the energy therapist's personal code of ethics. We have noted earlier the pervasive impact of intention on outcomes (Tiller, 1997). Attention to our personal attitudes and opinions is essential, and we must be willing to let our egos step out of the way and to empower clients in finding the solutions that are best for them.

COMPETENCIES REQUIRED FOR ENERGY PSYCHOTHERAPY

Multidimensional healing requires specific competencies, skills, and knowledge in addition to development of higher sense perception and intuition. Although the actual techniques given here are relatively easy to learn, the principles behind them and understandings for appropriate applications are quite complex. Training and supervision must be ongoing in such a newly developing field as energy psychotherapy. There needs to be clarity about physical touching and therapist movement in the client's biofield. Boundaries must be set to enhance the facilitator's personal effectiveness without compromising client needs.

Training and Supervision

There are many programs that teach energy psychotherapy in a variety of formats. These include easy-to-learn generic approaches such as Craig's Emotional Freedom Technique (EFT) and Nims's Be Set Free Fast (BSFF) as well as highly sophisticated, customized programs like Clinton's Matrix work, which utilizes the chakras to reach core issues, and Swack's Healing from the Body Level Up (HBLU), a combination of hypnotic techniques to heal events beyond the client's personal lifetime. Comprehensive, step-by step training for beginners who wish to learn diagnostic work such as that described briefly in the previous chapter is available through Gallo's EDxTM, Nicosia's TEST program, and Grudermeyer and Hover-Kramer's Individualized Energy Psychotherapy (IEP), which is a multilevel training that works with the entire human vibrational matrix. Resources and organizational information for these training programs are given in Appendix E.

Expertise in providing safe practice of energy healing develops during several years after training is completed. Therefore, ongoing supervision with colleagues and experts in the field is highly desirable and may need to become a requirement as the work expands. Learning about energetic interventions through personal experience is comparable to the supervised practice that is built into most counseling education programs. If we wish to develop true healership skills in this new domain, we must also have direct knowledge of our own breakthroughs in order to help clients chart their course through unknown territories. If we have no knowledge of our inner world, we would have no way of helping clients to integrate or understand their seemingly unusual experiences.

Every energetically oriented therapist must be personally willing to explore motivation, distractions, biases, and new learning. A list of advanced practitioners and supervisory resource persons in different regions of the world is available through the Association for Comprehensive Energy Psychology (ACEP).

Clarity about Physical Touch

Since we work in close proximity with our clients, clarity about physical touch and its appropriate use is essentail. Energy healing does not require physical touching despite the somewhat confusing name of "Therapeutic Touch," which actually works with the biofield beyond the body. Whenever possible, I encourage clients to perform any of the processes described in this volume on themselves. I work on my own related aspects along with the client to support the client and to strengthen my own matrix.

For muscle checking, limited touching by the therapist is needed, and agreement with the client about the use of this approach is required. The wise counselor clarifies client preferences regarding touch at the beginning of the therapeutic relationship. At the same time, we need to be astutely aware of ways touch may have been misused in the client's past, for punishment or inappropriate sexual contact, and use utmost care even when permission to touch is given. Within the framework of client-centered counseling, we recognize that while touch can be mis-used, there are also may times that it would be inappropriate *not* to touch. For example, a lack of touch might further exacerbate the sense of childhood abandonment or the sense of touch-deprivation among the elderly. In discussing ethics involving the use of new, innovative thera-pies, Taylor observes, "There are times when a therapist should not touch a client; therefore some have made it unethical ever to touch the client. This logic is flawed. It ignores those times when it is important to touch a client" (1995, p. 60).

At times, it is necessary for the facilitator to touch acupoints or move into biofield/chakra areas because the client is unable to reach those areas of the body or the field. As long as careful agreement about the therapist's presence in the client's field or acupoints has been made, it seems unethical not to use a technique that might facilitate client relief.

"Susan," for example, was a client for whom I moved beyond usual injunctions around touch. She was suffering from bilateral reflex sym-pathetic dystrophy, a debilitating condition affecting nerves, blood cir-culation, and muscles in both hands. The incredible pain of the condition caused her to have severe psychoenergetic imbalance. After I balanced Susan's field a few times with the Brush Down and Con-necting the Chakras, she was calmer and receptive to meridian work. I used the thigh muscle on the leg for muscle checking as the upper body muscles were too painful to touch. With this, I was able to determine sequenced pattern in the meridians that reduced the anxiety associ-ated with her pain. I tapped the identified acupoints for her, asking her to remember the sensation of the tapping for future reference. Then we made a tape to which she could listen at home while imaging the clear-ing and strengthening of the biofield and the tapping of selected acu-points. She reported that these self-care sessions gave her a strong sense of empowerment that she had never felt before in the dark days and nights of pain—the tape and its reminders became a beacon of hope for her.

Establishing and Maintaining Boundaries

Establishing and maintaining boundaries is essential when client and therapist have interactive fields, and especially when client's issues may resonate with related material in the counselor. We are, after all, human beings who sympathize vibrationally with others' experiences. If our field is not strong and balanced, we may find a form of "energy conta-gion" and feel weakened after an encounter with a difficult client. Charles Whitfield, addictions counselor, puts it this way: "If we have unhealthy boundaries, we can be like sponges that absorb the painful, conflicted material [of the client]" (1993, p. 248).

For example, a counselor with unclear boundaries may inadvertently become enmeshed in a client's third chakra issues. The client may ask for advice and appear helpless; the counselor, who wishes to be effective, begins to influence client decisions in covert ways and to offer solutions. Rather than teaching the client healthy ways of accessing third chakra empowerment, the therapist, in this case, inadvertently sets up a situation where power and control are established external to the client's system. Ultimately, this pattern leads to increased client dependency and encourages a sense of powerlessness.

I find it helpful to do energy balancing exercises before each client session and to practice releasing movements after each session. This prevents depletion of my energies and the possibility of my joining into a client's energy pattern. The aphorism, "Either the client gets better or the therapist gets worse," is a statement about poor boundaries and also about energy communication. Put another way, either clients are able to increase harmony of their fields through our centered presence, or we become more frazzled by joining into clients' dysfunctional patterns.

Other issues of boundary-setting include policies about session frequency and cancellations, after-hour telephone calls, and therapist availability should an emergency arise. In my experience, one telephone call per week is all I can handle without becoming resentful. I never return a call unless I have centered and meditated on the client's issue and have found a succinct answer to tide us over until the next face-to-face meeting. Constant, refreshing inner work is essential in order for us to set and keep healthy boundaries.

Appropriate Use of Intuitive Material

As presented in the assessment chapter, therapist intuition is a helpful ingredient of the energy therapist's resource kit. However, great care must be used if such material is ever shared with the client. Although many clients are eager to know our opinions and may even try to guess what they are, it is not productive to share our internal perceptions unless some good therapeutic reason warrants it. In working with clients who are very blocked or not at all attuned to their inner states, sharing of an intuitive guess without any judgment or criticism may be helpful. This must be done with care, in a spirit of acceptance and openness as well as willingness to let it go if it does not resonate for the client. We must constantly be aware of our own needs—perhaps our desire to be right or all-knowing—and how this may impact the client in unpredictable ways.

Muscle checking may be seen as intuitive perception shared between client and therapist. If client self-report and the muscle checked SUD levels differ, it is not wise to say, "Aha, I knew you were holding out on me!" A much more neutral comment, such as "How interesting," may be all that is needed to help the client face a useful inner truth. My best rule of thumb is "when in doubt, leave it out." It keeps me out of trouble, and prevents me from saying too much that may lead to confusion, misunderstanding, or regrets. As therapists we need to remember that because we are talking about patterns that are energetically held in the vibrational matrix, issues have a way or resurfacing; if an issue did not get addressed at a certain time, it will undoubtedly come up again.

Integration of Learning and Closure

Results with energy psychotherapy are often so quick and effective that we may neglect taking time for clients to integrate learning and to make sure proper closure is achieved. Since working with the biofield, chakras, or meridian acupoints can cause clients to have a slight shift in consciousness, return to ordinary, consensual reality may be difficult without our assistance. In my experience, it is helpful to allow a final 10 to 15 minutes of a session for discussion and closure.

Assimilation of learning seems so natural in energy work that clients may actually deny that anything unusual has happened—they simply no longer have the problem. Clients report, "I see the situation but it no longer bothers me," or "It seems as if there's a protective veil between me and the issue." To make sure that the therapeutic effect of the interventions consciously stays with the client, it is helpful to ask the client to be a good observer or researcher until the next session. Clients can be asked to test out their new perceptions in similar settings as those posed by the presenting problem, or simply to repeat the energetic treatment pattern that helped them during the session. Written homework assignments are another valuable tool to remind the client of new learning.

Making sure the client is in car-driving alertness before leaving is a therapeutic responsibility. We can encourage the client to move about, ground to the earth, and repeat one of the centering exercises to accomplish this. Good space-time orientation can be facilitated by having the client pay specific attention to the physical environment—for example, describing visual details of the office. A sense of gratitude toward the client's self, the part that is willing to learn and try new things, can also be a good closing ritual.

Chapter 10

Relieving Pervasive Psychoenergetic Disturbance

I am not interested in the ephemeral—such subjects as the adulteries of dentists. I am interested in those things that repeat and repeat and repeat in the lives of millions. —Thornton Wilder

THE ENERGY TREATMENT CONTINUUM

From the perspective of a truly comprehensive, integrated energy psychotherapy, treatment involves careful attention to assessing client *readiness*, discovering possible internal *objections*, and addressing *specific issues*. These aspects of treatment help us to see energy therapy as a continuum for healing that extends from the initial assessment to the time when clients' SUD levels regarding major life issues reach zero.

Pervasive psychoenergetic disturbance, which is a systemic form of energy imbalance, is the most severe level of distress since it impacts all parts of the human vibrational matrix. Because as therapists we want to alleviate client symptoms, massive energetic disturbance may be undetected unless we consciously choose to look for it with the assessment skills described in chapter 8 —therapist intuition, client self-report, and/or muscle checking. Unless severe imbalance is addressed with referral to specialized resources or some of the methods described in this chapter, few of the more specific interventions to clear internal objections or to treat the presenting problem will be effective or will hold over time. Understanding pervasive imbalance is one of the significant contributions of energy approaches to psychotherapy in general;

it assists practitioners in considering client issues that need to be addressed before issue-related therapy can begin. In effect, *readiness* of the energetic system for treatment is not established until pervasive psychoenergetic imbalance is assessed and treated.

Another major concern from an energetic perspective is identifying and relieving unconscious, internal *objections* that the client may have. Callahan (2001) named these patterns "psychological reversals," implying that some mental reason exists in the client's conscious desire for change that conflicts with unknown, internalized beliefs. Because I feel it is more accurate to speak of a psychoenergetic pattern that seems to be held in the vibrational matrix and possibly even cellular memory, I prefer the term "psychoenergetic reversals" in addressing these internalized treatment objections with clients. It also seems less blaming for clients to think of themselves as holding an old belief -pattern in the energy system rather than as having a mental block. We will be exploring reversals and their treatment in the next chapter.

When system readiness and relief from objections have been established, we are ready to move to the client's issues by utilizing a variety of energy-based resources. Issue-specific imbalances can again be noted and treated in all three aspects of the human vibrational matrix. In chapter 12, we will describe these methods in more depth.

For now, let us visualize an energetic treatment continuum (modified from Grudermeyer, 2000), moving from the most broad to more specific aspects, in the following linear manner:

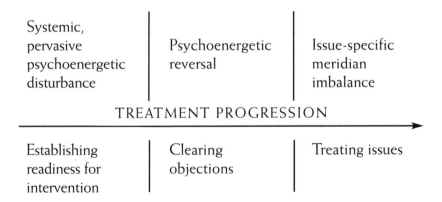

| Systemic, pervasive psychoenergetic disturbance | Psychoenergetic reversal | Issue-specific meridian imbalance |

TREATMENT PROGRESSION

| Establishing readiness for intervention | Clearing objections | Treating issues |

Our work is to assess client needs along the continuum and then determine the most effective intervention from the resources available through our understanding of the elements of the energy matrix. At each place along the treatment continuum, from dealing with the most general, pervasive imbalance, to addressing limiting beliefs and specific

issues, client distress level may diminish when pervasive energy disturbance, reversals, and issue -specific patterns are cleared.

Figure 10.1 gives another view of the treatment continuum, one that
may appeal to more holographic, visual thinkers. Again, we see movement from the general to the explicit, from the pervasive to a stated, particular problem. The funnel suggests the shift from the broad to more
specific issues. Our goal in assessing and treating each level of disturbance is to assist the client in reaching zero-distress levels and to move
from there to more creative options and high-level well-being.

Figure 10.1
THERAPY FROM AN ENERGETIC PERSPECTIVE

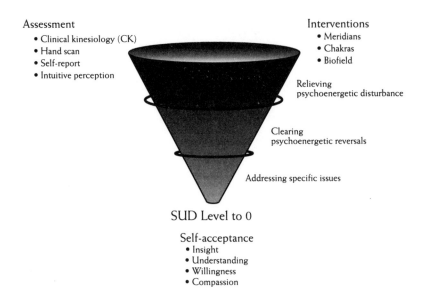

TECHNIQUES FOR TREATING PSYCHOENERGETIC DISTURBANCE

Biofield Interventions

We have already learned three techniques for treating pervasive psychoenergetic disturbance through the biofield—Centering, Brush
Down, and Central Alignment (see chapter 5). There are many more

ways of restoring balance to the biofield, but one of the most immediate is to introduce clients to biofield imagery. Since pictures seem to exceed verbal descriptors and allow most people an easy grasp of new concepts, I often use images of a balanced, symmetrical biofield to assist clients to "see" what they wish to create for themselves. You can expand on the imagery idea by using one or several of the following steps.

Exercise 1. Biofield Imagery

1. *"As you look at the image of a balanced field in front of you, while comfortably seated, release the breath and with it any tension you may be holding in your body. Imagine any darkness or depletion flowing out through the hands and feet."*
2. *"When you feel ready, take a full in-breath while bringing the image into your body. Feel the central core that flows from the top of your head to the base of your spine and through the feet."*
3. *"Sense the extension of your biofield beyond the physical body, feeling the connection from the earth that supports you and from the unlimited supply of energy in the heavens. Sense yourself as a vibrant being of energy."*
4. *"If you wish, allow a color or sound to flow through you, to soothe and harmonize with you. Feel a sense of safety each time you breathe fully."*
5. *"Imagine your field to be a protective sphere around you, one that can let supportive vibrations in and deflect anything that might be harmful to you. Sense the subtle but steady energy of this sphere."*
6. *"Gently let yourself come back to full awareness in this room while continuing to feel the harmony of your body, mind, and spirit."*

Chakra Interventions

Working with the chakras is another effective way of restoring harmony to the psychoenergetic system. One effective and enjoyable approach is using the Chakra Rotation (see chapter 6). Purposeful movement in general seems to "awaken" sluggish or disorganized energy bodies and to remind them of their natural proclivity for self-healing. For instance, encouraging clients to walk or dance with full attention to the feet, legs, and the root chakra at the base of the spine is an effective daily exercise for many who have blocked or stagnant energy patterns. In addition, we can encourage clients to add color and sound to their movement imagery. Red is the color vibration of the root, and a steady rhythm, like the patterns in drumming or Baroque music, supports client vitality.

Connecting the Energy Centers, described below, is helpful for clients who feel tired or depleted as well as for someone who is depressed or in grief. It can be done on a regular daily basis as a form of meditation or whenever needed to give extra support to the energy system. This technique incorporates some of the minor chakras at the joints of the legs in addition to the seven major chakras discussed in chapter 6.

Exercise 2. Connecting the Energy Centers

Begin by instructing clients to make sure they have a quiet place for 10 to 15 minutes. Intentionally finding quiet time for oneself may be a major therapeutic issue for many clients because of their hectic lifestyles. Then you might proceed with these instructions:

1. *"Making sure you are in a comfortable position while sitting or lying down, set your focus and intent toward yourself, your health, and well-being. Imagine your hands as the messengers to your body and energy system to bring about this intent."*

2. *"Place your hands above and below the foot on your nondominant side to bring warmth and a flow of life-supporting energy to it. Give your attention and appreciation to the foot for half a minute or so."*

3. *"When you feel a sense of caring and warmth in the foot, move one hand to the ankle and the other to the knee on the same side. Hold your focus on the ankle, knee, and the part of the leg in-between, until there is a sense of caring and warmth in the area."*

4. *"Let the hands then move to connect the knee and the hip, with one hand on each joint. Hold your focus on the knee, hip, and thigh until there is a sense of 'fullness' or warmth in the area."*

5. *"Repeat steps 2 through 4 on the dominant side of the body, connecting hands and your intention with the foot, the ankle and knee, and then the knee and hip."*

6. *"Now, hold both hips and allow the warm flow of your caring to fill the lower pelvis. After a while, you will get a sense of how long to hold each area, and also to notice any emotion that arises as you do this technique."*

7. *"Bring one hand to the root chakra at the base of the spine and place the other hand on the sacral area, letting the whole lower pelvis fill with light, warmth, and caring."*

8. *"Move the hands to connect the sacral and solar plexus centers. This is often an area where you may feel very vulnerable, so you might want to spend an extra half minute here and image a protective bubble or shield that holds the qi in place over the area."*

9. *"Move the hands now to connect the solar plexus and heart center, again holding as long as needed while sensing the protective bubble or shield over the area. "*

10. *"Place your hands over the heart center and throat while feeling your connection to self-expressive, creative energies."*

11. *"Connect the throat and brow centers while acknowledging your gifts for intuition and compassion."*

12. *"Finally, move your hands to connect the brow and crown centers to facilitate your connection to your higher self. Let one hand rest over the crown center while the other reaches above the crown and connects you to the transpersonal dimension, beyond the personal self."*
13. *"Feel the integration between body, mind, and spirit while affirming your right to be fully alive and present in this lifetime. Write down or share the insights that come to you."*

Meridian Interventions

The most direct meridian interventions that deal with pervasive psychoenergetic disturbance are those associated with the two central flows. Working with the central vessel gives us the Zip Up, while the Crossover Correction (both described in chapter 7) intersects with the middle meridians and connects the governing and central vessels via the tongue movements. In addition, we might think of the general affirmations with the pledge spot (see chapter 7) as another resource for treating pervasive or global disturbance.

Clear statements of clients' intention toward themselves also overcome psychoenergetic confusion. I find it helpful to ask clients to tap the thymus area in the upper mid-chest while they state their intention toward themselves. This helps to anchor the abstract idea of intention into the physical body and energy system. Often, it takes some discussion for clients to really be clear about their direction; general statements, such as "I want to be happy, wealthy, and wise," are not very useful unless the client is absolutely clear about the personal meaning of the phrase. Clarification may lead to more specific statements of intention—"I want to align myself with joy, I want enough resources to sustain me, and the wisdom to choose what is best for me."

The thymus area, related to the master gland of the immune system, is also the site for the Thymus Thump. Conceptualized and documented first by Diamond (1985) this is one of the many ways to give disorganized energy systems a jump start.

Exercise 3. The Thymus Thump

This exercise allows clients to lighten up and rebalance through laughter. Because it is so much fun, I enjoy doing it myself along with clients. Care must be taken, though, to make sure clients do not feel silly or exposed.

1. *"While seated, think of someone who unconditionally loves and accepts you and supports your efforts."* (*This may take a while for clients with severe energetic imbalance, and you may need to assist them in finding such resources.*)
2. *"Bring that person's energy into the palm of one your hands, and close your thumb inside that hand."*

3. *"Gently bring this hand to your upper mid-chest (thymus) area and tap lightly."*
4. *"As you exhale, use the syllable 'ha' several times to feel the support of the loved ones and your own energy."*
5. *"Try the syllable 'ho' several times and note how it feels to you; or try the syllable 'hee.' Is there a difference? Do you have a preference?"*
6. *"Enjoy this exercise as often as you wish. Joy and laughter are deep healers."*

A number of exercises, described below, from *Brain Gym* (Dennison & Dennison, 1982) and educational kinesiology are effective in addressing systemic energetic disturbance. Many of these approaches were initially developed by educators to help children with attention deficit disorders, and it is safe to say that many learning problems are associated with the presence of basic psychoenergetic disturbance.

Many adults who come to us as clients suffer from undiagnosed mild to moderate attentional deficits. Addressing these as a form of imbalance in the energy system is an important first step in their resolution. With muscle checking we can ascertain which exercise is most beneficial and the frequency with which the treatment needs to be made. This lends a client-centered approach to homework assignments practiced during the week. Unless psychoenergetic imbalance is due to a recent short-term event and therefore temporary, frequent repetition of the systemic balancing exercises over a number of weeks is needed for clients to feel better and more balanced.

Exercise 4. The Cross Crawl and Figure Eights

You may choose to do one or two of these steps with a client or to turn the whole exercise into a movement sequence.

1. *"While standing comfortably, set your intention for stimulating the right and left hemispheres of the brain through your movements."*
2. *"Move the right hand to the left knee and then alternate with the left hand to the right knee. Repeat this movement until you find a comfortable rhythm."*
3. *"While still moving, let your eyes go down to the left, and then the right. Move your eyes in big circles each way. Hum a tune, count out loud to five, hum again."*
4. *"Cross as many limbs in you body as you can."* (This might include moving the hands across the back, crossing legs and arms, crossing ankles, wrists, etc.)
5. *"Move your arms together to make a figure eight in front of you, swinging as far to the right and the left as possible. Move your whole body into a figure eight or just let your eyes make a figure eight by following a finger. Every time you cross the midline, you are establishing communication between the two brain hemispheres."*
6. *"Take another deep breath, release it fully, and notice how you feel."*

Exercise 5. The Belly Button Correction

This exercise stimulates several meridian points to help restore systemic balance: under the nose for the governing vessel, under the lip for the central vessel, at the collarbone for the kidney meridians, and at the base of the tailbone for the endpoint of the governing vessel. In addition, it uses the belly button as a connecting point, one that is familiar, comforting, and fun. Touching the fingertips to each other gives closure to the exercise and integrates right and left brain hemispheres.

1. *"While sitting or standing, take a deep breath, release it fully, and set your intent for allowing your system to move to balance."*

2. *"Place one hand on the belly button while moving the other hand to touch the points under the nose and under the lip. Rub lightly to stimulate each point and to set your vertical alignment." (This can also be done simultaneously with one finger on each of the two acupoints.)*

3. *"While keeping the hand on the belly button, move the other hand to the two collarbone points and rub lightly to set your horizontal alignment."*

4. *"Still keeping the hand on the belly button, move the other hand to the end of the tailbone, rubbing lightly to set alignment between front and back of your body."*

5. *"Switch hands, placing the other hand on the belly button and repeat steps 2 through 4."*

6. *Continuing to breathe fully, bring your fingertips together and hold for a few minutes to feel integration in your body, mind, and spirit."*

CREATIVITY IN SELECTION OF TREATMENT METHODS

Our clinician skill and creativity is the ingredient that transforms the exercises discussed here from mere techniques to effective treatment interventions. In selecting the resources that are most appropriate for a particular client's systemic imbalance, our knowledge, judgment, and intuition all come into play. In our dynamic interaction with clients, we may actually modify techniques or invent new approaches—there is a vibrant element of creativity in each client session.

The social sciences of counseling can be taught to some extent, but the subtle nuances required for moment by moment decision-making in therapy sessions are more correctly seen as an art form. Selecting the right intervention at the right moment requires our full creative energies and brings a sense of discovery and adventure to each client session.

Chapter 11

Addressing Psychoenergetic Reversals

To touch a suffering human being in the dark, hidden recesses of his inner wound requires the therapist's own willingness to open herself and reach out to the client from her own deepest core, fearlessly and without winning tricks of self-presentation or defensive tactics of self-concealment.
—Stephen Gilligan (2001)

A reversal is the energetic equivalent of an unconsciously held belief that influences the energy system and interferes with conscious changes the client wishes to make. While psychoanalytic theory holds that a person's unconscious beliefs sometimes move in opposing directions from conscious volition, our energy model suggests that reversals are associated with constrictions of qi flow in the biofield and chakras and may be related to reversed direction of electrical flows in the meridians. With either case, the result is some form of self-sabotage or counter-intention. Callahan (2001) has identified psychological reversals extensively and describes them as actions that are "contrary to what you say you want to do. You might say that you want to quit eating when you aren't hungry, and in your heart of hearts you really do want to quit overeating. But in reality you are continuing to overeat. You are sabotaging your own efforts, your feel helpless and you don't know why" (Callahan & Perry, 1991, pp. 40–41).

Another understanding of reversals comes from the work of psychologist Feinstein (2001; Feinstein & Krippner, 1997). He proposes that cultural myths and stories inform the sense of who we are, and that maturing into an individual personality requires facing and restructuring these myths. He also describes the personal myth as both a cognitive structure that is chemically coded in the brain and as a field of information held in our morphic, shape-generating fields. Dysfunctional, conflicting myths, both cultural and personal, can be addressed by treating psychoenergetic reversals.

Psychoenergetic reversals seem to emanate from underlying limiting beliefs that can affect the psychoenergetic informational network. It is certainly not in the person's conscious intent to sabotage cognitive decisions; neither are these subconscious patterns purely psychological in nature, for they do indeed have patterns that can be sensed in the client's vibrational matrix. Reversals, however, do constitute significant obstacles to positive treatment outcome, and many treatment failures stem from inability to identify and address reversals.

IDENTIFICATION AND TREATMENT WITH BIOFIELD AND CHAKRA APPROACHES

In the biofield, reversals may be sensed with the Hand Scan (chapter 8) as areas of density or congestion, thickness or depletion, heat or coolness over a particular area of the body, especially when the client attunes to a limiting belief. In the chakras, they are sensed either as a depletion or over-abundance of qi, too much or too little energy, either of which constitutes a form of imbalance. In addition to hand assessment, clinical kinesiology or pendulum dowsing, as described in chapter 8, can be used to assess physically such reversals. Balanced, open chakras influence the pendulum to spin in a clockwise direction, whereas a chakra impacted by a limiting belief pattern or reversal will literally be reversed—with the pendulum spinning counterclockwise or showing no movement at all. Most energy-healing practitioners also find ways of noting reversals through client self-report and intuitive sensing via meditation or internal imagery.

Because even one limiting core belief can influence many other patterns throughout a lifetime, some of the patterns that become established in the client's informational network are highly complex. Clinton's Seemorg Matrix Work (2001) is seminal in helping to identify the entire complex of core beliefs and in clearing psychoenergetic reversals through each aspect of the chakra system. There are many other ways of releasing reversals once a sense of rapport and connection is established between therapist and client. As the chapter quote suggests, we always tread carefully and with utmost respect when working with the hidden recesses of inner wounds that may underlie reversals.

In chakra/biofield approaches, reversals may be identified by asking clients to state a limiting belief that they or the therapist have identified. Then, the clients describe areas of the body where they experience the impact of that belief most intensely. This usually gives a strong indication of the most impacted chakra, since most people, with a little encouragement, have a sense of somatic awareness. Once the location of the distressing pattern is established, the client may or may not be able to access disturbing memories that created the reversal. If possible, I encourage clients to state the reversal as a currently known limiting belief that they wish to release. We then assist clients in releasing that limiting belief by having them perform strong counterclockwise spins over the chakra area in order to bring a more functional, empowering belief to the area.

Below are two exercises that further clarify biofield and chakra approaches to psychoenergetic reversals.

Exercise 1. Release of a Constricted Reversal Pattern in the Biofield

1. "While seated or standing comfortably, set your intention to learn about a limiting belief, or psychoenergetic reversal, in your biofield. Using internal imagery, scan your biofield to locate a constriction in the biofield that seems related to this old belief."
2. "Clear, smooth, or unruffle with your hands this congested area in the biofield. If it is held in the emotional body, for example, the pattern and its heaviness will clear with quick downward movements."
3. "You might wish to add the image of releasing this constriction to the earth so that it will be healed and transformed, and no longer burden you or anyone else. Notice any emotion associated with releasing, clearing movements."

Exercise 2. Release of a Reversal in the Chakra(s)

1. "While standing or sitting, identify a belief that you wish to release and notice where it is most felt in your chakra system."
2. "Since healthy, open chakras spin in a clockwise direction, the release of any disturbed or limiting pattern would most easily be effected with a counterclockwise spin over the specific chakra(s). While thinking of the pattern of which you wish to let go, move both hands over the most impacted chakra, first in a counterclockwise direction, while literally spinning it out and releasing the belief and the emotions associated with it."
3. "Sometimes more than one chakra is impacted by a limiting core belief, so you can also rotate the hands in counterclockwise direction over each center while releasing associated emotional distress as well."

Letting go and clearing is generally more effective working downward, from the crown toward the root chakra, or from the most impacted chakra downward. As we speak of installation of new patterns and treatment in the next section, we will note that these processes occur most naturally while moving one's consciousness upward.

Here is an example of clearing a reversal in the sacral chakra. "Nikki" stated numerous limiting beliefs about her so-called writer's block regarding her doctoral dissertation. These patterns included "I'm not good enough to write; people will judge me if I write; I will be misunderstood." After jotting down as many of her objections to writing as possible, I asked her where in relation to the physical body she most felt the impact of each belief. She repeatedly pointed to a "weak" sensation in the sacral area.

As she held her hands over the area, a whole flood of memories' emerged. The most damaging was a fourth-grade teacher who doubted her integrity. Nikki had written an unusually deep poem about friendship and read it to the class. So great was the trauma over the teacher's accusations of plagiarism before a classroom of children that Nikki resolved never to write again for any teacher. This definitely constituted a limiting belief for someone seeking a doctoral degree. When asked where in her body she felt most intense about this incident and its consequent decisions, Nikki continued to hold the sacral center, which is the center of consciousness for expressing feelings and making choices. Tears helped her to express and release the embarrassment and humiliation of the damaging classroom scene.

Treatment of the imbalance in the sacral chakra was relatively easy once the depth of the trauma had come to light. With several counterclockwise spins over the sacral chakra and expressive sounds, Nikki released the traumatic event. She added the image of sending the teacher to the light, to get more training in working with sensitive children. Nikki's field was then ready to bring in new, more effective beliefs about her writing and to repattern the structure of the chakra with her focused attention. She held her hands over the sacral area while stating her new empowering beliefs: "I deserve to write and complete the work I have begun; I am good enough; some people may misunderstand my writing or judge me, but I'm still okay."

IDENTIFICATION AND TREATMENT WITH MERIDIAN APPROACHES

The use of muscle checking, or clinical kinesiology, helps us to identify psychoenergetic reversals in general, as well as their many specific forms. Although these concepts of reversals began with Callahan's identification of psychological issues through muscle testing, they have grown into a whole compendium of specifically named reversals that can be identified and treated (Grudermeyer, D., 2000; Grudermeyer & Grudermeyer, 2001; Gallo, 2000). These include possible reversals around topics such as intention for treatment, future direction, deserving change for self or others, safety for self and others, motivation, deprivation, possibility, permission, benefit, and so forth. I will address some of thes topics below. As we check muscle strength to determine specific psychoenergetic reversals, we need to clarify that our goal is simply to discover what might interfere with treatment efficacy and to resolve possible conflicts. Just because reversals show up does not mean that clients believe them or are holding onto sinister secrets. Rather, clients' energetic fields hold patterns from previous experiences, myths, or trauma that simply may need updating.

IDENTIFICATION AND TREATMENT OF PSYCHOENERGETIC REVERSALS WITH MERIDIAN ACUPOINTS

Identifying and Treating "Intention" Reversals

Muscle-checking statements regarding the context for treatment and intention are as follows:

"I want to be over————this problem." (It is usually more effective if clients state the identified problem area using their own words.)

Alternate test statement: "I want to keep this problem."

Optimally, the first statement will show a strong response and the second, a weak response. However, there may be many conflicting ideas that this statement of intention brings up in clients, and we may get a weak response to the first statement and strong to the second—indeed, a reversal.

Gently offer the following treatment method: "While gently rubbing the nlr or pledge spot, please repeat three times, 'Even though I want to keep this problem, I deeply and profoundly accept myself.'"

We are not sure exactly how this process works internally, but after the client has completed the assignment, we retest the two initial muscle-testing statements. Most of the time, the second round of muscle checking will demonstrate clearing of the intention reversal. Clients often report a somatic or emotional shift when a reversal clears. Many treatment opportunities are, of course, present while addressing a reversal, as the case example on page 116 demonstrates.

Identifying and Treating Reversals about the Future

The contrasting statements to check for a possible "future" reversal are as follows:

"I will get over this problem/I will never get over this problem."

If a reversal is present, the treatment phrase is, "Even though I will never get over this problem, I deeply and profoundly accept myself." This is repeated three times while tapping under the nose. Then we recheck to assess if the reversal has cleared.

Identifying and Treating Reversals about "Deserving" to Make a Change

The contrasting test statements around a client's deserving to make a change are:

"I deserve to get over this problem/I don't deserve to get over this problem."

If the muscle check shows a reversal, the treatment statement is, "Even though I don't deserve to be over this problem, I deeply and profoundly accept myself." This is repeated three times while tapping under the lip.

Reversals related to deserving change are often associated with client shame stemming from trauma or violation and may open a large psychotherapeutic opportunity as they are identified. Additionally, "deserving" reversals are often held in relation to a significant other person—a parent, sibling, spouse, or boss—as a way of holding onto resentment. In effect, there may be a hidden wish, "I'll show them just how angry they make me." The holding of such a vengeful reversal can well sabotage treatment progress until it is cleared.

Test statements for a "deserving in relation to another person" reversal are:

"My————(insert name or relationship) deserves for me to be over this problem/My————does not deserve for me to be over this problem."

If a reversal is demonstrated, the treatment phrase is, "Even though————does not deserve for me to be over this problem, I deeply and profoundly accept myself." This is repeated three times while tapping under the lip.

Identifying and Treating "Safety" Reversals

As clients consider change, their basic beliefs about safety may be challenged. We check for safety reversals with the following test statements:

"It is safe for me to be over this problem/It is not safe for me to be over this problem."

If a reversal is present, it is treated with: "Even though it is not safe for me to be over this problem, I deeply and profoundly accept myself." This is repeated three times while tapping the side of the hand. Then we retest to make sure the reversal has cleared.

Codependent clients are often very concerned about what will happen to others if they make a change. Therefore, "safety in relation to others" can be another form of safety reversal. We test with:

"It is safe for————for me to be over this problem/It is not safe for————for me to be over this problem."

If a reversal shows, it is treated with: "Even though it is not safe for————for me to be over this problem, I deeply and profoundly accept myself." This is repeated three times while tapping the side of the hand.

Discussion

There are basic patterns to finding and treating reversals. First, while having the client make two contrasting statements, we use muscle checking to determine if a reversal is present. Then we treat the reversal by stating the truth of what the client's system has told us—i.e., even though this reversal is true for the moment, self-acceptance, self-respect, and forgiveness are greater. Often, clients wish to speak about their internal shifts while the treatment statements are being made, and following these client wishes leads to many opportunities for therapy and deeper integration for resolving reversals. Finally, we retest muscle strength to determine if the reversal has cleared.

The topics selected here to accompany the treatment phrases are the ones I have found most effective for each reversal mentioned. The perceptive reader will note that the nlr/pledge spot is often used for anchoring important general statements in the body and that "under the nose" and "under the lip" are the most accessible acupoints for the two midline meridians. The "side of the hand" corresponds to the small intestine meridian and is hence associated with releasing waste from the body. Callahan (2001) uses this acupoint almost exclusively to treat all reversals because of the presumed interrelationship between the physical and emotional releasing processes. Diamond uses treatment phrases (1985), whereas Callahan currently eshews verbalization and only uses tapping for reversal treatments. It is evident, then, that the suggestions given here are a hybrid, and the reader is welcome to develop alternate wording or treatment points, provided the intent of direct addressing of the reversal is met.

Sometimes, reversals that do not clear on one treatment point will clear readily on another. Skilled energy counselors can take the guesswork out of finding the best treatment point by using the trusty resource of muscle checking. Contrasting statements for each treatment acupoint may be formulated in the following way:

"The————point is most effective for me to clear my————

reversal/The————point is not most effective for clearing my————
reversal."

Again, the intention is for us to find what works best for a given client
rather than trying to establish patterns that work for everyone. As long
as rapport is strong and clients feel respected, we can use muscle checking as a refined, careful resource for truly client-centered therapy.

Case example

One of my long-term clients, "Sharon," had worked on numerous control issues, and we were able to treat many deeply held reversals. Then
a new crisis came along: Sharon's five -year-old daughter had been
rushed to the hospital with an asthma attack. Sharon assumed the hospital staff would be incompetent and anxiously anticipated that they
would be not know how to treat her child; she stared daggers at the
nurse who administered medication and felt ready to kill her because
the nurse moved somewhat slowly and did not seem to know much
about asthma. We carefully identified Sharon's treatment issue as "anxiety about others' different ways of doing things." The most anxiety-
producing scene was that of the slow nurse administering the
injections; Sharon rated it as a 8 on her distress scale, which was confirmed by muscle checking. As there were no signs of psychoenergetic
disturbance, I checked for reversals before moving to specific treatment
of the anxiety.

Since client intention is so vital for creating a meaningful therapeutic context, I checked for possible intention reversal first. I was totally
surprised to find that Sharon tested weak on "I want to be over this
problem" and strong on "I want to keep this problem." This was a clear-
cut reversal for sure. Despite her strong assertions about wanting to
release the anxiety, Sharon had something more powerful overriding her
goal. Almost immediately, Sharon was able to give the objection a
voice—there was fear that if she was not anxious, nothing would get
done to help her daughter. To compound these fears, Sharon had met
with a business customer that same week whose adult child had just died
after an asthma attack. The underlying fear of losing her daughter was
intensely disturbing and activated all the old concerns around controlling her daughter's health.

As Sharon attuned to these fears, which she rated at a 9+, psychoenergetic imbalance became activated. Sharon treated them by selecting
movement, root chakra spins, and the Crossover Correction. We were
then able to reformulate her treatment goal as overcoming fear of her
child's possible death. This time the intention was clear and no reversals were evident. Gradually, we were able to bring the distress level of

the fear to a lower intensity, and Sharon was able to identify the medical information she needed to ascertain that her child's life was not in immediate danger. She also recognized that she had much to learn about the early stages of asthma to prevent emergency-room dramas. Ultimately, several sessions later, she was able to turn the unknown aspects of her child's illness over to a higher power, through prayer and strong healing imagery.

Chapter 12

Treatment Applications for Working with Specific Emotional Issues

Just as energy medicine works to activate meridians and other energy sites in the body to heal illness, the technology of energy psychology may work through the psyche to help heal psychophysiological aspects of health imbalance.　　　—Maggie Phillips (2000)

After pervasive psychoenergetic disturbances and reversals have been cleared, the vibrational matrix is ready to deal directly with the client's specific issues. The distress (SUD) level, via both client self-report and muscle checking, may have already decreased by several points or actually come to a zero; it is helpful to recheck client discomfort levels after addressing the broader aspects of the healing continuum to denote any changes.

Working with the major aspects of the vibrational matrix gives us a number of creative options to assist clients with identified problems. While meridian work proceeds with eliciting a treatment pattern, or algorithm, via muscle checking or intuition, chakra/biofield work proceeds with direct interventions to the affected part of the informational network.

TREATMENT OF SPECIFIC ISSUES WITH BIOFIELD/CHAKRA INTERVENTIONS

A simple dialogue with an affected, asymmetrical part of the biofield may yield sufficient insights for psychological processing and insight. For instance, "Terry" was a client who found a strong imbalance between the right and left sides of her biofield when she assessed herself with the Hand Scan. Terry reported that her left side was in constant pain from an old back injury while the right side seemingly moved her forward as a busy industrial consultant and caregiver of her aging mother. I noted an area of intense heat over the left shoulder, to which she could attribute nothing more than carrying a purse that was too heavy. Nonetheless, this was information—while the right side was free to do as it pleased, the left side got the extra burden on top of an already overwhelmed life. I asked Terry's right and left sides to speak with each other. At first, this was almost inconceivable to Terry. With encouragement, however, she began to understand how all the pressure, tension, and shadow material got "dumped" on the left side and thus became hidden from awareness except for the presence of hip pain. Over time, Terry acknowledged her lagging side and found ways to ease the overall burdens. Terry also smoothed, cleared, and then held her focused attention over the most painful areas of her left side to give them her active concern. Interestingly, the physical pain, which doctors felt would require surgery, diminished markedly over the course of several months with this simple process.

Establishing dialogue with unknown parts of ourselves can be seen as part of a psychoenergetic process that can be used in a stepwise fashion (Hover-Kramer & Shames, 1997, pp. 83–96). After assessing imbalance or depletion of qi over the biofield or a specific chakra, we ask clients to hold their hands over the affected area and to note any image, color, or memory that comes to mind. Often, spontaneous recall of material imbedded in the vibrational matrix will surface. In therapeutic settings, we support the safe expression of such memories and their full emotional impact. Then we help the client to step back from the historical material by externalizing, or creating a *Gestalt* (Perls, 1969) of the person or specific event. While clients speak, with counselor encouragement, to each person that contributed to a traumatic event, they continue to clear, brush, sweep, or pull away congestion from the identified area. Strong expulsive breaths and sounds further assist full release of emotional constrictions. Sometimes, many layers of imbedded material need to be released before clients can move to new integration and insight.

Once full clearing of specific issues has been effected, we encourage clients to connect with their resources for resolution of the issue of concern in a manner that is creative and congruent for them. Clients assist the rebalancing or modulation of qi over the most impacted chakras by holding the hands and focusing attention over the injured area. The intention is to assist the healing and rebalancing

of the energetic disturbance. We complete this pychoenergetic healing sequence by having clients view the process from the perspective
of their higher self and breathing deeply, experiencing the deep inflow
of qi.

As each chakra has a specific psychological dynamic, a dialogue can
ensue with a closed or reversed center. The treatment goal would be not
only to increase awareness of a limiting core belief but to assist the client
in finding new, more functional patterns. For each limiting or negatively
phrased belief, new and positively phrased patterns can be installed.
This is usually most effective if we move upward through the chakra
sequence, from the most basic aspects of ourselves to the most forgiving
and spiritually aware aspects. Holding focus over each chakra in the
sequence while recognizing the new pattern, tapping the area, or spinning clockwise helps to strengthen the intervention.

For example, a limiting pattern around, say, public speaking may
have a message for each chakra via a new pattern that the client selects.
A new desired belief, such as "I own my birthright to speak effectively
and to be heard" has relevance not only for the throat center of self-
expression but for all of the chakras. Beginning with conscious intent
and hands held over the root, clients can address basic survival needs
with, "I now safely own my birthright to find my voice and to speak
effectively." As images of insecurity or fear related to the issue arise,
they can be readily released from the chakra with the clearing movements. Then we can proceed to the sacral center with the same message, but this time with awareness of feelings and the need to
discriminate between appropriate and inappropriate settings for self-
expression. Each chakra in turn can release, let go of its reversed, limiting patterns so that the desired belief can be installed and felt
throughout the energy system. We will discuss this work in more detail
in chapter 14.

The psychological quality of each center can help us in designing a
helpful mantra, or repeated phrase, to aid clients attune to changes
they are making. For instance, we can assist clients in clearing intense
fears related to survival and safety by encouraging dialogue with the
root chakra. Wording might be phrased in the following manner: "I want
you (root chakra) to hear me and make sure all parts are in agreement. .
. . I am releasing my old belief that there is not enough food, money, or
love for me. . . . I release all parts that made this old agreement in the
past from responsibility for holding this belief. . . . I accept that my
sense of security lives within me. . . . With every breath, I increase my
sense of safety."

TREATMENT OF SPECIFIC ISSUES WITH STIMULATION OF MERIDIAN ACUPOINTS

Eliciting an Algorithm Through Muscle Checking

When we have established psychoenergetic balance and released rever-sals, we are ready to find the specific pattern in the client's meridian sys-tem that helps to balance any weak or constricted flows of qi. Muscle checking should show that there is significant weakness when the client simply thinks of the selected distressing issue. Because some clients have difficulty staying attuned, or connected to their problem, the therapist can assist by using reminders such as *seeing* the setting of the problem, *hearing* what is being said or listening the *sounds* associated with the situ-ation, *feeling* the distress in the body, or *focusing* on the most intense aspect of the issue.

Since memory of the problem creates *weakness* in the entire psy-choenergetic system, we want to find out which of the 14 possible meridian acupoints are most affected by the problem and need to be *strengthened*. We elicit these points by muscle checking each acupoint (given in Figure 7.2) as the client clearly attunes to the debilitating issue. While the client touches an acupoint and attunes to the problem issue, the acupoint in need of treatment will test *strong*. In other words, it is the acupoint of the meridian where the electromagnetic system has short-circuited or decreased functioning except when the point is touched or treated to provide additional circuitry. The points that test weak as the client attunes to the issue will not need to be treated as they are not directly impacted by the problem. As we elicit the several acupoints for strengthening, we are establishing a treatment recipe or algorithm. The points can then be tapped, held, or imaged to stimulate or arouse the meridians affected by the client's problem. This diagnostic method for eliciting the client treatment sequence can be easily learned in one or two intensive weekend courses and is totally client-centered since all the information is obtained through muscle checking that reflects the client's inner knowing and psychoenergetic system.

Callahan, ever the innovator, has determined that there are specific algorithms, or acupoint patterns, for many treatment issues (2001). Thus, acupoints under the eye, under the arm, and at the collarbone rep-resent the most frequently used algorithm to relieve anxiety (2001, p. 110). He lists a compendium of dozens of algorithms to "cure" phobias, love pain, fear, compulsions, and even physical pain. The technician can simply look up an algorithm, or formula, and apply it like a recipe.

My experience has taught me that eliciting treatment sequences by muscle checking is more individualized and clinically effective. In truth, there are always clients who will not respond to a given recipe but will get immediate relief from an algorithm that they generated with the help of their therapist in a counseling session. Furthermore, I see the therapeutic environment as a creative interaction in which the dynamic between client and therapist establishes unique forms of energetic communication.

Below is an issue-specific treatment sequence that you can use with clients. It involves assessing the client's distress level, diagnosing the meridians that need treatment, and treating them with tapping in a sandwich-like format—first, we treat by tapping the elicited algorithm; then, we tap on a specific acupoint of the tri-heater (aka thyroid, triple stimulator, or triple-warmer) meridian, to help generalize the new program throughout the psychoenergetic system; and then we repeat the algorithm. As always, we recheck the client's SUD level to see if change has occurred, how much, and in what direction.

I like to inform clients of what I will be doing as we go along. The language of the exercise is therefore given in a way that you might share with clients.

Exercise 1. Diagnosing and Treating Meridian Imbalances

1. *"While seated comfortably, please think of your issue while I check your indicator muscle."* (Muscle should test weak as client attunes to the issue.)
2. *"Please think of your issue while I check for the treatment points that will be most helpful to you. Please touch the eyebrow and think of the problem while I check your muscle."*
3. *"If the muscle check is strong while you are attuned to your issue, it means that this point is affected by the problem and needs to be treated. I will ask you to treat the eyebrow acupoint by tapping 10 to 15 times while thinking of the problem. If it is weak, that means it is unaffected by the issue, and we can go on to the next point, at the outer eye, to see if it needs treating."*
4. *"Each time after we have treated an acupoint, I will recheck your indicator muscle without your touching a point to ascertain if the whole system has become strong even while you're thinking of the problem."*
5. *"I will write down the algorithm that we get as we treat each of the points so that we can come back to this recipe after we work with the valley spot acupoint of the tri-heater meridian."*
6. *"The middle part of the sandwich is as follows: While you tap on the valley spot between the last two knuckles of your hand, I will ask you to do several things that help to integrate the right and left brain hemispheres. These steps are to close the eyes, open the eyes, bring the eyes to the left (without moving your head), bring the eyes to the right, make a full circle with the eyes, now circle*

> in the opposite direction, hum a tune, count out loud to five, and hum a tune again."
>
> 7. "Then we will repeat the sequence I wrote down; all the while you will be attuning to the issue."
>
> 8. "When we finish, allow yourself to take a deep breath and release fully. Tell me the intensity of your distress on a scale of 0 to 10."

If the client's SUD level has dropped by two or more points after doing this treatment sequence, we can infer that this method is helpful, and we can repeat the process in order to find additional treatment points (and tap them with the same sandwichlike sequence) until we get to a zero distress level.

If the client's distress level remains the same, escalates, or diminishes just a little, we can infer that something else is happening, such as emergence of a new issue, presence of a secondary gain, or possible activation of a reversal or even a new psychoenergetic disturbance. In each case, we can use muscle checking to identify the nature of the problem, to clear reversals, or to treat more pervasive disturbance.

Exercise 2. Checking for a True Zero and Closure of a Treatment Session

> 1. "When we get to zero in your perception of distress in relation to the identified problem, we want to make sure it is a true zero. I will ask you to think of the most difficult aspect, the most painful memory, or the most unnerving future aspect of the problem that might occur. As you attune to this, I will recheck your indicator muscle strength. (If the muscle is strong without touching any acupoint, it means the your system is strong in relation to the issue. If the indicator muscle tests weak, we will go through another round of assessing and treating acupoints.)"
>
> 2. "If we have a true zero, let's end by using a simple yoga technique. Please bring your eyes to the floor while tapping on the valley spot. Let your eyes roll slowly (counting to 10 seconds) up toward the ceiling without moving your head. Breathe deeply and fully while feeling the relaxation, close your eyes if you wish, and then let the eyes relax in the middle. Stop tapping and thank yourself for the work that you have done."

Naturally, time constraints enter into issue-specific treatment sessions—clients may need to stop before a true zero has been reached on the SUD scale. The eye roll technique just given in step 2 is ideal for giving a sense of completion at the end of a session when there still is some distress about an issue. Especially if clients have not reached a true zero, I like to give homework assignments for them to practice until the next session.

Completely Level Reversals and Their Treatment

At times, the effective, rapid decrease of distress levels during an algorithm treatment sequence generates another form of reversal. A "completely level" reversal is simply one that arises during treatment. It is as if the client's system says, "Wait a minute! I'm not so sure I want to be completely over this problem just yet." Completely level reversals are often apparent when client progress toward problem resolution suddenly slows or reaches a plateau. Muscle checking can be done to assess for each of the possible reversals at this stage, just as we did in the previous chapter, except that this time we add the word "completely" to the contrasting test statements.

Thus, we have the following statements to check for such reversals:

Intention: "I want to be completely over this problem/I do not want to be completely over this problem."

Future: "I will be completely over this problem/I will never be completely over this problem."

Deserving: "I deserve to be completely over this problem/I do not deserve to be completely over this problem."

Safety: "It is safe for me to be completely over this problem/It is unsafe for me to be completely over this problem."

Treatment of the completely level reversal involves stating the truth of what the muscle check demonstrated just as we did in our discussion of reversals in the previous chapter. This time, however, the word "completely" is also added. For example: "Even though I do not want to be *completely* over this problem, I deeply and profoundly accept myself." This is repeated three times while rubbing the pledge spot. Then we retest to assess if the reversal has cleared. Each completely level reversal can be treated in a style similar to the phrases described in the foregoing chapter while including the word "completely" to let the client's system know that we are working toward full resolution of the problem rather than just a partial decrease in affective symptoms.

Identifying and Treating Psychoenergetic Disturbance Activated During Issue-Specific Treatment

Even more pervasive than a completely level reversal is the sudden reappearance of systemic psychoenergetic imbalance that can occur during issue-specific treatment. For example, during a workshop I held, "Walt" was receiving algorithm treatment for performance anxiety. His SUD level dropped to a comfortable 1 in the last practicum. Then I suggested that Walt imagine speaking on his topic in front of the workshop participants. He looked shocked and paled, his pupils dilated, his discomfort scale soared to a 9; it was as if all his circuits blew out at once. Muscle checking was undifferentiated because his system was temporarily totally imbalanced; proceeding with further elicitation of algorithms would have been meaningless. Walt's psychoenergetic system needed to be realigned: he proceeded to make a clear statement of his intent, took some deep breaths, and used the Brush Down to clear his "baggage" around public speaking. Once he was rebalanced, Walt quickly cleared several completely level reversals with the aid of his classmate, and finally moved to a true zero. He even practiced standing in front of the class during a break to get the actual feel of public speaking in an *in vivo* setting. At present, he is a successful presenter at ACEP conferences.

As we can see, work with the human vibrational matrix is a dynamic process that is psychologically sound and effective. It does not require labels of pathology. Often, traumas or repressed memories are stored, held energetically in a chakra/biofield areas, or are the cause of constriction and imbalance in one or more meridians. Because most trauma occurs very quickly and without words (van der Kolk, McFarlane, & Weisaeth, 1996), or happens in stages of life before verbalization even took place, the psychoenergetic resources of meridian, chakra, and biofield work can be effective therapies for accessing preverbal or "unthinkable" dilemmas. Comprehensive energy psychology is truly an expansion of the art of counseling beyond words.

Part IV

Integrative Energy Psychology Interventions for Accessing Creativity

Chapter 13

Expanding Our View of Energy Psychotherapy

*The exclusive focus on pathology that has dominated so much of out dis-
cipline results in a model of the human being lacking the positive features
that make life worth living.*

—Martin Seligman and Mihaly Csikszentmihalyi (2000)

The energy therapies seem to plant good seeds. In contrast to more traditional orientations that treat what is wrong with the client, the emphasis in energy therapy is on what is right and what can be learned to activate the self-healing capacity of the client's psychoenergetic system. The energy approaches exemplify the philosophy of the well-known Buddhist teacher Thich Nhat Hahn (1997), who writes, "The only moment available . . . is the present moment. If you can get into this moment deeply, then you can fix the things done in the past and also take good care of the future. . . . I would like to propose that we all reflect on the human capacity to connect with what is wonderful and healing in the present moment." Rather than being overwhelmed with the dismal state of our clients' problems and lives, we can use energy-oriented metaphors to help clients understand themselves more fully and to expand our resources as helping professionals as well.

From the very first energy therapy session, there is an emphasis on a positive therapeutic alliance to learn about patterns held in the client's energy system and to find the most helpful resources. With the energetic support of the counselor, clients learn self-care as they assess and treat their own chakras, biofields, and meridian acupoints. In addition, there is an inevitable sense of hope when clients actually experience relief from intensely held negative emotions and begin to see new options. Furthermore, many clients appreciate learning about their vibrational matrix—it's as if whole new dimensions of self-understanding open up.

Certainly, talking about psychoenergetic disturbance, reversals, and ways of treating specific issues from energetic perspectives seems to be more encouraging than addressing client needs from the framework of psychopathology and *DSM-IV* diagnosis, a model that is intended to parallel the predominant medical emphasis on pathology. Clients who have experienced this model often internalize self-defeating beliefs about themselves. We may hear these phrases from clients: "The doctors say they cannot do anything more for me; I probably need more medication; I have to learn to live with my problem"; or, simply, "I was told it's all in my head." None of these conclusions seems to offer helpful alternatives, solutions for self-care, or directions for the future. I personally would rather work with the not yet fully understood energetic metaphor than to limit my thinking to these perceptions. I believe we have something to offer that is self-empowering to each individual, even if full symptom relief is not possible, as in the case of chronic pain or long-term illness. For those whose distress is primarily emotional, the energy approaches offer a rich variety of resources for ongoing healing and high-level wellness.

Even though we do not yet fully understand the dynamics of psychoenergetic interventions, we can demonstrate remarkable changes in clients' conditions with the methods discussed in the previous chapters. Someone with severe emotional pain finds relief; even intractable physical pain is reduced or manageable. A person with anxiety is able to decrease its intensity and consider other options. Another, who holds long-term resentments and grudges, is able to forgive. Phobias literally seem to disappear, never to return. Severely traumatized individuals can reduce the emotional intensity of the trauma and access new beliefs about themselves and the world around them. These are powerful changes, which go beyond our usual experiences in counseling settings and move clients beyond symptom relief.

Using a model of therapy for full-energy living, let us now explore possibilities for ongoing change in clients' lives that exceeds dealing with presenting problems. Then, in the following two chapters, we will discuss specific considerations for expanding clients' creative potentials—a quality that the energy therapies seem to generate and empower.

EXPANDING OUR MODEL OF THERAPY FOR FULL-ENERGY LIVING

Figure 13.1 shows a schematic model of integrative energy psychology for full-experience living and high levels of well-being. We have discussed the various tools for energetic assessment (in chapter 8) and described the variety of maneuvers that can be used to treat psychoenergetic disturbance and reversals, as well as specific issues using meridian, chakra, and biofield interventions (in chapters 10 through 12). Our goal time has been to help clients move their distress levels to a true

Figure 13.1
THERAPY FOR FULL-ENERGY LIVING

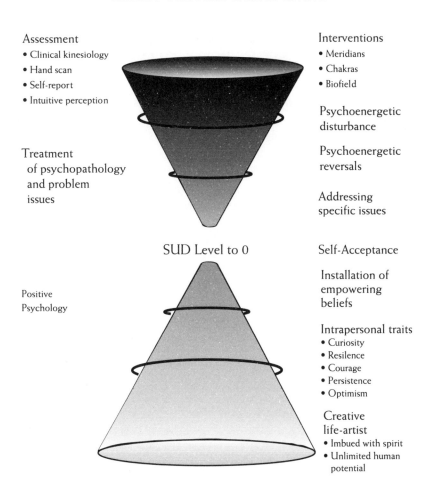

Assessment
- Clinical kinesiology
- Hand scan
- Self-report
- Intuitive perception

Treatment
of psychopathology
and problem
issues

SUD Level to 0

Positive
Psychology

Interventions
- Meridians
- Chakras
- Biofield

Psychoenergetic
disturbance

Psychoenergetic
reversals

Addressing
specific issues

Self-Acceptance

Installation of
empowering
beliefs

Intrapersonal traits
- Curiosity
- Resilence
- Courage
- Persistence
- Optimism

Creative
life-artist
- Imbued with spirit
- Unlimited human
  potential

zero while affirming deep and profound self-acceptance, forgiveness, appreciation, and self-esteem.

As the schematic suggests, however, treatment of pathology, diminished self-esteem, or problem issues is only a portion of a full-energy spectrum. Positive psychology, as posited and developed in the work of major theorists (Seligman & Csikszentmihalyi, 2000), represents a vast terrain for exploring human potential and creativity. Once clients diminish their distress ratings in the treatment continuum of the upper funnel represented in the schematic, they begin to integrate true sense of self-appreciation and are able to move into the open-ended domain of the lower funnel. This expanding vortex includes installation of empowering beliefs, development of the intrapersonal traits identified in positive psychology, and becoming the creative artists of their own lives.

INTRAPERSONAL TRAITS IDENTIFIED IN POSITIVE PSYCHOLOGY

Positive psychology emphasizes building on client strengths—"Our message is to remind our field that psychology is not just the study of pathology, weakness, and damage; it is also the study of strength and virtue. Treatment is not just fixing what is broken; it is nurturing what is best" (Seligman & Csikstezsmihalyi, 2000, p. 7). In truth, psychology is not just another branch of medicine, but rather an exploration of experiences such as insight, love, satisfaction, and play that make life worth living. Just as health is more than the absence of disease symptoms, so psychological health requires evolving ever fuller life potentials. Positive psychology has identified the following personal traits as essential to full-dimensional living:

- hope, optimism
- courage, curiosity
- autonomy, self-regulation
- responsibility, self-determination
- perseverance, resilience
- future mindedness
- wisdom, interpersonal skills, tolerance
- happiness, sense of satisfaction, altruism
- creativity, originality, sense of flow
- spirituality

These intrapersonal traits—and ways we might aid clients in developing them—are just now being studied in this new realm of positive psychology. For example, Seligman has shown that cancer patients with "optimistic explanatory styles" had significantly greater survival rates and probably better quality of life than those who lacked optimism (Seligman, 1990). In the experience of energy therapy practitioners, positive personal traits sometimes emerge spontaneously when the heaviness of client distress lifts. At other times, these qualities can be encouraged with simple reminders from the counselor. Above all, we seek to amplify client strengths and increase coping capacities. In the end, we begin to perceive that it is not so much what happened to clients, but rather how they interpret what happened to them and how they move forward with their lives that is most significant.

To interpret life events, such as trauma, in this new light requires a shift in perception, an expansion that becomes possible once we move our counseling skills toward the arena of assisting clients to full-energy living. Building a sense of hope, encouraging responsible self-care, supporting resilience and perseverance, enhancing relationship skills, opening to full human potentials—these are some of the powerful outcomes possible with energetic approaches to emotional healing. We will discuss each of them and their relationship to positive psychology traits as we continue.

BUILDING A SENSE OF HOPE

Some clients seek out energy therapies after they have already experienced more traditional approaches with limiting perspectives. For these clients, the idea that they might diminish their distress through an effective mind/body approach comes as a relief and offers hope. As they learn about and work with their energy system, they are delighted with the new resources available for healing.

Other clients come to therapy for the first time feeling like victims of events they cannot control. The personal optimism inherent in the energy approaches—i.e., "You can learn to help yourself by activating your own energy resources"—offers a beacon of hope. We further help to establish a sense of hope by sharing case examples of successful resolution and by building on clients' curiosity. Sharing information about the meridians, for instance, and how stimulation of specific acupoints can bring symptom relief may bring out clients' courage and willingness to experience something new.

ENCOURAGING RESPONSIBLE SELF-CARE

The self-care aspects of energy therapy are ideal for developing the sense of autonomy and self-regulation that are so essential to positive psychology. After we introduce the possibility of using energy psychology resources, clients choose the direction they wish to go and the issues they wish to address. The additional resource of muscle checking further supports a sense of self-determination. As soon as distressing events come into client's awareness, they are encouraged to take responsibility by treating the emotional effects of a situation directly.

Blaming others for personal distress is all too easy in many fragmented families; counselors must beware of falling into the trap of supporting clients' displaced anger and blaming mechanisms. As an example, "Dana" would spend the first part of each session berating her husband for his many faults. Each time, after sufficient venting had occurred, the therapist reminded Dana that she needed to treat her anger in order to avoid harming her physical body. The husband was not available for change, but she was. The exercise of rubbing the pledge spot while stating, "Even though I have intense anger about——
——, I deeply and profoundly accept myself," became a daily mantra for Dana. Gradually, she gave up wishing that her husband would change and came to appreciate her own personal strengths and abilities. Accepting appropriate self-responsibility opened the door to new thinking about her life and long-term goals.

SUPPORTING RESILIENCE AND PERSEVERANCE

Resilience is the ability to bounce back from difficulties without ignoring them or being overwhelmed. It requires a certain tenacity, a willingness to postpone immediate gratification in deference to future outcomes. Success, despite its portrayal in movies and television, usually does not come instantly: it comes from repeatedly trying to learn and work at something. The energetic approaches support such perseverance through daily exercises and the sense of empowerment that comes from doing personal assignments.

Let us continue with Dana's story. She worked for her husband, in his physician's office, but he was often emotionally abusive. The possibility of finding a different job totally overwhelmed her with fear. We treated this fear with a mantra similar to the one she used before: "Even though I am afraid of working in a different place, I deeply and profoundly accept myself." And, of course, we cleared numerous reversals around her deserving a better situation and then used acupoint tapping to diminish the sense of fear. Then she went through strength-building exercises such as listing her skills and writing a resume. Her persistence began to pay off, and she found job-listings that corresponded to her skills. Dana recognized that she was free to make new choices at the pace that was right for her.

ENHANCING RELATIONSHIP SKILLS

According to a recent psychological study (Sheldon, Elliot, Youngmee, & Rasser, et al. 2001), relatedness—that feeling of closeness with others—is one of the four most essential ingredients for happiness and satisfaction. The three other ingredients for personal satisfaction, not surprisingly, are autonomy (feeling that activities are self-chosen), competence (feeling that one is effective in one's activities), and self-esteem. To be effective in helping clients find their paths to happiness and full-energy living, then, we need to help them to address relationship issues from an energetic perspective. Fortunately, the energy modalities offer rich resources for bringing a sense of wisdom, tolerance, satisfaction, and altruism into interpersonal relationships.

Often, in beginning work with couples, I teach several psychoenergetic balancing exercises that partners can do with each other. The partner who is the most flexible on a given day becomes the one that reminds the other to begin centering practices together. Conflicts invariably de-escalate when partners commit to using focusing methods with each other. Since much of energy therapy invites attention to intentionality, finding out the intention behind even very botched communications is helpful. As each person in a family takes responsibility for his or her feelings and for lowering distress levels, there is room for joy, sharing adventures, play, and collaboration.

Let's look in on Dana again. She clearly had relationship issues with her husband, "Rick." He finally agreed to come for only one session and seemed to cower in front of me, waiting to be chastised for his wrong doings. I suggested that both Dana and Rick talk about their intentions in their communications and that once those were understood, they might like to use some energy concepts to keep their intentions clear. Dana asserted that she wanted to work for Rick to help him to succeed but that she now had enough confidence to realize she could get other jobs. Rick admitted that he "might be hard on her at times" because he wanted to succeed in his business so Dana could have the lifestyle she wanted as a physician's wife. Both seemed to want to help the other but the goal had become lost in their day-to day irritations. I stated that reprogramming would require concerted efforts on both their parts—a willingness to validate each other, to reiterate intention, to ask for what each person needed, and a commitment to performing daily centering practices together. Rick was encouraged by the positive outcome of the session and started his own intensive therapy. Dana continued to develop her job skills so that she could move forward if needed. At this time, Dana and Rick are still together and report being considerably less angry in the workplace; prognosis for the relationship over time is admittedly guarded.

OPENING TO FULL HUMAN POTENTIALS

Personal thriving seems to engender creativity and originality. This is not possible, or remains very limited, when clients are stressed with internal or relationship conflicts. Opening to one's full potential becomes possible only when inner balance is restored; it becomes actualized when clients consciously choose to express themselves and to access their inner wisdom. The outcome of such a perspective may simply mean enjoying life more, taking time to connect with nature, or developing spiritually through the sense of being connected to something greater than the personal self.

As Dana began to value herself, she announced quite spontaneously one day that she would spend the next weekend "crafting." The idea of playing with long-forgotten craft items surfaced when she became more balanced and started to access new self-esteem. It was astounding to see the results of Dana's handicraft once the generative impulse surfaced: the formerly mousy, oppressed wife produced exquisite paintings on clothes and gradually developed a personal wardrobe of unusual beauty. With pride Dana told me one day that she literally sold a shirt off her back to an enthusiastic passerby for $150. With her self-esteem so affirmed she was on her way to inner satisfaction and healing.

One of the most rewarding aspects of good psychotherapy is helping clients to discover the hidden treasures within. Opening to full-energy living is the ultimate goal of creative therapies.

Chapter 14

Releasing Limiting Beliefs and Installing Desired Beliefs

Everyone makes for himself his own segment of world and constructs his own private system, often with air-tight compartments, so that after a time it seems to him that he has grasped the meaning and structure of the whole. But the finite will never be able to grasp the infinite.

—Carl Gustav Jung (1971)

Redirecting limiting patterns toward a more effective behavioral styles can be surprisingly easy if we allow psychoenergetic approaches to assist. Work with the chakras, the biofield, and the meridian acupoints—the major aspects of the human vibrational matrix—give delightful resources for daily self-care, which can extend well beyond the scope of traditional counseling sessions. It is our goal to enable clients to address their patterns of distress and, on a daily basis, to transform these patterns into new ideas and resources.

CORE BELIEFS AND CLUSTERED PATTERNS

Just one issue may generate awareness about a host, or complex, of limiting beliefs that clients hold. These core patterns may have been imbedded in the vibrational matrix during early life trauma and now inform the entire personality, leading to other dysfunctional beliefs and spawning psychoenergetic imbalance and reversals (Clinton, 2001). Examples of such negative core beliefs are "I don't accept myself; I am confused; I am betrayed; I am powerless, helpless; I deserve failure; I have nothing to live for; the world is dangerous." It is easy to see how any one of these broad generalizations could generate many related negative thinking-patterns along with a lifetime of mistrust and unhappiness.

In my work with musicians, issues around performance inevitably surface. When I ask them to list their most absurd and limiting beliefs, patterns around self-esteem and personal confidence surface quickly. Furthermore, we may find perceptions that were internalized during childhood trauma or inferred from powerful adults at a time when the person had few, if any, defenses or coping mechanisms.

Often, I simply begin by asking musicians to list all their awful thoughts about performing. "Mark," who was also a physician, came up with his list rapidly: "If I perform, I might make a mistake. . . . If I make a mistake, I will be wrong. . . . If I'm wrong, I will not be a good doctor. . . . If I'm wrong, I will be a poor role-model for my children. . . . If I'm wrong, my father will punish me. . . . If I'm wrong, everyone in the family will laugh at me." I could see him accessing sheer terror as his list unfolded and grew longer. The core issues that emerged from this simple exercise were not just Mark's adult identity around being a physician and father but also his childhood family structure of felt intimidation and embarrassment.

Mark sensed the terror of public performance in all three of his lower chakras, so I asked him to release the most powerful old belief from each of the three centers with a vigorous counterclockwise spin. He chose "My family will laugh at me" as the most damaging core issue and released it with vigorous expulsive sounds from each center. As he released the family's jeering, Mark began to see them smiling, cheering him on in a more kindly fashion. I asked which new thought or affirmation would be helpful to him in overcoming the old image and bringing in the new one. Within a moment, he had it—"If I make a mistake, my family supports me." He anchored the new belief into his body by holding his hands over each chakra in turn and giving each one a clockwise spin. Just to make sure, we added the Thymus Thump (chapter 10), with each supportive family member, both present and past, safely tucked into his fist.

Alternate ways of releasing limiting beliefs is to use meridian-based protocols (Grudermeyer, Grudermeyer, & Hover-Kramer, 2000). One way is to establish the extent to which the limiting belief is true for the client on a scale of 1 to 7, followed by tapping the Generic Sequence (chapter 7) while having the client state, "I now release——
—" at each acupoint. Retesting should show that the truth of the limiting belief has diminished significantly, especially if the client has accessed repressed material from traumatic experiences in the releasing process. In another approach, we can use muscle checking to determine which acupoints are the strongest while the client attunes to a limiting

belief. We then have the client tap only those affected points, to let go of the dysfunctional thought. Again, muscle checking should demonstrate a decrease of the client's validation of the limiting belief. Now there will be room for installation of more functional patterns. A third approach would be to ask the client to rub the pledge spot while stating three times, "Even if I make a mistake, I deeply and profoundly accept myself." Possibly, the words, "I deeply and profoundly forgive myself" would be even more effective for guilt-laden individuals like Mark. In either case, the intent is to overcome erroneous beliefs about making mistakes or being wrong.

The human creative process requires looking at our mistakes and moving forward with the insights we have gained (Cameron, 1992). People who want to live fully accept the reality of daily repeated risking and reorganizing—visual artists paint 20 pictures before selecting the one they wish to display; musicians practice over and over to perform and share with audiences, wrong notes and all; photographers shoot 10 rolls of film to find the right angle for their subjects; good architects design and redesign hundreds of times until they master the discipline and develop their own style.

IDENTIFYING LIMITING BELIEFS AND ACCESSING NEW POSSIBILITIES

The work of identifying and releasing limiting beliefs and their powerful influences is only partial; it still needs the installation of new, more functional patterns. We must let go of the old disruption or constriction before a new idea, balance, or harmony can fill its place. Once distress has cleared out, the creative human mind has the magical capacity to attract what it wishes and make it real with a single word, phrase, or image.

"Nikki," whom we met earlier in chapter 11, was a doctoral student lost in the mire of university requirements as well as self-doubts about her own writing. We spent most of a whole session identifying all her dysfunctional patterns around writing. Needless to say, it was a heavy session with tears and memories of childhood trauma. As I opened the possibility that each limiting belief could have a more empowering counterpart, things began to brighten. We came up with a list similar to that given in Table 14.1, with the column on the left listing the old beliefs and the column on the right accessing the desired possibilities.

As described in chapter 11, we can simply take a limiting belief and release it from the chakra in which it is most intensely felt by the client. In addition, we might go through a psychoenergetic release process as

Table 14.1 SAMPLE OF LIMITING BELIEFS AND DESIRED NEW BELIEFS ABOUT WRITING

Limiting Belief	Desired, New Belief
I'm not good enough to write.	I am good enough to write.
I'm not special enough to write.	I am ordinary enough, and special enough, to write.
Writing is only for extraordinary people.	Writing is for everyone.
If I become a writer, I will be doomed to a life of poverty.	If I become a writer, I will fulfill my destiny.
If I show who I really am, I will be criticized.	If I show who I really am, I may be criticized or praised.
If I express myself, it will be dangerous.	When I express myself, I can plan for my safety. I will feel good.
When I express myself, I will be dangerous.	When I express myself, I can be a safe person.
If a reader does not like what I say, it will be my fault.	If readers do not like what I say, it is their choice.
I am afraid of ridicule.	I can deal with ridicule. I don't have to like it.
If the teacher does not like my poem, I will never write another.	If the teacher does not like my poem, it will be her choice.
I can only write a few poems.	I can choose to write as many poems as I wish.
Writing about the ordinary is stupid.	Writing about ordinary things can communicate great meaning.
If I express myself, I will be misunderstood.	If I express myself, I can learn to be understood. Some will understand and some will not; it is their choice.
If I follow the university rules, I will be stupid.	If I follow the rules and graduate, I will be free to write as I please.
If I write badly, I will never get better.	If I write badly, I can learn how to write better.

Table 14.1 continued	
Limiting Belief	Desired, New Belief
I am embarrassed to write about myself.	I can learn much about myself if I write about myself.
No one is interested in my writing.	Some persons may find what I write to be interesting.
I can't learn new things about writing.	I can always learn new things about writing.
I dislike making mistakes in my writing.	I can learn from my mistakes in writing. Not learning from my mistakes is the greatest wrong.

described in chapter 12. Alternately, we can work with the meridian acupoints to stimulate the points where the belief is most fully held and thus release these beliefs.

Installation of a belief that is more desirable and empowering for the client could be accomplished in similar ways. One way would be to bring attention to each chakra, starting at the base, while stating the desired new belief and letting the unique energy of each chakra support and enhance the new belief. Another would be to tap all the meridians while stating the new belief as an affirmation. Alternately, we could use muscle checking to determine the validity of the new belief to the client on a 1–7 scale, install the belief with the acupoints that test most strong with the new statement, and recheck the muscle for any change.

The following exercises further clarify the approaches we might use to identify and release old patterns and install more functional and desirable beliefs. Establishing psychoenergetic balance through centering practices (given in chapters 5 through 7), always precedes specific work such as this.

Exercise 1. Releasing Dysfunctional Beliefs through the Chakras and Biofield

1. "While standing or sitting comfortably, please think of a belief that you have around your creativity (or an identified issue). Notice where in your body you most feel it."
2. "Bring your hands to this area while thinking of all the related beliefs or iden-

tified memories that you may be holding there. Consider anything that may be holding you back from letting go of these limiting ideas."

3. "With the hands over the affected area, please rotate to the right to sweep out the pattern that you wish to release. Stating the old belief and using expressive, expulsive sounds and movements will further enhance this work."

4. "Notice and describe any images or thoughts that come to you now. When you have done this, you will then be ready to bring in new, more desirable beliefs."

Exercise 2. Installing Desirable Beliefs through the Chakras and Biofield

1. "Please think of an empowering belief that you would like to have about your creativity (or an identified issue). Notice where in your body you most feel it."

2. "Beginning at the base of the spine, please bring your hands to each energy center while stating the new belief as an affirmation for the center and its energy. (For example, for the the root chakra, 'I am safe and secure in my whole being while reading my poetry in front of critics.' For the third chakra, 'I feel my power and effective assertiveness while reading my poetry to audiences.')"

3. "Sense your whole being filling with the light of this new belief in each center; breathe fully and stretch your arms wide to the outer dimensions of your biofield."

4. "Notice related beliefs that you might want to add; install them in a similar fashion. Make a poster or chart of the most empowering beliefs. Enjoy your new images, talents, and abilities!"

Exercise 3. Releasing Dysfunctional Beliefs through the Meridian Acupoints

1. "As you sit or stand comfortably, think of an old belief regarding your creativity (or an identified issue), please rate the truth of it for you on a scale of 1–7. (A rating of 1 means it is not very true at all; 7 means it is very true at this time.)"

2. "I will check your indicator muscle to learn from your psychenergetic system about the rating as well."

3. "While attuning to the limiting belief, I will check your muscle strength to find which acupoints are most associated with the belief."

4. "While stating the belief, tap the acupoints that we have identified as most associated with the belief. This will release it from your energy system." (An option here would be to make this a sandwichlike sequence, as described in chapter 12.)

5. "Please state the truth of the belief for you on the 1–7 scale. I will recheck your muscle as well to confirm." (Truth of the limiting belief should be a 1; if not, another release pattern may need to be elicited through the muscle checking.)

Exercise 4. Installing Desirable Beliefs through the Meridian Acupoints

1. "Now think of the new belief regarding your creativity (or stated issue). Tell me how strong it is for you on a scale of 1–7. Through muscle checking I

will also confirm the validity of the new belief for you. (If the new belief is less than a 7, we will want to continue with this exercise.)"

2. *"Through muscle checking we will now find out which acupoints most strengthen the desired belief."*

3. *"Please tap on the acupoints that we have identified as most strengthening the belief, while stating the belief out loud." (The option of making this a sandwichlike structure is also available.)*

4. *"Now we will recheck the validity of the new belief through your self-report and muscle checking. Please describe how you feel and any thoughts or ideas that come to you." (Muscle checking and self-report of the truth of the belief should be at a 7, i.e., very true; if not, another installation pattern could be elicited through muscle checking.)*

Exercise 5. The Temporal Tap for Changing a Psychological Habit

This exercise was originally used for pain control in the East, but is also every effective in breaking emotional habit patterns and establishing new resources. It accesses the resources of the right and left hemispheres by alternating a statement of negative belief, while tapping on the left side of the head, with a positively stated belief while tapping on the right side, and is described in further detail by Donna Eden (1998, pp. 332–338). The exercise involves elements that are powerful for accessing change—repetition, auditory and kinesthetic sensory processing, autosuggestion, neurological reprogramming, and stimulation of numerous meridians on the head. As always when working with client beliefs, the words must be stated in the same way that clients talk and think and be in harmony with clients' core beliefs and values.

1. *"Starting at the temple, tap the left side of your head from front to back below the ear with a few fingers of your left hand. State the limiting belief that you wish to change by tapping front to back at least five times while attuning clearly to the words."*

2. *"Now tap with the right hand on the right side of your head while stating the positive version of the belief. Repeat this about five times, while attuning to the meaning of the words."*

3. *"Repeat this procedure several times during the day. The more you tap in the positive affirmation, the more you will change the old habit pattern."*

LEARNING TO TRUST INNER WISDOM

When we introduce these concepts to clients, they may comment, "Oh, I already knew that; you just helped me to remember it." It is one of the joys of interactive therapy that we can help clients to find what they already sensed at a deeper level but could not fully bring into conscious awareness. Assisting clients to formulate language patterns for their new beliefs is wonderfully empowering—both for them and for us. Blocks to creativity in the form of limiting belief patterns are usually self-imposed; but as the impediments are removed, vibrant energy for new endeavors can emerge. It is like a renewing breath of fresh air when clients permit themselves to see again the true jewel that resides within.

Most training programs related to creativity in adults first address the vast repository of self-doubt and criticism that resides within most of us and hobbles our every human capacity for enjoyment. *Finding What You Didn't Lose* (Fox, 1995) is a powerful book about learning to express one's truth and creativity through poem-making. More important, it is simply good therapy to cease negative self-talk, make some kind of acceptable peace with the inner critic, and begin whatever we have been putting off.

Since we have never really lost our capacity for playing with words, paint, clay, dirt, rocks, musical instruments, or clothes—becoming a life-artist means recovering the playfulness we always had. During the 100 years of war in medieval times, villagers who wanted to protect their churches' treasures covered them with ugly lead. Later generations were able to peel off the lead and rediscover the gold underneath. Similarly, clients and therapists alike can find the "gold" within themselves by learning to trust their sense of "inner knowing."

Jung relished exploring nonlinear, alternate ways of knowing by studying divination, intuition, and synchronicities (Jung, 1965). We can consider his work to be the psychological basis for our growing understanding of unconscious processes through exploration of affirmations, symbols, images, and the whole realm of energy psychology. He predicted that future generations would be working more and more with the human vibrational matrix because of its roots in cross-cultural healing practices, which he had studied extensively. Although clinical kinesiology had not yet come into use, Jung would be delighted at our discovery of noninvasive means to access feedback directly from the client's psychoenergetic system.

Energy therapies offer a number of client-centered approaches to accessing intuitive wisdom. One is simple the acknowledgment of self-acceptance repeated in the affirming self-statements for psychoenergetic balancing: "I deeply and profoundly accept myself with all my talents, gifts, and abilities to love." Another is the recognition of other ways of knowing—for example, through muscle checking and basic respect for every client's unique patterns. Attention to centering practice is a further way of connecting with inner wisdom. In effect, the focusing techniques bring clients' scattered, disorganized thinking into coherence. By way of analogy, centering is the energetic equivalent of switching from a incandescent electrical light source to a laser—incoherent light with random emissions becomes highly focused and directed. If the emissions from a simple light bulb were turned into a laser beam of coherent light, they could burn holes into thick sheets of metal. So too, the human mind can become powerful, directed, and inventive when its energies are brought to coherence.

As clients learn to trust their inner wisdom and access increasingly effective new beliefs for themselves, they become the conscious co-creators of their lives—the life-artists they were meant to be. We will explore this creativity—the pinnacle of full-energy living—in our next chapter.

Chapter 15

Becoming a Life-Artist

Survival no longer depends on biological equipment alone but on the social and cultural tools we choose to use. The inventions of the great civilizations—the arts, religions, political systems, sciences and technologies— signal the main stages along the path of cultural evolution. To be human means to be creative.   —Mihalyi Csikszentmihalyi (1996)

In his analysis of 95 famous, highly creative persons, Csikszentmihalyi (1996) distinguishes between the sense of personal creativity that is potentially available to everyone and the Creativity (with a capital "C") of those few individuals who are actually recognized as changing the world of knowledge. Creativity requires not only dedicated mastery of a chosen discipline but also the ability or good fortune to gain the recognition and support of established leaders in the field. For example, Einstein could not have become the physicist that changed our understanding of the world about us without validation from experts in his field and the greater scientific community.

Personal creativity, on the other hand, is available to all of us. Its development requires mastery of a at least one domain and the nurturing of specific personal traits such as openness and resilience. The chosen domain may be gardening, knitting, singing, playing an instrument, writing, counseling, or interior design, to name only a few. Exploring a domain in depth eventually may bring about recognition from other contributors and the larger field of the domain. But for most people, the ability to put things together in innovative ways and to live creatively is simply a better way of finding personal fulfillment. It is enriching to explore a domain and master it, whether or not we ever find public recognition.

Unfortunately, many of our clients are disconnected from this opportunity for personal fulfillment and live rather lackluster day-to-day lives, letting random, disorganized thoughts dominate. Full healing requires both reclaiming the potential for personal creativity and reconnecting with the innate human capacity for inventiveness and playfulness. Beyond recovery from life's challenges through effective psychotherapy, clients can learn to access high-level well-being through their expressions of personal creativity.

A good place to start accessing principles of creativity is to watch how young children open to the world around them: almost anything new is fascinating and attracts their curiosity. As they explore, they may play, question, move, shove, and put things together in new ways. They seem to derive pleasure and satisfaction from building something, then tearing it down with glee and building something even grander. They are in a flow, just doing something for its intrinsic pleasure and satisfaction. There is no thought about the future or what others might think—they are totally in the moment.

Few adults maintain this sense of flow—simply enjoying an activity for its own worth—and, with it, the possibility for discovery and invention. We may rightly ask how we can help clients recover the spontaneity they once knew as children. We might also ask how playful, explorative, imaginative youngsters could become burdened, colorless adults who may even dislike their chosen careers.

From a psychological point of view, we may point to early life trauma, not only loss or violation but also lack of recognition and validation, as major factors influencing clients' core beliefs. Thus, young persons may come to think of themselves as stupid, incapable, or unworthy. In addition, limiting beliefs about innovation and creative activity are repeated in our social environments. Beliefs, such as "Oh, I can't carry a tune; I can't draw; I'm too awkward to dance; I'm not creative like so and so; girls can't do math," become so internalized that we are hardly conscious of their presence. They are powerful influences, nonetheless, and may require intensive, committed work to reprogram. Fortunately, through the psychoenergetic resources that we considered in chapter 14, there are means for releasing limiting beliefs and for accessing more functional, empowering thought patterns to nurture innate abilities and creative zest.

AN EXAMPLE OF PERSONAL CREATIVITY

In the film *Cast Away*, Tom Hanks captures the psychological truth of human response to loneliness and peril on a deserted island. Much like the generations of early humans living millennia ago, Hanks first secures his life by finding food, establishing shelter, and making a fire. Although he is quite alone, he cheers out loud when he succeeds in fire-making. He then draws pictures, even a calendar, on the walls of his dark cave. The pictures become symbols of his connection with life and his friends. They become points of comfort in the desperate silence.

Another development is the establishment of communication with "Wilson," a soccer ball retrieved from a washed-up package. The lonely man draws a face on the soccer ball, and Wilson becomes our hero's friend, allowing social conversations to take place. Wilson serves as a form of alter ego, a way of reflecting inner thought, and as a way of tapping into personal intuition. Since the soccer ball is a symbol to which Hanks attributed personal meaning, the loss of Wilson causes an emotional cataclysm for the hero later on.

Although we assume Hanks will ultimately be rescued, his will to make it happen is a truly creative act. Viewers may have a sense of utter futility when Hanks unwraps washed-up packages filled with irrelevant items like ice skates and video tapes. But, as things proceed, we learn that ice skates make great knives, and videotape becomes an effective substitute for rope. The ultimate new resource, which eventually frees our hero, is the arrival of two sides from a plastic outhouse. Putting ideas together in unusual ways, the castaway turns the outhouse into a shelter and, finally, an effective sail with which to leave his entrapment.

Observers might say that our hero was lucky to escape from the wave-locked island after four years, but one must also note his tremendous resourcefulness. He made new associations between objects, allowing seemingly useless items to become tools. He created symbols that empowered him during the many difficult times and dark nights. He even generated a friend with whom to talk. He made a map of his location and a calendar based on the times of the year for optimal travel. When the opportunity of the two-sided outhouse debris showed up, he was ready to respond and make the most of his preparations.

TRAITS OF CREATIVE PEOPLE

Discoveries in human history appear to have an element of luck. But the careful observer will note the years of preparation, the willingness to explore possibilities, and the openness that allow an inventor to move froward when an opportunity presents itself. Creative synthesis may follow years of determined effort. For example, it is well-known that Thomas Edison developed over 200 models of the incandescent light bulb before he found one that would work. We can only imagine the persistence and vision that was required for Edison to continue his quest through so many seeming failures.

The research of highly successful people who become beacons to their professional domain shows that they, indeed, have extraordinary persistence. Although these leaders have unique talents as well, it is how they persevere, deepen their knowledge, and ultimately respond to fortunate opportunities that is most significant (Csikszentmihalyi, 1996).

The traits of continuing in the face of adversity, of being resilient, of enjoying each day fully, of living courageously, of following new leads with curiosity—these positive traits are available as a potential to all of us, including our most constricted clients. These traits form the human essence to which we give the name "creativity." Accessing creative self-expression is an important direction in all healing processes and brings clients to new understandings of themselves and who they are in the world. Psychologist Whisenant (1994, p. 355) hypothesizes that "during and for a time after the creative act, the overcharged and under-charged meridians balance their energies. . . . More often the true healing takes place when that person finds the creative voice calling from within, heeds it, and follows it."

SELF-INVENTORY OF PERSONAL CREATIVITY

To explore personal creativity and direction, let us consider the qualities that support originality and generativity. The hallmark of highly creative people, according to Csikszentmihalyi's research, is their willingness to think outside of established, accepted parameters. Rather than being oddballs or outsiders, though, creative people are those individuals who go deeper and venture further than the ordinary person. Most important, they seem to be on a lifelong quest of learning and growing. They are able to direct and focus their energies toward their interests in an enthusiastic search for knowledge and excitement. These same qualities can be cultivated in each of us and our clients as we learn to note strengths and deficits, identify limiting beliefs, and open up to more desirable possibilities.

Exercise 1. Personal Inventory

1. *"As your review the partial listing of characteristics for personal creativity given here, you may wish to note which areas you have already incorporated into your lifestyle, and which areas need further development."*
2. *"Using the following list, check the areas you would like to develop more fully and note the areas to which you are already paying attention."*

3. *"Some of the personal qualities that are essential to developing your own creativity are as follows:*

- Be curious about something everyday. Enjoy surprises.
- Explore what is mysterious to you.
- Maintain a sense of openness and wonder.
- Consider the many subject areas that attract you. List at least five.
- Find at least one area to explore in depth. Master as much available information about it as possible.
- Be persistent in learning the subject area and in increasing your skills and level of complexity.
- Be willing to learn from everything, even what may appear to be a mistake or a wrong turn.
- Actively engage in divergent thinking—produce as many ideas as possible, make them as different as possible, consider things from the opposite way of your usual way of thinking.
- Be flexible. Pay attention to feedback so that you can correct your course as you go.
- Organize the mundane aspects of daily life (like knowing where your car keys and glasses are) so your train of thought is not continuously interrupted by looking for things.
- Take charge of your schedule.
- Cultivate a sense of flow. Take time to reflect. When something sparks your interest, follow it.
- Develop the aspects of your personality that are lacking. If you are predominantly rational, put conscious energy into developing your intuitive knowing.
- Know what you like and don't like. Enjoy who you are."

To continue with this as a self-exploratory exercise, we might help clients to select the trait(s) that seem most difficult at the moment. For example, taking charge of one's schedule to have time for reflection and inner quiet may trigger several limiting beliefs: "I am at the mercy of others' schedules. There is never enough time for my needs. I don't deserve to run a schedule for me. I am incapable of controlling my time." As a divergent thinking exercise, we could ask the client to generate four totally opposite thoughts that can form the basis of desired, more empowering beliefs. Examples might be as follows: "Others' schedules affect me only as I choose. I now make time for my needs. I decide and take charge of my schedule. I am capable and effective in controlling my time." As we can see, each of these new, desired beliefs generates a host of related possibilities and requires decisions that need intentional work.

Traits leading to more original, innovative thinking can be enhanced by increasing aesthetic perception, connecting with nature, engaging in divergent thinking, and opening up to the transpersonal, or spiritual, dimension. We will consider these possibilities and related exercises as we continue.

FINDING BEAUTY

During a life-threatening childhood illness, writer Michael Ventura credits his recovery to seeing a few lowly pigeons outside his hospital-room window. "It's impossible to prove," he writes, "but I believe that my intake, my inspiration of the elegance, the beauty of the birds and the sky gave me strength and saved my life. This, at least is sure: from that time on I have been extraordinarily gratefully susceptible to, and conscious of, the beauty of the physical world, even in the bleakest of places—like Brooklyn" (Ventura, 2001, p. 32). He goes on to describe how we are influenced by the "dull ugliness" of most urban environments without understanding how this is affecting us energetically. The lack of beauty may be causing the sense of personal alienation, disconnection, and dissatisfaction so prevalent in today's world. "The experience of beauty is always one of expansion, of opening, of inclusion. . . . So beauty is not merely decorative; its primary function is to connect—beauty connects our innermost being to the world " (Ventura, p. 33).

As our clients open to new potentials within themselves, we encourage awareness of what is special, worthwhile, and beautiful in their experience. Because of the many distortions in our culture, individuals literally need help in discernment, in learning to see, hear, and feel more fully again. The following exercises are ways of expanding clients' consciousness and sense of appreciation of the world around them. They may be used one at a time or as a sequence.

Exercise 2. Noticing Beauty

1. *"Please describe the first time you noticed that something was beautiful in your life. Notice the events around you, the colors, the sounds, the feelings of that time. Let those feelings become even stronger and note where you sense them in your body."*

2. *"Imagine walking through your home. Notice the places of beauty. Describe them to me. If you do not see any such place, tell me how you might create one. Describe how you might increase the sense of beauty and comfort in your home."*

3. *"Tell me what is beautiful in your life right now. Tell what it is that you do to enjoy and remember special times, people, and places."*

4. *"As you relax or close your eyes in this office, tell me what objects you remember. Describe colors, textures, pictures, sounds, shadows, lights, shadings, things of interest, and feelings. Enjoy the present moment fully."*

The first part of this exercise often brings up nostalgia and unresolved past issues, good material for psychoenergetic interventions. The second part gives clients new ways of thinking about their surroundings and how to make their surroundings match their new lifestyles. The last item has the immediacy of shared experience between client and therapist and allows the client to open more fully into the present moment. Often, clients are so unaware of their surroundings that they do not even remember items of furniture or wall decorations in the room where they are sitting. Without any judgment or criticism, the exercise helps clients to widen their perceptual style.

As clients respond with more awareness of their surroundings, they often report sorting through closets, discarding the ugly and mundane, to make room for something more pleasing. Those with plants may discard old stragglers, buy colorful, more encouraging blooms, rearrange pots, or restructure an area—all signs of regeneration and increased vitality. I encourage clients to arrange objects in their homes and create meaningful, aesthetically pleasing areas, meditation places, or altars. This is especially helpful in giving grief full expression or in acknowledging important events. Becoming aware of surroundings begins to celebrate the deeper sensitivities of the psyche, while shaping and creating beauty nurtures the soul.

CONNECTING WITH NATURE

For most urban dwellers, there is a distinctive disconnection from nature. We may go from home to work, and back again, without ever seeing the sun, let alone seeing a sunrise or sunset. Cycles of the moon are almost forgotten. The blossoming of groves of trees and their smells and seasonal changes go unnoticed—unless there is a concerted, intentional effort to seek out natural settings.

Connecting with nature brings us into palpable psychoenergetic harmony and connects us with the creative energy of the world about us. One client told me she was afraid to be outdoors. Part of her healing process included sitting safely outside my office just enjoying each shade of green she could see in the grass and trees. The warmth of the sun nurtured her unlike anything she had ever felt from her dysfunctional parents. She was at peace and satisfied for a whole hour—something quite remarkable for her, and for the many who are too busy or harried to make time for such an opportunity.

Exercises can help to enrich the experiencing of nature so that being outdoors becomes a time of nurturing and comfort. Again, these suggestions are starting places for your own creative energies to begin flowing with clients as they open to the many gifts that surround them.

Exercise 3. Increasing Enjoyment of Nature

1. *"Tell me about a recent time you were outside. What did you notice, what pleased you, what comforted you? What surprised you? What did you have to do to make sure you had this time? What would you need to do to make sure you have this time again?"*

2. *"Think of the four directions of the sun. Where does the sun rise in your home? Where does the sun set? As you imagine standing in your home, align to the four directions of the sun as if you were a compass. Envision the direction of your loved ones; face toward it and send them your blessings."*

3. *"Let's take a walk outside for 10 minutes or so in silence. Allow yourself to notice all the colors you see, hear all the sounds around you, and sense the textures of various objects. Just enjoy the moment and then we'll share." (This exercise becomes even more powerful if clients close their eyes and agree to trust you to guide them safely.)*

4. *"Tell me how you experienced your connection with Higher Power (or a sense of the transpersonal) recently. List five things for which you are grateful. Now name five more. Notice how gratefulness builds on itself. Notice how you feel as you move into the vibration of gratitude."*

5. *"Hug a tree. Touch the earth. Notice how healthy energy moves within you while breathing fully, in and out. Now shake, stretch, skip, and bounce to release any stagnation or blockage."*

ENGAGING IN DIVERGENT THINKING

Ideational fluency grows as we engage in divergent thinking. While the left hemisphere of the brain holds functions that are predominantly linear and analytical, the right hemisphere delights in imagery, confluent and divergent thinking, and making associations. Skills in right and left hemispheric integration grow with the Crossover Correction and other Educational Kinesiology exercises described in chapter 12. In addition, we can help clients to access their inner flexibility and imaginations by encouraging them to make word associations, keep a journal about their feelings, explore their dreams, and create helpful imagery. Our sense of vitality and energy follows thought. Much has been written about journalizing, use of the imagination, creative imagery, and dream analysis. So, a useful assignment might be to have clients visit a neighborhood bookstore and peruse its offerings on these topics, and then select the books that most speak to them.

Numerous workshops in various forms of art-making are offered in every part of the country. They can become opportunities for personal discovery and adventure. In remote Ramona, California, well-known European artist Marie-Louise Ertle offers silk painting workshops for adults who have never held a brush in their hands. "When we paint, and when we can let go, the brush begins to dance," she says. "It is our inner beauty that we meet in the long run" (personal communication, May, 2001). There are also numerous tapes available on art-making (Seaton, 2001). Even writing poetry as a form of therapy has been developed and has its own national association, resources, and conferences (Fox, 1995; Mazza, 1999).

The following exercise may help you and your clients get started in creative play with words. Once clients begin to experience this dimension, they usually come up with more resources of their own.

Exercise 4. Playing with Language for Increased Internal Flexibility

1. *"Please think of three words that have no seeming relation to each other. (This could be a food item, something from nature, and a man-made structure, i.e., ice cream, tree, White House). Describe how each word impacts you; use as many words as possible to describe each item. Now tell me how the three items could be related for you."*

2. *"Come up with as many words as you can that rhyme with clunk. Put in a few words to connect the rhymes so you have a fun poem about the whole world of clunk."*

3. *"Think of a recent dream that created a good feeling in you. Give three possible messages that the unconscious may want to communicate to you with this dream. (One way to approach this is to list each item in the dream and make as many associations as possible with each of the dream symbols.)"*

4. *"Think of an individual who gives you a sense of personal empowerment, an idea, or has a quality that you would like to emulate. Quickly write down everything you can think of that relates to the person you have chosen. Now think of those people who don't have these characteristics—the "critics"— and leave the critics on a telephone pole. Tell them you will call them when you need them—much, much later. Notice how you feel connecting to the person that you have chosen. Now be that person; bring in his or her qualities into your own energy field."*

CONNECTING WITH THE HIGHER SELF

Playfulness and generativity invariably connect clients with parts of themselves that are unexpected and surprisingly better than they presumed. In effect, they come to realize, "I am much more than my problems, my history, my family legacy, my long-term patterns."

As the higher, wiser, deeper self emerges, there is often a sense of connecting to the creative mind, the unifying force in the order of nature. We may speak of good orderly direction (GOD) as a personal being or as a transcendent quality of universal qi. Life-artist Julia Cameron connects creativity with human energy in this way: "Creativity is God energy flowing through us, shaped, by us, like light flowing through a crystal prism. When we are clear about who we are and what we are doing, the energy flows freely and we experience no strain" (Cameron, 1992, p. 163).

Life is meant to be lived with enthusiasm. The word "enthusiasm" is from the Greek and literally means to be filled with God or to have a god within (Heritage Dictionary, 1992). Those who allow themselves to be filled with inner light as they align with their life purpose shine forth in wonder-filled ways. They become treasures to their small community of family and friends, a blessing to all whose lives they touch. Some shine brightly throughout history. Franz Joseph Haydn, the composer of over a 100 symphonies and father of the string quartet, was unabashedly connected to his creator when he expressed his muse. He wrote in his journals, "When I think upon God, my heart is so full of joy that the notes dance and leap, as it were, from my pen, and since God has given me a cheerful heart it will be pardoned me that I serve Him with a cheerful spirit" (quoted in ACMP, 1999, p. 4).

MODEL FOR AN ONGOING HEALING PROCESS

It remains now for us to develop a conceptual model for the kind of ongoing healing process that incorporates release of distress and moves clients forward to help them generate new choices, new connections, images and symbols, meaning, and a sense of flow. Figure 15.1 is a schematic of such an ongoing dynamic.

As we can see, this dynamic for full-energy living is not limited to the context of therapy sessions. Instead, it reflects a daily choosing to let go of an identified distress by focusing intention with psychoenegetic balancing, releasing limiting beliefs, and treating for specific issues with self-help algorithms or chakra/biofield patterns that clients have learned. As clients integrate learning and diminish their personal distress by releasing, they are able to install empowering beliefs, enjoy more creativitiy, and participate in ever-expanding self-awareness. The connecting line with the arrow and movement through the layers suggests that this work can happen quickly, even with a single intentional movement, rotation, or spin of the entire body to release stagnation or blockage. Like children, who experience the world with fresh perceptions

Figure 15.1
ONGOING DYNAMIC OF FULL-ENERGY LIVING

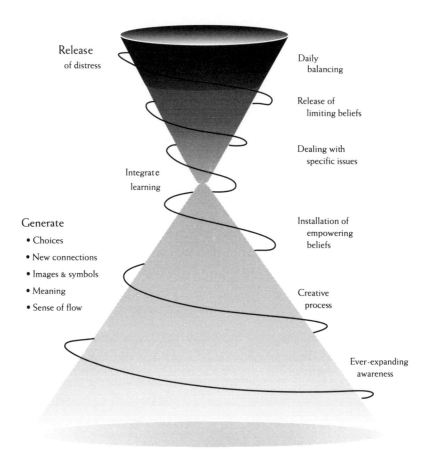

through their play, we can participate in an ongoing process of assembling, forming, dissembling, letting go, reforming, and recreating ourselves and our lives. We continue lifelong expansion into unlimited potentials.

Chapter 16

Future Directions for Creative Energies

It is something to be able to paint a picture, carve a statue and make objects beautiful. But it is far more glorious to carve and paint the atmosphere in which we work, to effect the quality of the day—this is the highest of the arts.   —Henry David Thoreau

As we conclude our journey of exploring energy-related healing, we see the importance not only of addressing client problems but of helping clients to move into the domain of ongoing personal vitality and creative self-expression. Optimal living flows through the innovative life-artist who effects the quality of each day—the client who is willing to install empowering beliefs and generate new choices, connections, images, and symbols. Such clients begin to find deep meaning in their personal lives and enjoy a sense of just being in the moment, with whatever activity, challenge, or playfulness they choose.

The energy-related therapies seem to lend extraordinary resources for such optimal functioning. As we have seen in the model of therapy in Figure 13.1 and the ongoing dynamic for full-energy living in Figure 15.1, the methods of releasing distress and accessing new awareness are readily available through the therapeutic and self-care resources of the energy modalities. As clients learn to repeatedly release their own distressful situations, they access an image of their own "future mind" (Lee Pulos, personal communication, May 2001). No longer content to see themselves as dragging around a rusty barge of past issues, they can visualize and step into their desired state, perhaps as a graceful cruise liner with all possible amenities.

As we consider future developments of creative energy therapy, we will, I believe, see a tremendous expansion of ideas for clients' healing. This will, hopefully, be balanced with a commitment to valuing and protecting the inner artist since we live in a time of impersonal technology and ever-expanding sameness. In addition, we therapists will need to learn to transmute quickly the emotional pain to which we are exposed into viable, life-giving potentials through careful attention to our own energy hygiene. Another factor in future developments will be expansion of the holistic, integrative emphasis in health care. Finally, I believe we will see the growth and development of the whole field of energy psychology and its gradual acceptance into mainstream counseling practices. This will likely be grounded in the growing research base and the fact that, simply said, energy concepts are highly effective for many clients.

COMMITMENT TO ONGOING HEALING

Creative self-expression is the ultimate healing. In this book, we have seen numerous tools for evaluating clients' distress and for assisting them in acknowledging the psychoenergetic components of their defined issues. In addition, clients learn how to establish their own systemic balance through centering practices, release of dysfunctional beliefs, and treating themselves with acupoint and chakra/biofield methods. As clients move to self-acceptance, they can shift to new, more powerful language and affirm new directions in their lives. They may celebrate new-found strengths with dancing, art-making, symbols, images, or activities such as lighting a candle, burning incense, listening to music, writing a poem, or beating a drum—activities that are innately nurturing.

Psychologist Gilligan writes (2001, p. 55), "Our clients are each in his or her own way individual poems. . . . As therapists, we are the sponsors—or human impresarios—to the inner poetry that is at the core of our clients' lives. Indeed we might better regard therapy as a kind of rigorous poetic practice, rather than as a science." Therapy directed toward the outcome of personal creativity is an art in itself, and it is well-grounded in the history, theory, and knowledge base of the energy-healing approaches we have explored here.

VALUING AND PROTECTING THE INNER ARTIST

We basically live in a culture that is hostile to most forms of personal inventiveness. Consider, for example, the expanding scene of endless malls in North America with the same franchise stores. One could be in any urban area, from Seattle to Miami, Toronto to San Diego, and purchase essentially the same products in stores that look alike. There seems to be little value attached to the unique, the special, the out-of the-way. Although the arts admittedly add quality, depth, and opportunities for cross-cultural communication to our lives, funding for the arts is always the first to be cut when the national budget is being considered.

Suggesting to clients that they make something from within themselves that is innately satisfying will require careful nurturing of the inner artist. Since we all once had the capacity for playing with paint, clay, color, and words as children, we might say we are all recovering artists as we attempt to make something or give a sense of purpose to our daily surroundings. Much like work with the inner child, developing a relationship with the inner artist requires daily inner dialoging and attention. For most artists in recovery from early life criticism, the creative aspect is very young, easily offended, and prone to withdrawal. The seedlings of new attempts at self-expression must be greeted with "the eyes of the heart" (Seaton, 2001), gentleness, and kindness.

Attention to intuition is one way of valuing and nurturing new ideas that emerge from clients. We can give our students permission to honor the wisdom from within themselves as it unfolds. Bringing the imaginal into form is seldom easy, but we can assure clients that each endeavor gets better with repeated practice and will improve over time. It's all right to be doing something just to enjoy the sense of flow and inner harmony it brings. It's all right to make a mess, to take risks, to start over—in other words, to be engaged in an ongoing process of generating new possibilities and achieving a sense of personal satisfaction.

As creative therapists, we also benefit from developing our intuitional skills. For example, a friend reported thinking about a client, an overworked architect. He had not heard from "Jamie" for weeks and knew she was traveling frequently, especially on Mondays. He meditated about Jamie on a Monday afternoon and saw her at home in his mind's eye. On this hunch, he picked up the phone; she answered on the first ring saying, "I was just thinking about you." Coincidence? Nonlocal mind interaction? Connection of interactive energy fields? Remote viewing supported by the vibration of caring? Whatever our explanation (all are correct from a multidimensional perspective), such incidents can occur more frequently as we practice looking within ourselves for answers concerning clients. Life as a whole becomes more interesting and enjoyable as we open to intuition and take responsibility for our own daily energy balancing.

EXPANSION OF HOLISTIC, INTEGRATIVE EMPHASIS

In 2000, the Office of Alternative Medicine, founded in 1992 within the National Institutes of Health (NIH), expanded to form the National Center for Complementary and Alternative Medicine (NCCAM), which will be a fully funded, separate department (Stokstad, 2000). The over $90-million budget will foster research into complementary modalities such as acupuncture and herbal treatments for depression and arthritis. A new investigation of "frontier medicine" has also been funded to study therapies for which there are no known biological mechanisms, such as work with magnets, energy healing, and homeopathy.

Another milestone was the establishment of the White House Commission on Complementary and Alternative Medicine in July 2000. Headed by James S. Gordon, M.D., a well-known leader in mind/body modalities, the Commission will generate a profound impact on medical practice and education in the 21st century. The report, when completed in 2002, will parallel the impact of the 1910 Flexner report that shaped medical school curricula for most of the 20th century. Dr. Gordon writes, "At the beginning of the 21st century, congress and the president are asking a commission of conventional physicians and researchers, complementary and alternative medicine pioneers, citizen advocates, and business people—men and women of many colors and ethnic backgrounds—to design a new blueprint for a new medicine that is both scientific and inclusive" (2000, p. 28).

Clinics and centers like the Center for Integrative Medicine at the prestigious Scripps Hospitals in La Jolla, California are developing nationwide. In conjunction with the Ornish Cardiology Center at Scripps, Healing Touch is one of the many complementary modalities used to assist cardiology patients to develop new lifestyles. This multi-modal program may be one of the arenas chosen for frontier medicine studies (personal communication, Phyllis Mabbett, April 2001).

Since psychotherapy and counseling in general are regarded as alternative therapies, i.e., not within the present mainstream medical model, the development of a more holistic and integrative emphasis within medicine itself will open doors to expanded models of health care. The energy therapies will undoubtedly take their rightful place in mind/body emphasis, given their ready efficacy for releasing distress and attaining high-level wellness.

DEVELOPMENT OF AN INTEGRATIVE ENERGY PSYCHOTHERAPY

Energy therapy, which includes work with the meridians, chakras, biofield, and other aspects of the vibrational matrix, will presumably expand in the next decades. Research further corroborating the effectiveness of methods explained here will continue, especially with the coordination of the strong research arm of the Association for Comprehensive Energy Psychology. A rich variety of books and articles will continue to expand our knowledge base. The publication of *Energy Psychology in Psychotherapy: A Comprehensive Source Book*, slated for release in 2002, will be another milestone. It is edited by the well-known author Fred Gallo and will contain over 20 contributions from visionary leaders in the growing field of energy psychotherapy.

We can further hypothesize that the interrelationship between matter, energy, and consciousness will be more fully understood as scientific breakthroughs continue to unfold. Physicists may find the long-sought-after unified field theory, or more fully comprehend Tiller's ten-dimensional universe (1997). Perhaps, in time, we will grasp a model of the world that allows us to understand from a much larger perspective how the effects of energetic interventions are in harmony with the laws of nature. Current models may develop into proven, operating theories to explain these effects. For the present, we hypothesize that the stimulation of an aspect of the vibrational matrix while simultaneously attuning to a traumatic issue creates a form of reciprocal inhibition, a paradox, or a form of symptom prescription (by asking clients to focus on what they are doing anyway—thinking about their problem) (Gallo, 2001). This dynamic may loosen set paths within the limbic system of the brain and permit clients to access new, more adaptive and functional levels of integration.

IN CONCLUSION

When we see our therapeutic interactions with clients as communication between biofields and watch our clients heal, we increase our sense of the numinous and transformative. In addition, the energy therapies seem to facilitate the alignment of both therapist and client to the resources of the higher self, the transpersonal perspective, and the pervasive qi of the universe. Alignment with intuition allows accessing of potentials for the highest good of the client, an opening to rich, new dimensions from within both healer and healee. We come to see therapy as the creative blending of both science and art.

Here is a poetry meditation that came to me while thinking about energy-based communication with clients:

> *You come to me with trust*
> *That I can be of help,*
> *Relieve your pain.*
> *I come to you with artist eyes*
> *And learned skills, models, ideas,*
> *To meet you in this vital new*
> *Healing moment*
> *That awaits discovery by us both.*
> *In the instant of my intent*
> *And your reaching out for peace*
> *Comes the healing—*
> *Interacting fields*
> *Chakras spinning*
> *Meridians balancing*
> *Energies dancing*
> *Flows restoring*
> *Realigning*
> *To the center*
> *For full-energy living.*

References

Achterberg, J., Dossey, B., & Kolkmeier, L. (1994). *Rituals of healing: Using imagery for health and wellness.* New York: Bantam.

Amen, D. G. (2001). *Healing attention deficit disorder: The breakthrough program that allows you to see and heal the 6 types of ADD.* New York: Putnam.

American Association for Marriage and Family Therapy. (1991). *Code of ethics.* Washington, DC: Author.

American Heritage dictionary of the English language (3rd ed.). (1992). New York: Houghton Mifflin.

American Psychological Association. (1992). *Ethical principles of psychologists and code of conduct.* Washington, DC: Author.

Aron, E. N. (1997). *The highly sensitive person.* New York: Broadway.

Association for Comprehensive Energy Psychology (2001). *Standards of care and Code of ethics* [On-line]. Available: www.energypsych.org.

Association for Comprehensive Energy Psychology (2001, May). *Ethics at the leading edge: A position paper.* Paper presented at the Third Annual International Energy Psychology Conference, San Diego, CA.

Association for Holotropic Breathwork International. (1994). *Ethical agreements for holotropic breathwork practitioners.* Santa Cruz, CA: The Inner Door.

Association of Chamber Music Players. (1999, September). *ACMP Newlsletter.* New York: Author.

Baker, H., & Siegel, L. (2001, May). Preliminary findings using EFT with animal phobias. *Proceedings of the Third Annual International Energy Psychology Conference.* San Diego, CA: ACEP Publications.

Bandler, R. O., & Grinder, J. (1975). *Patterns of the hypnotic techniques of Milton H. Erickson.* Cupertino, CA: Meta.

Beardall, A. G. (1995). *Clinical kinesiology laboratory mannual.* Portland, OR: Human Bio-dynamics.

Becker, R. O. (1985). *The body electric.* New York: Tarcher/Putnam.

Becker, R. O. (1990). *Cross currents: The perils of electropollution, the promise of electromedicine.* New York: Tarcher/Putnam.

Bell, J. S. (1964). On the Einstein Podolsky Rosen paradox. *Physics, 1*(4), 195.

Benor, D. (2001). *Spiritual healing* (Vol. 1). Southfield, MI: Vision.

Benson, H. (1996). *Timeless healing: The power and biology of belief.* New York: Simon & Schuster.

Braud, W. G., & Schlitz, M. (1989). A method for the objective study of transpersonal imagery. *Journal of Scientific Exploration, 3*(1), 45–60.

Brennan, B. (1988). *Hands of light.* New York: Bantam.

Brennan, B. (1993) *Light emerging: The journel of personal healing.* New York: Bantam.

Bruyere, R. (1989). *Wheels of light.* Sierra Madre, CA: Bon.

Burch, J. L., Mende, S. B., Mitchell, D. G., Moore, T. E., Pollock, C.J., Reinisch, B. W., Sandel, B. R., Fuselier, S. A., Gallagher, D .L., Green, J. L., Perez, J. D., & Reiff, P. H. (2001). Views of earth's magnetoshpere with the IMAGE satellite. *Science, 291,* 619–626.

Burr, H. (1972). *Blueprint for immortality: The electric patterns of life.* Essex, England: C. W. Daniel.

Callahan, R. (1985). *Five minute phobia cure.* Wilmington, DE: Enterprise.

Callahan, R. (1996). *Thought field therapy and trauma.* Indian Wells, CA: Author.

Callahan, R. (2001). *Tapping the healer within.* Lincolnwood, IL: Contemporary.

Callahan, R., & Perry, P. (1991). *Why do I eat when I'm not hungry?* New York: Doubleday.

Cameron, J. (1992). *The artist's way.* New York: Putnam.

Capra, F. (1977). *The tao of physics.* New York: Bantam.

Carringon, P. (2001). *Book of meditation.* New York: HarperCollins.

Chamberlain, D. (1998). *The mind of your newborn baby.* Berkeley, CA: North Atlantic Books.

Cho, Z. H., et al. (1998). New findings of the correlation between acupoints and corresponding brain cortices using functional MRI. *Proceedings of the National Academy of Science, 95,* 2670–2673.

Cleary, T. S., & Shapiro, S. I. (1995). The plateau experience and the post-mortem life: Abraham Maslow's unfinished theory. *Journal of Transpersonal Psychology, 27*(1), 1–24.

Clinton, A. (2001). *Seemorg matrix training manual.* Princeton, NJ: Author.

Cornell, J. (1994). *Mandala: Luminous symbols for healing.* Wheaton, IL: Quest.

Craig, G., & Fowlie, A. (1995). *Emotional freedom techniques: The manual.* Sea Ranch, CA: Author.

Creswell, J. W. (1994). *Research design: Qualitative and quantitative approaches.* Thousand Oaks: Sage.

Csikszentmihalyi, M. (1996). *Creativity: Flow and the psychology of discovery and invention.* New York: HarperCollins.

Dale, C. (1998). *New chakra healing.* St. Paul, MN: Llewellyn.

Davidson, R. J., Marshall, J. R., Tomarken, A. J., & Henriquest, J. B. (2000). While a phobic waits: Regional brain electrical and autonomic activity in social phobics during anticipation of public speaking. *Biological Psychiatry, 47,* 85–95.

Dennison, D., & Dennison, G. (1982). *Brain Gym.* Glendale, CA: Educational-Kinesthetics.

Diamond, J. (1985). *Life energy.* New York: Dodd, Mead.

Dossey, L. (1989) *Space, time, and medicine.* San Francisco, CA: Shambala.

Dossey, L. (1993). *Healing words.* New York: HarperCollins.

Dossey, L. (2000). Creativity: On intelligence, insight, and the cosmic soup. *Alternative Therapies, 6*(1), 12–17, 108–117.

Durlacher, J. V. (1994). *Freedom from fear forever.* Tempe, AZ: Van Ness.

Eden, D. (1998). *Energy medicine.* New York: Tarcher/Putnam.

Eden, D. (2001). The radiant circuits. In W. Lammers & B. Kircher (Eds.), *Proceedings of First European Energy Psychology Conference.* Lucern, Switzerland: Institute for the Application of Social Sciences.

Eisenberg, D. M., Davis, R. B., Ettner, S. L., Appel, S., Wilkey, S., Van Rompay, M., & Kessler, R. (1998). Trends in alternative medicine use in the United States, 1990–1997: Results of a follow-up national survey. *The Journal of the American Medical Association, 280*(18), 1569–1575.

Erikson, E. (1970). *Stages of life development.* New York: W. W. Norton.

Fahrion, S. L., Wirkus, M., & Pooley, P. (1992) EEG amplitude, brain mapping, & synchrony in and between bioenergy practitioner & client during healing. *Subtle Energies, 3*(1), 19–52.

Feinstein, D. (2001). *Myth and the energy body.* Paper presented at the Third Annual International Energy Psychology Conference, San Diego, CA.

Feinstein, D., & Krippner, S. (1997). *The mythic path.* New York: Tarcher/Putnam.

Figley, C. R., & Carbonnel, J. L. (1995). *The "active ingredients project": The systematic clinical demonstration of the most efficient treatments of PTSD.* Tallahasse, FL: Florida State University Psychological Stress Research Program and Clinical Laboratory.

Fox, J. (1995). *Finding what you didn't lose.* New York: Tarcher/Putnam.

Freeman, I. M. (1990). *Physics made simple.* New York: Doubleday.

Furman, M. E. & Gallo, F. P. (2000). *The neurophysics of human behavior: Explorations at the interface of brain, mind, behavior, and information.* Boca Raton, FL: CRC.

Gagne, D., & Toyne, R. (1994). The effects of therapeutic touch and relaxation techniques in reducing anxiety. *Archives of Psychiatric Nursing, 8*(3), 184–89.

Gallo, F. P. (1998). *Energy psychology: Explorations of the interface of energy, cognition, behavior, and health.* Boca Raton, FL: CRC.

Gallo, F. P. (2000). *Energy diagnostic and treatment methods.* New York: W. W. Norton.

Gallo, F. (2001, May). *Getting on the same page: The big picture.* Plenary address to the Third Annual International Energy Psychology Conference, San Diego, CA.

Gallo, F. (Ed.). (in press). *Energy psychology in psychotherapy.* New York: W. W. Norton.

Geddes, N. (2002). Research in healing touch. In Hover-Kramer, D. (Ed.), *Healing touch: Guidebook for practitioners.* Albany, NY: Delmar.

Gerber, R. (2001). *Vibrational medicine.* Rochester, VT: Bear.

Gilligan, S. (2001). Getting to the core. *Psychotherapy Networker, 25*(1), 22–29, 54–55.

Gordon, J. S. (2000). The White House Commission and the future of healthcare. *Alternative Therapies, 6*(6), 26–28.

Goswami, A., Reed, R. E., & Goswami, M. (1995). *The self-aware universe: How consciousness creates the material world.* New York: Tarcher/Putnam.

Goswami, S. S. (1999). *Layayoga.* Rochester, VT: Inner Traditions.

Gough, W. C., & Shacklett, R. L. (1993). The science of connectiveness. Part III: The human experience. *Subtle Energies, 4*(3), 187–214.

Greyson, B. (1996). Distance healing of patients with major depression. *Journal of Scientific Exploration, 10*(4).

Grudermeyer, D. (2000). *The energy psychology desktop companion.* Del Mar, CA: Willingness Works.

Grudermeyer D., & Grudermeyer, R. (2001). *Individualized energy psychotherapy (IEP) level I: Training manual.* Del Mar, CA: Willingness Works.

Grudermeyer, D., Grudermeyer, R., & Hover-Kramer, D. (2000). *Individualized energy psychotherapy (IEP) level II: Training manual.* Del Mar, CA: Willingness Works.

Harpur, T. (1994). *The uncommon touch: An investigation of spiritual healing.* Toronto, Ontario: McClelland & Steward.

Healing Touch International Research files (2001). *Listing of ongoing research projects.* Lakewood, CO: 12477 W. Cedar Dr., Suite 202, 80228; www. healing-touch.net

Heidt, P. (1981). Effect of therapeutic touch on anxiety levels of hospitalized patients. *Nursing Research, 30*(1), 32–37.

Herbert, N. (1985). *Quantum reality: Beyond the new physics. An excursion into metaphysics and the meaning of reality.* New York: Doubleday.

Hoffman, E. (1988). *The right to be human: A biography of Abraham Maslow.* Los Angeles: CA: Tarcher.

Horowitz, J. M., (2001, April 16). The man with magic fingers. *Time, 65.*

Hover-Kramer D. (1993). *Energetic impressions of ancient Egypt.* Poway, CA: Behavioral Health Consultants.

Hover-Kramer, D. (2001). *Ancestral dreams: Notes from a spiritual pilgrimage to the High Andes.* Poway, CA: Behavioral Health Consultants.

Hover-Kramer, D., Mentgen, J., & Scandrett-Hibdon, S. (1996). *Healing touch: A resource for health care professionals.* Albany, NY: Delmar.

Hover-Kramer, D., & Shames, K. (1997). *Energetic approaches to emotional healing.* Albany, NY: Delmar.

Hughes, P. P., et al. (1997). Therapeutic touch with psychiatric adolescent patients. *Journal of Holistic Nursing, 14*(1), 6–23.

Hunt, V. (1995). *Infinite mind: The science of human vibrations.* Malibu, CA: Malibu.

Joseph, L. M., & Greenberg, M. A. (2001). The effects of a career transition program on reemployment success in laid off professionals. *Consulting Psychology Journal, 53*(3), 169–181.

Judith, A. (1996). *Eastern body, western mind.* Berkeley, CA: Celestial Arts.

Jung, C. G. (1965). *Memories, dreams and reflections.* New York: Vintage.

Jung, C. G. (1971). In Campbell, J. (Ed.) *The Portable Jung.* New York: Penguin, 23.

Kaptchuk, T. J. (1983). *The web that has no weaver: Understanding Chinese medicine.* New York: Congdon & Weed.

Katz, R., Biesele, M., & St. Denis, V. (1997). *Healing makes our hearts happy.* Rochester, VT: Inner Traditions.

Kemeny, M. (1998). *Chronic fatigue immune deficiency syndrome.* Philadelphia, PA: CFIDS Association.

Kemeny, M. (2001, February). *The immune system.* San Diego, CA: CorTexT Educational Seminar.

Kendall, H. O., & Kendall, E. M. P. (1949). *Muscles—Testing and function.* Baltimore, MD: Williams & Wilkins.

Kieffer, G. (1988). *Kundalini for the new age: Selected writings of Gopi Krishna.* New York: Bantam.

Krieger, D. (1979). *The therapeutic touch.* Englewood Cliffs, NJ: Prentice-Hall.

Krieger, D. (1990, September). Therapeutic touch: Two decades of research. *Imprint,* 83–88.

Krieger, D. (1993). *Accepting your power to heal.* Santa Fe, NM: Bear.

Lambrou, P., & Pratt, G. (2000). *Instant emotional healing.* New York: Broadway.

Lambrou, P., & Pratt, G. (2001, May). Energy psychology in magnetoencephalogram brain scans. *Proceedings of the Third Annual International Energy Psychology Conference.* San Diego, CA: ACEP Publications.

Lambrou, P., Pratt, G., Chevalier, G., & Nicosia, G. (1999, October). Thought energy therapy: Quantum level control of emotions and evidence of effectiveness of energy psychotherapy methodology. *Proceedings of the International Forum on New Science* (pp. 169–170). Fort Collins, CO: International Association for New Science.

Le Shan, L. (1976). *Alternate realities: The search for the full human being.* New York: Evans.

Leadbeater, C. W. (1927). *The chakras.* Wheaton, IL: Theosophical Publishing.

Levy, S. (1999, October/November). Built-in compass. *National Wildlife,* 33–39.

Li, Z. (1996). [The experimental demonstration of the "isothermal meridian courses"]. *Zhen Ci Yan Jiu, 21*(1), 76–78 (original in Chinese).

Lindley, D. (1996). *Where does the wierdness go? Why quantum mechanics is strange, but not as strange as you think.* New York: Basic.

Litscher, G., & Wang, L. (2000). [Cerebral near infrared spectroscopy and acupuncture—results of a pilot study] *Biomed Tech* (Berlin), 45(7–8), 21–28 (original in German).

Luthke, M.F., & Stein-Luthke, L. (2001). *Beyond psychotherapy: Introduction to psychoenergetic healing.* Chagrin Falls, OH: Expansion.

Maslow, A. (1961). *Existential psychology,* New York: Random House.

Maslow, A. (1971). *The farther reaches of human nature.* New York: Penguin.

Mazza, N. (1999). *Poetry therapy: Interface of the arts and psychology.* Boca, Raton, FL: St. Lucie.

McCraty, R., Atkinson, M., & Tiller, W. A. (1993). New electrophysiological correlates associated with intentional heart focus. *Subtle Energies,* 4(3), 251–268.

Merejildo, J. A. (1997). *The awakening of the puma: Evidences of archeo astronomy in the Andes.* Cusco, Peru: Imprenta.

Monti, D. A., Sinnott, J., & Kunkel, E. J. S. (1999). Muscle test responses to congruent and incongruent self-referential statements. *Perceptual and Motor Skills,* 88, 1019–1028.

Moreland, K. (1997). *The lived experience of receiving the chakra connection of women with breast cancer who are receiving chemotherapy.* Lakewood, CO: Healing Touch International.

Motoyama, H. (1981). A biophysical elucidation of the meridians and ki energy. *International Association for Religion and Parapsychology,* 7(1).

Motoyama, H. (1986). Before polarization of current and the acupuncture meridians. *Journal of Holistic Medicine,* 8, 15–26.

Motoyama, H. (1995). *Theories of the chakras.* Wheaton, IL: Quest.

Motoyama, H. (1997) *Treatment principles of Oriental medicine from an electrophysiological viewpoint.* Tokyo: Human Science Press.

Motoyama, H. (1999). *Comparisons of diagnostic methods in Western and Eastern medicine.* Tokyo: Human Science Press.

Murphy, M., & Donovan, S. (1997). *The physical and psychological effects of meditation.* Sausalito, CA: Institute of Noetic Sciences.

National Association for Music Therapy. (1994). *Code of Ethics.* Silver Springs, MD: Author.

National Institutes of Health. (1997). *Report on the effectiveness of acupuncture for certain medical conditions.* Washington, DC: Author.

North American Nursing Diagnosis Association. (1996). *NANDA nursing diagnoses.* Philadelphia, PA: Author.

Nurse Healers–Professional Associates, Inc. (2001). *Compendium of therapeutic touch research to date.* Reston, VA; 11250 Roger Bacon Dr. Suite 8, 20190; www.therapeutic-touch.org

Olson, M., & Sneed, N. (1995). Anxiety and therapeutic touch. *Issues in Mental Health Nursing,* 16(2), 97–108.

Olson, M., Sneed, N., LaVia, M., et al. (1997). Stress-induced immunosuppression and therapeutic touch. *Journal of Alternative Therapies,* 3(2), 68–74.

Oschman, J. (2000). *Energy medicine: The scientific basis.* Edinborough, Scotland: Churchill Livingstone.

Oschman, J. L. (1998). What is "healing energy?" *Journal of Bodywork and Movement Therapies,* 2(1), 117–122.

Ouzman, S., & Loubser, J. (2000). Art of the apocalypse. *Discovering Archeology*, 2(5), 38–45.

Pavek, R. (1993). *Manual healing methods: Physical and biofield.* Washington, DC: NIH–Office of Alternative Medicine.

Pearsall, P. (1998). *The heart's code.* New York: Broadway.

Peck, S. D. (1997). The effectiveness of therapeutic touch for decreasing pain in elders with degenerative arthritis. *Journal of Holistic Nursing, 15*(2), 176–198.

Perls, F. (1969). *Gestalt therapy verbatim.* Lafayette, CA: Real People.

Pert, C. (1997). *Molecules of emotion.* New York: Charles Scibner's Sons.

Phillips, M. (2000). *Finding the energy to heal.* New York: W. W. Norton.

Prudden, B. (1986). *Pain erasure,* New York: Ballantine.

The Italian iceman. (2000, February 2) San Diego, CA: Public Broadcasting System.

Pulos, L. (in press). The integration of energy psychology with hypnosis. In F. Gallo (Ed.), *Energy psychology in psychotherapy.* New York: W. W. Norton.

Quinn, J. (1984). Therapeutic touch as energy exchange: Testing the theory. *Advances in Nursing Science, 6*(2), 42–49.

Quinn, J. F. (1992). Holding sacred space: The nurse as healing environment. *Holistic Nursing Practice, 6*(4), 26–36.

Quinn, J., & Strelkauskas, A. J. (1993). Psychoimmunologic effects of therapeutic touch on practitioners and recently bereaved recipients. *Advances in Nursing Science, 15*(4), 13–26.

Radin, D. (1998, Summer). Mind moving matter. *Noetic Sciences Review, 46,* 21–25, 58–61.

Radin, D. I., Rebman, J. M., & Cross, M. P. (1996). Anomalous organization of random events by group consciousness: Two exploratory experiments. *Journal of Scientific Exploration, 10*(1), 143–168.

Radomski, S. (2001, May). Energy psychology to treat allergy-like symptoms. *Proceedings of the Third Annual International Energy Psychology Conference.* San Diego, CA: ACEP Publications.

Radomski, S. (2001). *Manual for dealing with allergy-like symptoms from an energetic perspective.* Philadelphia, PA: Author.

Rama, S., Ballentine, R., & Ajaya , S. (1981). *Yoga and psychotherapy.* Honesdale, PA: Himalayan International Institute.

Rawnsley, M. M. (1985). Health: A Rogerian perspective. *Journal of Holistic Nursing, 3*(1), 13–26.

Rogers, M. E. (1970). *The science of unitary man: An introduction to the theoretical basis of nursing.* Philadelphia, PA: Davis.

Rose, B. H. C., & Keegan, L. (2000). "Exercise and movement," in Dossey, B. M., Keegan, L., & Guzetta, C. E. (Eds.), *Holistic nursing* (3rd ed.). Gaithersburg, MD: Aspen.

Rossman, M. (1987). *Healing yourself: A step-by-step program for better health through imagery.* New York: Wahlen.

Seaton, J. (2001). *Artlife: Twelve creative journeys for life healing.* Boulder, CO: Sounds True.

Seligman, M., & Csikszentmihalyi, M. (2000, January). Positive psychology. *American Psychologist, 55*(1), 5–14.

Seligman, M. E. P. & Csikszentmihalyi, M. (January, 2000). Positive psychology: An introduction. *American Psychologist, 55*(1), 5.

Seligman, M. E. P. (1990). *Learned optimism.* New York: Simon & Schuster.

Selye, H. (1978). *The stress of life.* New York: New American Library.

Shapiro, F. (1995). *Eye movement desensitization and reprocessing.* New York: Guilford.

Sheldon, K. M., Elliot, A. J., Youngmee, K., & Rasser, T. (2001). What is satisfying about satisfying events? Testing 10 candidate psychological needs. *Journal of Personality and Social Psychology, 80*(2).

Sheldrake, R. (1981). *A new science of life: The hypothesis of formative causation.* Los Angeles: Tarcher.

Sheldrake, R. (1988). *The presence of the past.* New York: Time Books.

Simington, J. A., & Lang, G. P. (1993). Effects of therapeutic touch on anxiety in the institutionalized elderly. *Clinical Nursing Research, 2*(4), 438–450.

Simonton. C., Mattthews-Simonton, S., & Creighton, J. L. (1981). *Getting well again.* New York: Bantam.

Slater, V. (2000). Energetic healing. In B. Dossey, L. Keegan, & C. Guzzetta (Eds.), *Holistic nursing.* Gaithersburg, MD: Aspen.

Smith, L. L. (2000). *Called into healing.* Arvada, CO: Healing Touch Spiritual Ministries Press.

Stefano, G. M., Frichiore, G. L., Slingsley, B. T., & Benson, H. (2001). The placebo effect and relaxation response: Neural processes and their compliance to constitutive nitric oxide. *Brain Research Review, 35*, 1–19.

Stockstad, E. (2000). Stephen Strauss' impossible job, *Science, 288,* 1568–1570.

Stravena, J. A. (2000). Therapeutic touch coming of age. *Holistic Nursing Practice, 14*(3), 1–13.

Swingle, P., Pulos, L., & Swingle, M. (2001). *Neurophysiological correlates of successful EFT treatment of post traumatic stress disorder.* (Manuscript submitted for publication). Available from University of British Columbia, Vancouver, BC.

Synderman, R. (2000). CAM (complementary alternative medicine) and the role of the academic health center. *Alternative Therapies, 6*(6), 93.

Taylor, K. (1995). *The ethics of caring.* Santa Cruz, CA: Hanford Mead.

Teeguarden, I. M. (1996). *A complete guide to acupressure.* Tokyo: Japan Publications.

Thich Nhat Hanh. (1997). *Teachings on love.* Berkeley, CA: Parallax.

Tiller, W. (1997). *Science and human transformation.* Walnut Creek, CA: Pavoir.

Turner, J. G., Clark, A. J., Gauthier, D. K., & Williams, M. (1998). The effect of therapeutic touch on pain and anxiety in burn patients. *Journal of Advanced Nursing, 28*(1), 10–20.

Upledger, J. E. (1997). *Your inner physician and you: Cranio-sacral therapy and somato emotional release.* Berkeley, CA: North Atlantic Books.

van der Kolk, B. A., McFarlane A. C., & Weisaeth, L. (1996). *Traumatic stress: The effects of overwhelming experience on mind, body, and society.* New York: Guilford.

Ventura, M. (2001, January/February). Beauty resurrected. *Psychotherapy Networker, 25*(1), 30–35.

Veth, I. (1949). *The yellow emperor's classic of internal medicine.* Berkeley, CA: University of California Press.

Villodo, A. (2000). *Spirit medicine: Shamanic healing practices of ancient America.* New York: Random House.

Wang, P., Hu, X., & Wu, B. (1993). [Displaying of the infrared radiant track along meridians on the back of the human body] Fujian Institute of Traditional Chinese Medicine, Fuzhou, China. *Zhen Ci Yan Jiu, 18*(2), 90–93 (original in Chinese).

Watson, A. (1997). Quantum spookiness wins, Einstein loses in photon test. *Science, 277,* 481.

Wells, S. (2001, May). Comparison of diaphragmatic breathing and EFT for phobias. *Proceedings of the Third Annual International Energy Psychology Conference.* San Diego, CA: ACEP Publications.

Whisenant, W. F. (1994). *Psychological kinesiology: Changing the body's beliefs.* Kailua, HI: Monarch Butterfly Productions.

Whitfield, C. (1993). *Boundaries and relationships.* Deerfield Beach, FL: Health Communications.

Wilson, E. S. (1993). The transits of consciousness. *Subtle Energies, 4*(2), 171–186.

Wirth, D. (1990). The effect of non-contact therapeutic touch on the healing rate of full thickness dermal wounds. *Journal of Subtle Energies, 1*(1), 1–20.

Zachos, J., Pagani, M., Sloan, L., Thomas, E., & Billups, K. (2001). Trends, rythms, and aberrations in global climate 65 ma to present. *Science, 292,* 686–693.

Zhang, D., Fu, W., Wang, S., Wei, Z., & Wang, F. (1996). [Displaying of infrared thermogram of temperature character on the meridians] Institute of Acupuncture and Moxibustion, Beijing, China. *Zhen Ci Yan, Jiu, 21*(3), 63–67 (original in Chinese).

Zimmerman, J. (1990). Laying-on-of-hands healing and therapeutic touch: A testable theory. *BEMI Currents, Journal of the Bio-Electro-Magnetics Institute, 2*(8), 1–17.

Glossary

applied kinesiology (AK) Method developed by Goodheart for evaluating strength of a client's organ system or meridian function by testing an indicator muscle with gentle pressure; if the client's system is strong in relation to the meridian being touched, the indicator muscle will hold strong; if the client's system has dysfunction in relation to the meridian, the indicator muscle will be weaker.

acupoint A specific node or point along a meridian that has slightly less resistance and serves as a minute relay of electrical energy along the meridian. Most meridians have numerous acupoints.

acupressure A method of working with the meridians through direct pressure, tapping, or holding of an acupoint, rather than stimulating it with needles or heat. Meridian-based psychotherapy is a form of emotional acupressure.

acupuncture A method known in ancient China for over 5,000 years of aiding the body to rebalance by the stimulation of acupoints by insertion of fine needles or use of heat and herbs.

aura Metaphysical term for the human energy field, or biofield.

balancing Term used to describe the realignment of the biofield to its natural, highest vibrational function and potentials.

biofield A scientific term for the vibrational emanations that surround and extend beyond the human body, as measured by SQID (Super-conducting Quantum Interference Device) and demonstrated through the mechanism of Kirlian photography.

centering The process of focusing one's attention and intention to be fully responsive and present to one's client, setting aside personal issues and outcome expectations.

chakra Sanskrit word, meaning spinning wheel, used to name the human energy centers that spin like rotating vortices. Also known as centers of consciousness, owing to the psychological and developmental properties of each center.

ch'i Preferred spelling is **qi** and is pronounced "chee." Chinese term for energy or vital life force that acts as nourishing subtle flow through the chakras, the meridians, and the biofield. Also called *prana, ki,* or *spiritus.*

clearing The facilitator's hand movements above the biofield that facilitate the release of energy blockage. Synonymous with releasing, letting go, smoothing, or unruffling of the biofield.

clinical kinesiology (CK) Term coined by Beardall to described muscle testing in psychological settings.

comprehensive energy psychology (CEP) Psychotherapeutic interventions that combine all aspects of working with the human vibrational matrix to assist emotional, cognitive, and spiritual healing. The human vibrational matrix includes the biofield, the chakras, and the meridians and their related acupoints, as well as other flows.

desired beliefs Beliefs that are productive and functional for the individual, as opposed to limiting or constricting choices; for example, "I am a lovable and capable person."

energy blockage A general term that refers to the interruption or constriction of the natural flow patterns in the human vibrational matrix. May refer to a closed or diminished chakra, asymmetry in the biofield, or nonpolarity and reversal in the meridian flows.

energy center Same as chakra, a specific center of consciousness in the human vibrational matrix that allows inflow of qi to the human organism from the Universal Energy Field, and outflow of excessive qi from the human body/mind.

energy healing Broad term used to describe interventions that address the releasing of energetic blockage or imbalance, followed by repatterning, balancing, and aligning of the human vibrational matrix to higher levels of functioning.

etheric layer The layer of the human energy field that is closest to the body and creates the interface between the body and its more subtle other dimensions.

focusing The holding of positive intent in relation to a specific aspect of the biofield or a chakra to allow for repatterning, balancing, and modulation of energy; this focusing or holding of intent can be assisted by placing the hands over the area and is generally done after clearing maneuvers.

grounding Connecting to the earth and earth's energy field to calm the mind and balance the energy system.

healing The ongoing evolution toward ever higher levels of functioning in the multidimensional human being.

human energy system The entire interactive dynamic of human subtle energies consisting of the chakras, the multidimensional field, and the meridians, and their acupoints; the human vibrational matrix of subtle energy.

human vibrational matrix Same as human energy system.

intention Holding one's inner awareness and focus to accomplish a specific task or activity; being fully present in the moment. A specific form of directed consciousness.

limiting beliefs Often unconsciously held beliefs that limit human potential; examples, "I am not capable; I am flawed; I am a victim."

muscle testing/muscle checking Same as applied kinesiology or clinical kinesiology.

psychoenergetic healing A form of healing practice that interrelates psychological insights with understanding of the human vibrational matrix.

psychoenergetic disturbance A form of pervasive distortion in the human vibrational matrix that limits the whole person from obtaining psychological relief from stressors; also called non-polarization and pervasive, or systemic imbalance.

psychoenergetic reversal A form of distress where conscious and subconscious thinking are in conflict. This may be represented in the energy field as a blocked area, a chakra spinning counterclockwise or not at all, and a limiting belief pattern that no longer serves the person.

qi Same as ch'i. Term for the vital life force in the Chinese traditions.

subtle energy Term coined by Einstein to describe the invisible, unmeasurable energies that radiate from living organisms and are in constant interrelationship with matter.

subjective units of distress (SUD) rating scale commonly used to describe intensity of a felt emotion, as in, "On a scale of 0 to 10, where does your distress about this issue lie?"

tapping Repeated percussion on an acupoint to stimulate it into full functioning. Stimulation of an acupoint can also be accomplished by holding an acupoint or using internal imagery.

transpersonal Term coined by Drs. Abraham Maslow, Anthony Sutich, and Stanislav Grof, founders of the Association for Transpersonal Psychology, to describe the psychological realm beyond the purely personal, reaching to the wider, spiritual dimension of human experience.

universal energy field Term to describe the infinite resource of unlimited energy that surrounds and interpenetrates all aspects of the Universe.

unruffling Term coined by Dr. Dolores Krieger to suggest the clearing or smoothing of a ruffled, disturbed area in the biofield.

Bibliography of Selected Readings

PHYSICS OF ENERGY-ORIENTED PSYCHOTHERAPY

Bentov. I. (1977). *Stalking the wild pendulum*. New York: Dutton.

Bohm, D. (1980). *Wholeness and the implicate order*. London: Routledge.

Eisenberg, D. (1995). *Encounters with qi*. New York: W. W. Norton.

Freeman, I. M. (1990). *Physics made simple*. New York: Doubleday.

Herbert, N. (1985). *Quantum reality: Beyond the new physics*. New York: Doubleday.

Goswami, A. (1993). *The self-aware universe: How consciousness creates the material world*. New York: Tarcher.

Sheldrake, R. (1988). *The presence of the past: Morphic resonance and the habits of nature*. New York: Random House.

Tiller, W. (1997). *Science and human transformation*. Walnut Creek, CA: Pavoir.

ELECTROMAGNETIC NATURE OF THE HUMAN BODY

Becker, R. O. , & Selden, G. (1985). *The body electric: Electromagnetism and the foundation of life*. New York: William Morrow.

Becker, R. O. (1990). *Cross currents: The perils of electropollution, the promise of electromedicine*. New York: Tarcher.

Burr, H. S. (1972). *Blueprint for immortality: The electric patterns of life*. Essex, England: C. W. Daniel.

Moss, T. (1972). *The body electric*. Los Angeles, CA: Tarcher.

Oschman, J. L. (2000). *Energy medicine: The scientific basis.* Edinborough, Scotland: Churchill Livingstone.

MIND/BODY INTERACTIONS

Childre, E. D. L. (1994). *Freeze frame.* Boulder Creek, CA: Planetary (Institute of Heart Math).

Cousins, N. (1991). *Anatomy of an illness as perceived by the patient.* New York: Bantam.

Dossey, B., Keegan, L., & Guzzetta, C. (2000). *Holistic nursing: A handbook for practice,* 3rd ed. Gaithersburg, MD: Aspen.

Diamond, J. (1978). *Behavioral kinesioloy and the autonomic nervous system.* Valley Cottage, NY: Archaeus.

Diamond, J. (1979). *Your body doesn't lie.* New York: Warner.

Durlacher, J. V. (1994). *Freedom from fear forever.* Tempe, AZ: Van Ness.

Fleming, T. (2001). *Reduce traumatic stress in minutes: The Tapas acupressure technique (TAT) workbook.* Torrance, CA: Author.

Namudripad, D.S. (1993). *Say goodbye to illness.* Buena Park, CA: Delta.

Paddison, S. (1992). *The hidden power of the heart.* Boulder Creek, CA: Planetary (Institute of Heart Math).

Pearsall, P. (1998). *The heart's code.* New York: Broadway.

Pert, C. (1997). *Molecules of emotion.* New York: Charles Scribner's Sons.

Radomski, S. (2001). *Treating allergy-like symptoms.* Jenkinstown, PA: Author.

Rochschlitz, S. (1995). *Allergies and candida.* Mahopac, NY: Human Ecology Balancing Sciences.

ENERGETIC APPLICATIONS FOR PHYSICAL HEALING

Beinfield, H., & Korngold, E. (1998). *Between heaven and earth.* New York: Ballantine Wellspring.

Eden, D. (1998). *Energy medicine.* New York: Tarcher.

Gerber, R. (2001). *Vibrational medicine.* Rochester, VT: Bear.

Hover-Kramer, D. (2002). *Healing touch: Guidebook for practitioners.* Albany, NY: Delmar/Thomson International.

Krieger, D. (1993). *Accepting your power to heal.* Santa Fe, NM: Bear.

Macrae, J. (1999). *Therapeutic touch: A practical guide.* New York: Knopf.

Motoyama, H. (1997). *Treatment principles of Oriental medicine from an electrophysiological viewpoint.* Tokyo: Human Sciences.

NONLOCAL HEALING

Benor, D. (2000). *Spiritual healing* (Vol. I). Southfield, MI: Vision.

Dossey, L. (1993). *Healing words: The power of prayer and the practice of medicine.* San Francisco, CA: Harper/Collins.

Dossey, L. (1996). *Prayer is good medicine.* New York: HarperCollins.

Dossey, L. (1999). *Reinventing medicine: Beyond mind-body to a new era of healing.* San Francisco, CA: Harper.

Hunt, V. (1995). *Infinite mind: The science of human vibrations.* Malibu, CA: Malibu.

Targ, R., & Katra, J. (1998). *Miracles of mind: Exploring nonlocal consiousness and spiritual healing.* New York: New World Library.

ENERGETIC APPLICATIONS FOR EMOTIONAL HEALING

Callahan, R. (2001). *Tapping the healer within.* Lincolnwood, IL: Contemporary.

Clinton, A. (2001). *Seemorg matrix training manual.* Princeton, NJ: Author.

Craig, G. (2001). *Emotional freedom technique (EFT) manual.* Sea Ranch, CA: Author.

Diepold, J. (1998). *Touch and breathe.* Moorestown. NJ: Author.

Gallo, F. (1998). *Energy psychology.* Boca Raton, FL: CRC.

Gallo, F. (2000). *Energy diagnostic and treatment methods.* New York: W. W. Norton.

Gallo, F., & Vincensi, H. (2000). *Energy tapping.* W. W. Norton.

Gallo, F. (Ed.). (in press). *Energy psychology in psychotherapy.* New York: W. W. Norton.

Gudermeyer, D., Grudermeyer, R., & Hover-Kramer, D. (2001). *Individualized energy psychotherapy (IEP) training manuals,* I & II. Del Mar, CA: Willingness Works.

Grudermeyer, D. (2000). *Energy psychology desktop companion.* Del Mar, CA: Willingness Works.

Hover-Kramer, D., & Shames, K. (1997). *Energetic approaches to emotional healing.* Albany, NY: Delmar/Thomson International.

Lambrou, P., & Pratt, G. (2000). *Instant emotional healing.* New York: Broadway.

Nims, L. (2001). *Be set free fast (BSFF) training manual.* Orange, CA: Author.

Swack, J. (2001). *Healing from the body level up (HBLU) manual.* Needham, MA: Author.

METAPHYSICAL APPROACHES

Bloom, W. (1995). *Meditation in a changing world.* London: Gothic Image.

Bloom, W. (1997). *Psychic protection: Creating positive energies for people and places.* New York: Fireside.

Brennan, B. (1987). *Hands of light.* New York: Bantam.

Brennan, B. (1993). *Light emerging.* New York: Bantam.

Bruyere, R. (1987). *Wheels of light.* San Madre, CA: Bon.

Kunz, D. (1991). *The personal aura.* Wheaton, IL: Quest.

Luthke, M. F., & Stein-Luthke, L. (2001). *Beyond psychotherapy: Introduction to psychoenergetic healing.* Chagrin Falls, OH: Expansion.

Van Praagh, J. (1997). *Talking to heaven: A medium's message of life after death.* New York: Dutton.

Appendices

Appendix A: Sample Intake Sheet

Date

Identifying Data
    Name   Telephone #
    Street address
    City, State, Zip
    Profession
    Referred by   Date of birth

Physical Status
    Presenting symptoms
    Current medications
    Pertinent medical history, including surgeries
    Known allergies

Emotional Status
    Current stress in personal life
    Current stress in professional life
    Current sources of pleasure
    Self-rating of emotional health

Mental Status
    Predominant thought patterns
    Meditation experience
    Effectiveness of inner practices
    Self-rating of mental health

Spiritual Awareness
    Sense of connection to Higher Power
    Spiritual practices used
    Effectiveness of spiritual practices

Energetic Assessment
    Areas of energy field disturbance/imbalance
    Condition of the major chakras
    Intuitive perceptions of practitioner

Appendix B: Sample Treatment Consent for Use of Energy Psychotherapy Approaches

I have been informed about the new group of psychotherapeutic approaches, called energy psychotherapy, that work with the human energy system and are understood to effect the body/mind interconnection. I have also been informed that clinical experience and scientific studies are confirming that these approaches can significantly reduce conditions such as phobias, anxiety, and post-traumatic stress symptoms. I have also been advised that there are currently no known side-effects to energy psychotherapy treatments when properly administered and that the research to date confirms the efficacy and safety of energy-oriented psychotherapy.

I understand that, because energy psychotherapy consists of relatively new approaches to treatment, the extent and breadth of its effectiveness as well as possible side-effects, its risks and benefits, are not yet fully known. I have been advised of the following:

- Previously vivid or traumatic memories may fade. This could adversely impact the ability to provide detailed legal testimony regarding a traumatic incident.
- Reactions may surface during the treatment that neither my therapist or I can fully anticipate, including strong emotional or physical sensations, or additional, unresolved memories.
- Emotional material may continue to surface after a treatment session and give indication of other incidents that may need to be addressed.
- Light touch may be involved in diagnosis with clinical kinesiology, and I will be learning how to perform self-treatment through working with my own energy system.

I have considered the above information before selecting to receive energy psychotherapy treatment and have obtained whatever additional information or professional advice I considered necessary to make an informed decision. I choose to participate in energy psychotherapy of my own free will and know I have the right to cease using this approach at any time. I further agree to take full responsibility for my self-care in the physical, emotional, mental, and spiritual dimensions of my life.

My signature on this form acknowledges my choice to consent to the innovative approaches of energy psychotherapy. My consent is free from pressure or influence from any person or group.

Client Signature:_____ Date:_____

Appendix C: Standards of Practice in Comprehensive Energy Psychology

PART ONE: PRACTITIONER-FOCUSED STANDARDS

I. Professional Education and Personal Development

Standard of Care #1:
Practitioners of Comprehensive Energy Psychology shall be committed to professional growth.

Standards of Practice: Practitioners of CEP shall . . .
1. Participate in continuing education in the rapidly developing field of energy psychology treatments, as well as in the areas of theory and research.
2. Develop skills to facilitate a sense of centering and intention in their professional practice.
3. Explore and develop awareness of how their vibrational matrix has impact in facilitating the therapeutic environment.
4. Preceptor other professionals in their growth as practitioners of Comprehensive Energy Psychology.

Standard of Care #2:
Practitioners of Comprehensive Energy Psychology shall be committed to personal development.

Standards of Practice: Practitioners of CEP shall . . .
1. Continue their own personal development to assure expertise in their practice of energy psychology interventions.
2. Possess a sense of hope and confidence in approaching issues regarding the client's situation.
3. Have a clear intent for their caring interventions and ensure that they are not depleted, by regularly seeking out adequate support and replenishment.
4. Consciously participate in the evolutionary process of their lives

with the understanding that crisis can provide opportunity for learning.

II. Community and Global Involvement

Standard of Care #1:
Practitioners of Comprehensive Energy Psychology shall participate in establishing and promoting conditions in society that facilitate integration, health and wholeness.

Standards of Practice: Practitioners of CEP shall . . .
1. Become aware of relevant local, state, national, and international organizations that actively focus on development of Energy Psychology concepts at various levels.
2. Become politically active, in ways that have personal integrity, concerning issues that impact health and wellness from an energy-oriented perspective.

Standard of Care #2:
Practitioners of Comprehensive Energy Psychology shall participate in the ethics of caregiving and identify a linkage of caring to public policy.

Standards of Practice: Practitioners of CEP shall, in ways that have personal integrity . . .
1. Become involved in policy development related to psychoenergetic health.
2. Value and promote activities and policies that support an energetically sound human environment.
3. Advocate for the well-being of the global community's education and ethical norms.

PART TWO: CLIENT-FOCUSED STANDARDS

III. Caring for the Multidimensional Client and Significant Others

Standard of Care #1:
Clients and significant others experience the practitioner of Comprehensive Energy Psychology as a helpful presence, offering shared humanness, a sense of connectedness, and attention to the unique qualities of each person.

Standards of Practice: Practitioners of CEP shall . . .

1. Focus care on the whole multidimensional client, beyond only the current presenting symptoms or energy psychology treatment protocols.
2. Respect clients' rights and choices, ensure client awareness of risks and benefits of CEP treatments, and act as an advocate for the client.
3. Make decisions about the process of comprehensive care based on a thorough assessment and integrated understanding of the needs of the client.
4. Seek to be guided by the client's innate wisdom to know what is appropriate for him/her.

IV. Education for Effective Lifestyles and Mutual Decision-Making

Standard of Care #1:
Clients and their relations possess the knowledge they want and need in order to be involved in decisions about treatment and lifestyle planning.

Standard of Care #2:
Clients and their relations receive care based on priorities of treatment focus that contribute to their desired outcomes.

Standard of Care #3:
Clients and their relations are active partners in lifestyle planning and decision-making based on their desires and needs.

Standards of Practice: Practitioners of CEP shall . . .
1. Use sound principles of teaching and learning to provide assessment, education, and treatment of their clients, and to develop a map of their clients' knowledge-base pertaining to diagnosis, treatment planning, anticipated outcomes, and self-care activities.
2. Collaborate with other healthcare providers with the client's knowledge and consent.
3. Engage the client in collaborative planning for goals, treatment, practice at home, and follow-up care, drawing out clients' self-wisdom regarding their diagnosis, treatment -planning decisions, appropriate outcome goals, and choices of self-care activities.
4. Be persistent in responding to environmental or cultural barriers to the delivery of integrated goal-oriented care, taking risks, if necessary, to advocate for the client.

5. Support the client's sense of, and development of, personal responsibility, and support the client's desired outcomes.
6. Be flexible, willing, and able to give up attachment to specific treatment interventions or outcomes, in order to provide true client-centered care.
7. Engage clients in problem-solving discussions in relation to significant lifestyle changes as a result of new insights, healing, or anchoring of new client-desired beliefs.

V. Cross-Cultural Care

Standard of Care #1:
Clients and significant others shall receive care consistent with their cultural backgrounds, health beliefs, and values.

Standard of Care #2:
The client's cultural diversity and its importance to the global community will be respected, protected, and enhanced.

Standards of Practice: Practitioners of CEP shall . . .
1. Gain knowledge of cultural practices of clients in their care, particularly with respect to working with the energy system.
2. Integrate this knowledge into planning interventions.
3. Use appropriate community resources.
4. Recognize the critical nature and value of diversity to the global community.

VI. Self-Care

Standard of Care #1:
Clients and significant others shall be encouraged and supported in managing self-care to maximize quality of life.

Standards of Practice: Practitioners of CEP shall . . .
1. Plan with clients and families for self-care by assisting in identifying goals.
2. Provide information on Comprehensive Energy Psychology as appropriate to the client's understanding.
3. Initiate referrals and provide access to resources in urgent situations.
4. Maintain contact as necessary and ethically appropriate, with significant others, and with other health team members involved in the client's care.

VII. Spiritual Care

Standard of Care #1:
Clients shall receive care that is consistent with their beliefs.

Standard of Care #2:
Clients and significant others shall receive support for spiritual growth that is consistent with their beliefs.

Standards of Practice: Practitioners of CEP shall . . .
1. Assess clients' values and beliefs in planning of individualized care.
2. Provide an environment conducive to reflection, insight, and accessing the client's inner resources and wisdom.
3. Actively support the client's search for meaning and purpose in life.

VIII. Care of the Environment

Standard of Care #1:
Clients shall receive treatment in an environment that is as safe, toxin-free, respectful, and supportive as possible.

Standards of Practice: Practitioners of CEP shall . . .
1. Practice according to policies and procedures in relation to environmental safety and preparedness for emergencies.
2. Practice in accordance with the CEP practitioner's understanding of nourishing and toxifying energy field conditions.
3. Respect privacy, confidentiality, and the client's need for peacefulness.

IX. Theory and Research

Standard of Care #1:
Clients shall receive care based on theory and conceptual models related to Comprehensive Energy Psychology.

Standard of Care #2:
Clients shall receive interventions based on recognized research findings in the field of Energy Psychology.

Standards of Practice: Practitioners of CEP shall . . .
1. Be involved in systematic inquiry related to clinical issues by engaging in research that is congruous with the practitioner's interests.
2. Support, remain up-to-date about, and utilize recognized research by others.

3. Provide research information to clients as appropriate.

X. Comprehensive Energy Psychology Treatment Process

Standard of Care #1:
Clients shall continuously be assessed in an integrated, comprehensive manner.

Standards of Practice: Practitioners of CEP shall . . .
1. Demonstrate competency in communication skills to establish and maintain rapport.
2. Demonstrate competency in energetic assessment of the client's biofield, centers (chakras), and pathways (meridians).
3. Gather pertinent bio-psycho-social-spiritual data from the client, his/her health team members, and significant others as ethically appropriate, as well as using and validating one's own intuition.
4. Collaborate with other health team members, review database as new information becomes available, and document pertinent data in the client's record.
5. Utilize data collected to understand patterns that validate known problems, and provide clues about potential unidentified problems.
6. Make referrals as appropriate.

Standard of Care #2:
Practitioners of CEP shall develop appropriate treatment plans based on the client's assessed needs.

Standards of Practice: Practitioners of CEP shall . . .
1. Develop a plan of care in collaboration with the client, significant others as ethically appropriate, and other heath team members.
2. Determine appropriate interventions for each issue as well as note overall opportunities for enhancing well-being.
3. Incorporate interventions that communicate acceptance of the client's values, beliefs, and culture.
4. Incorporate client input in ways that communicate the seeking and valuing of the client's internal wisdom.
5. Provide ongoing evaluation and collaborative reassessment.
6. Revise and communicate the plan of care as appropriate, and record interventions implemented.

I wish to thank the Association for Comprehensive Energy Psychology for permission to publish its standards of care.

Appendix D: Code of Ethics for Practitioners of Comprehensive Energy Psychology

I. Standard of Ethical Consideration #1 in Relation to Self:

Practitioners of Comprehensive Energy Psychology shall maintain the integrity of their personal human energy system, or vibrational matrix.

Standard of Practice:

1. Practitioners of CEP have growing and sensitive awareness of their personal issues in the physical, emotional, mental, and spiritual dimensions of their vibrational matrix.
2. Practitioners of CEP seek appropriate help for physical, emotional, mental, or spiritual needs as soon as they become aware of any disturbance.
3. Practitioners of CEP trust their own inner wisdom and commit to independent thinking, thus avoiding over-involvement, dependency, or over-attachment to any one person's point of view.
4. Practitioners of CEP commit to continuing education and updates in the field of Energy Psychology.

II. Standard of Ethical Consideration #2 in Relation to the Client:

Practitioners of Comprehensive Energy Psychology consider the client's needs in physical, emotional, mental, and spiritual dimensions as a priority when providing care.

Standards of Practice:

1. Practitioners of CEP set their intent for the highest good of the client, relinquishing any attachments, personal agendas, or desire for specific outcomes.

2. Practitioners of CEP ensure that their own sense of personal gratification is derived from sources other than the client.
3. Practitioners of CEP shall provide the highest quality of care possible based on the theory and knowledge-base concerning the human vibrational matrix.
4. Practitioners of CEP continually evaluate client outcomes and revise their plan of care accordingly, seeking supervision as needed.

III. Standard of Ethical Consideration #3 in Relation to Colleagues:

Practitioners of Comprehensive Energy Psychology treat their colleagues with respect and honor.

Standards of Practice:
1. Practitioners of CEP refrain from publicly or privately disparaging remarks concerning other CEP practitioners, researchers, or innovators (and other people as well). They encourage and support professional discussion of relevant research and theory.
2. Practitioners of CEP discuss personal differences or concerns regarding a colleague's professional conduct, directly and privately with the person involved, avoiding third-party conversations or triangulation.
3. If direct discussion does not bring resolution, practitioners of CEP seek arbitration, mediation, or intervention of appropriate ethics boards, beginning with local resources, then state, regional, or national levels, as needed for resolution.

IV. Standard of Ethical Consideration #4 in Relation to Referrals and Consultants:

Practitioners of Comprehensive Energy Psychology readily utilize referral and consultant resources to maximize the client's well-being.

Standards of Practice:
1. Practitioners of CEP are clear with themselves and their clients about the limits of their expertise and what they may ethically do for their clients within the scope of their professional license.
2. Practitioners of CEP identify client needs that are beyond their scope of practice and refer such clients to appropriate resources as quickly as possible.
3. Practitioners of CEP take responsibility for defining and clarifying their practice to the local professional community.
4. Practitioners of CEP collaborate with other professionals who

refer clients for Comprehensive Energy Psychology, communicating frequently, and returning the client to the primary caregivers as soon as appropriate.

5. Practitioners of CEP establish and describe the interventions, underlying theory, and supporting research to appropriate professional organizations in their communities.

6. Practitioners of CEP donate a portion of their time for making public contributions to enhance general awareness of the discipline of Comprehensive Energy Psychology.

V. Standard of Ethical Consideration #5 in Relation to the Practitioner's Licensure:

Practitioners of Comprehensive Energy Psychology adhere to all ethical guidelines set forth by the profession in which they practice and by the licenses they hold.

Standards of Practice:

1. Practitioners of CEP are familiar with, and conduct themselves within, the code of ethics for their profession that are set forth by the bodies responsible for governing that profession.

2. Violations of ethics within the practitioner's profession automatically constitute a violation of ethics as a CEP practitioner.

3. CEP practitioners therefore immediately seek help and guidance with any and all ethical questions or dilemmas that may arise in the performance of their professional responsibilities.

I wish to thank the Association for Comprehensive Energy Psychology for permission to publish its code of ethics.

Appendix E: Organizational Resources for Further Information

Energy Psychology

Association for Comprehensive Energy Psychology (ACEP)
c/o Dr. Dorothea Hover-Kramer
12307 Oak Knoll Road, Suite B
Poway, CA 92064
Tel. (858) 748-5963; Fax (858) 748-3119
Administrator: Rutherford Associates
P.O. Box 910244
San Diego, CA 92117-0244
DRGrudermeyer@willingness.com; Dorotheah@aol.com
www.energypsych.org

Fred Gallo, Ph.D.
40 Snyder Road
Hermitage, PA 16148
(724) 346-3838
www.energypsych.com

Emotional Freedom Techniques (EFT)
Gary Craig
P.O. Box 398
The Sea Ranch, CA 95497
(800) 231-6132
www.emofree.com

Subtle Energy Medicine

International Society for the Study of Subtle Energies/Energy Medicine (ISSSEEM)
356 Golden Circle
Golden, CO 80403
(303) 278-2228

Healing Touch (HT)

Colorado Center for HT (CCHT)
12477 W. Cedar Drive, Suite 206
Lakewood, CO 80228
Tel. (303) 989-0581; Fax (303) 985-9702;
ccheal@aol.com
www.healingtouch.net

Therapeutic Touch (TT)

Nurse Healers–Professional Associates, Inc. (NH–PAI)
760 South Highland Drive, Suite 429
Salt Lake City, UT 84106
(801) 942-5900
RMGOOD@worldnet.att.net
www.therapeutictouch.org

Holistic Nursing

American Holistic Nurses' Association (AHNA)
P. O. Box 2130
Flagstaff, AZ 86003-2130
Tel. (800) 526-AHNA; Fax (520) 526-2752
AHNA-Flag@Flaglink.com
www.ahna.org

Appendix F:
Beyond Ground Zero—
Energy Concepts for Addressing
Shock, After-Effects of Trauma, Grief,
and Future Anxiety

The unexpected, massive trauma that occurred on September 11, 2001 brings us to look at applications of energy therapy concepts for treating emotional distress related to current and unfolding world events. While all the exercises discussed in this book are relevant, I want to identify approaches that can be most effective for specific needs. These needs range from treating initial shock, as one is faced with traumatic news either directly or on television, to dealing with the long-term sequelae of large-scale trauma, to resolving grief in its many forms, and to addressing anxiety about the uncertain future.

It is clear that we are living through an experience that is unprecedented in the United States. It is an experience that may lead many of us to reorder our values. It is an experience that holds opportunity for personal growth in each of us as therapists and for assisting the lives of our many clients. Further, it is an experience that asks us to act locally within our family and friendship circles while learning to think globally as an international community. In time, we may look on this as a turning point, a time when outmoded thinking of warfare could give way to new alliances and world order. There is always a high creative potential in such times of crisis, but first we must heal ourselves and others so creative potentials can follow.

The energy therapies are especially relevant in these times of crisis and rapid change. They can be easily taught in the step-by-step fashion outlined in this book and implemented for ongoing personal self-care. The techniques can be used by individuals or shared in group settings. Thinking from an energetic perspective helps us to understand the vast influence of global imbalance and the daily need for returning the human energy system to harmony. Then, specific issues, such as anxiety or grief, can then be identified and treated to bring relief, and the treatment can be repeated as often as necessary until symptoms ameliorate.

DEALING WITH SHOCK

The initial shock of an unexpected event can be as traumatizing for those who are directly involved as for those who are vicariously watching. Traumatic shock waves appeared to go around the earth as people watched in horror the events of September 11 on their televisions. While those who had to run for personal safety felt the turbulence directly in their bodies, all but the most emotionally closed felt some somatic response, such as a sick feeling in the stomach, or a sense of disbelief, "It just can't be true." Feelings of unreality, disconnection, and denial are well-known initial reactions to a catastrophe. People may wander about, forget their tasks, or lose concentration. Another shock reaction is to lash out in anger at others without thinking. Feelings of helplessness and hopelessness may become pervasive in the days and weeks after trauma occurs.

The severity of shock responses, whether somatically felt or psychologically experienced, can be diminished with the quick resources of energy psychotherapy. For example, the treatment acupoints for the two central meridians—under the nose and under the lip—can be rubbed, alone or together, as soon as personal safety is established or there is a moment to take a deep breath. This maneuver, along with the entire Belly Button Correction, described in chapter 10, establishes a direct, calming link within the physical and energetic bodies. In addition, the Thymus Thump, the Cross Crawl, and Figure Eight movements, also explained in chapter 10, give additional means to balance oneself in the face of immediate trauma by integrating brain hemispheres and stimulating the immune system. Other biofield resources for treating shock are Centering and the Brush Down given in chapter 5. All of these techniques can be safely used without instrumentation or medication. Clear intention to help oneself is the only basic requirement.

Affirmations, with the engagement of conscious thought, are very useful; these can be stated out loud to oneself, written down, or shared with others as appropriate. Samples that deal with shock reactions are as follows:

- "Even though I feel numb in the face of this event, I deeply and profoundly accept myself."
- "Even though I can't figure out what to do, I deeply and profoundly accept myself."

- "Even though I feel hopeless and afraid, I deeply and profoundly accept myself."

Combining such affirmations with rubbing the neurolymphatic reflex (nlr) or "pledge" spot adds a powerful somatic anchor for self-acceptance and inner peace.

In my experience, it is vitally important to consciously do something rather than to freeze into a shock reaction and its more long-term effects of depression, irrational anger, or withdrawal. Whatever can be done in the first few moments, no matter how simple, can help to create a pattern within the vibrational matrix that moves the person to harmony, positive intention, and healing in later stages of trauma resolution.

I always encourage helping professionals to treat themselves first so that they can bring their sensitive, caring presence to others. This approach has been repeatedly tested over the last decades in many emergency settings where nurses used Therapeutic Touch, Healing Touch, or other energy healing modalities. Energy therapists worldwide used the concepts of personal self-healing for treating shock and shared their outcomes through the Association for Comprehensive Energy Psychology newsletters after the terrifying incidents.

ADDRESSING THE AFTEREFFECTS OF TRAUMA

The aftereffects of massive trauma are difficult to estimate. Just like the sequelae of a physical accident or life-threatening illness, the effects of trauma can impact personal attitudes, beliefs, and sense of identity over a whole lifetime. Through the experiences of Viet Nam veterans, we learned that posttraumatic stress symptoms can be far-reaching and reverberate through the very fiber of one's psychoenergetic matrix. Acute symptoms that may be repeated daily are flashbacks, nightmares, reliving of the trauma, and physical impairment. Long-term symptoms include a sense of despair, unending grief, emotional irritability and lability, loss of hope, and severe psychological disturbance.

Treating these symptoms is possible with energy psychotherapy using the concepts described in this book. A place to start can be to assess the most disturbing symptom, establish the client's rating of its intensity, both by self-report and muscle-checking, and to determine the part of the body in which the symptom is most felt. This lends a baseline that allows the therapist to assess the efficacy of each intervention for the client. The sequence suggested—treating the most systemic or pervasive, biofield disturbance first (chapter 10), followed by addressing psychoenergetic reversals (chapter 11), and moving to specific interventions with meridian point algorithms or chakra releasing work (chapters 12 to 14)—is probably most logical. However, a client with frequent flashbacks or nightmares, may first need to obtain immediate relief through a generic sequence targeting the elements of the event or by the use of positive affirmations to establish a sense of hopefulness and calm. Therapist skill and careful attention to client rapport are needed to find the best avenue of approach.

In working with a client who was held up at gunpoint in her own home, I used two general energetic interventions, the Brush Down to smooth the biofield, and the affirmation, "Even though this happened to me, I deeply and profoundly accept and respect myself." The emotional release of these two actions helped the client to be able to describe the incident, and I was able to elicit treatment algorithms for each element of the hold-up that could be treated, one after the other—hearing the assailant rustle through the leaves, feeling the gun touch her head, hearing the assailant's death threats, seeing her purse as she gave it to him, and so forth. After each layer of the trauma cleared, new elements seemed to emerge, including traumatic experiences from her childhood. In this way, the treatment of the presenting trauma became an opportunity to clear old, repressed material and heal many levels of psychoenergetic disturbance.

ACCEPTING AND EXPRESSING GRIEF

The reality of intense grief in New York City is palpable and may be present for some time to come. Everyone has a story; everyone knows someone who was affected by the events. They feel the need to tell their stories to be heard, understood, and comforted. In addition to supportive listening, creative therapists of all backgrounds can enhance grief work by encouraging self-expression through poems, songs, art-making, and journal writing.

Since the grief in this situation relates to entire groups of persons in large environments, we are in a sense all touched by the energetic imprint of grief. This imprint is a decrease in a flow of vital life force, or qi, to the organism that over time can result in decreased immune function and development of health problems. Diminished qi can be counteracted with daily balancing of the qi of each individual, whether one is personally involved in loss or not. Thus, Centering, Brush Down (chapter 5), Crossover Correction (chapter 7), and Belly Button Correction (chapter 10) are effective ways to bring the system to a higher vibrational frequency. I have personally found the Chakra Rotation (chapter 6) and Connecting the Energy Centers (chapter 10) very valuable in grief resolution. These exercises brought vitality to my entire system since the chakras seem to act as energetic forms of step-up transformers.

Less visible, and more subtle than personal grief, is the mourning of a nation that has lost its most obvious myths in one catastrophic day. The old beliefs—such as unlimited expansion of wealth, security and safety, protection within our shores, the idea that we can have it all without paying a price—are shattered. Slowly, and with hope, we must learn to tolerate uncertainty and trust that there can be a gradual evolution to new, more viable beliefs about ourselves and who we are in the world. This will take time and incredible patience in a nation that is used to quick solutions. The exercises in chapter 14 can be helpful in releasing old, dysfunctional beliefs and installing more desirable, functional beliefs. For example, using the Temporal Tap, we can release on the left side, "I no longer crave quick solutions" and tap in on the right side, "I am now open to my personal qualities of patience and resilience." Alternatively, we can release "I do not demand instant gratification from my national leadership" and bring in "I seek and honor qualities of wise counsel for long-term solutions in my leaders."

Prayer and meditation can be our most direct energetic resources in times of national mourning and reshaping of the national image. From an energy perspective, each positive thought of goodwill creates a vibrational frequency that elevates the imbalanced or diminished energies of disturbed areas. All of us can contribute to the expanding energy vortex of human consciousness through our individual intentions.

ANTICIPATING FUTURE ANXIETY

Anxiety about the uncertain future is perhaps the most pervasive of the effects of terrorist attacks. It is impossible to think realistically about the future without trepidation when the aim of terrorism is to create a climate of fear and uncertainty, and numerous terrorist networks are known to exist worldwide.

Historically speaking, the future has always been uncertain. No amount of security forces can guarantee safety. What is possible however, is to look at our internal sources of calming, to consider our attitudinal choices on a moment-by–moment basis, and to trust in the transpersonal presence of Higher Guidance in whatever form is comfortable for each of us.

The effects of fear and pervasive anxiety on the human energy system are constriction of the biofield, diminished or closed chakras, and disrupted meridian circuits. Thus, daily intentional practices are needed to counteract these energetic blockages. Specifically, future anxiety can be treated daily with the self-centering exercises for the whole energy body found in chapters 5 to 7 , such as Centering, Brush Down, Central Alignment, Chakra Rotation, Zip Up, and Crossover Correction. In addition, affirmations spoken out loud and repeatedly while stimulating the neurolymphatic reflex (nlr) point are quick and effective. Examples are as follows:

- "I deeply and profoundly accept myself although there is no certainty in an uncertain world."
- "Even though I feel anxiety about the future, I deeply and profoundly accept myself."
- "Even though I feel unsafe, I trust my inner wisdom and Higher Guidance."
- "Even though there is tension in those around me, I choose to be open and flexible."

More specific ways to address anxiety involve treating a specific chakra or using algorithms. For example, the root chakra at the base of the spine is most essential for treating fear or issues of personal safety. Grounding through the feet and base of the spine to feel connection with the supporting earth is helpful. By the same token, exercise, walking, dancing, and movement help to release tension through the root and keep the inflow of qi into the energy body steady. Work with all three of the lower chakras through Connecting of the Energy Centers, described in chapter 10, allows the heart center to hold clear intention for responding to others from a place of caring rather than from fear or constriction.

While a generic tapping sequence of all 14 meridian acupoints, as given in chapter 7, could be effective for future anxiety, shorter and more direct algorithms have been used to address anxiety. The most frequently used sequence consists of tapping the eyebrow points, under eye points, and collarbone points while attuning to a specific anxiety-producing thought or image about the future. This algorightm can then be blended into a sandwichlike sequence described in chapter 12, exercise 2.

Since safety is such a deep concern to many, psychoenergetic reversals around safety can be treated by working with the lower three chakras or by tapping the side of the hand which is the most frequently used treatment point for treating safety reversals as described in chapter 11. The specific treatment words appreciate the reality of safety concerns, stating self-affirmation, while tapping the side of the hand as follows:

- "Even though I feel unsafe, I deeply and profoundly accept myself."
- "Even though it does not seem safe for me to travel, I deeply and profoundly accept myself."
- "Even though my world seems unsafe to me, I deeply and profoundly accept myself."

The profound challenge in this era of human history is to keep our energies as balanced as possible so we can quickly integrate change and help our clients and loved ones to be resilient in the face of external pressures. Our integrity and centered presence can be of great comfort to those in need, and, more than ever, we are asked to be beacons of hope to those many in distress. It appears we must consciously choose whether to yield to the constrictions of fear and anxiety or to offer useful alternatives. Human intention and will can make a difference—the difference that counts—when we are faced with fate and chance events beyond our control. The creative resources of energy psychotherapy offer a vital link to the new levels of self-understanding that will be required.

Here is a meditation that came to me as I consider our choices:

The darkness of a few disturbed minds
Has exploded a potential shockwave
Of darkness within each of us.
The old national myths—
    innocence, unlimited futures,
    safety for travel, work, and play—
Are bent forever
Like the twisted metal of the debris.

We are called now to find a new myth,
A new sense of order,
A guiding image of who we are as individuals
And as a nation
Who live within the certainty of uncertainty,
In the valley of the shadow of death.

We have the choice now
To resonate with the expanding vibration of caring
Or the constrictions of fear and anxiety.

(continued on next page)

Each of us must choose—
Compassion   or isolation
Facing reality   or dissociating from it
Reaching out   or going to numbness
Centered thinking   or irrational frenzy
Meditative prayer   or giving in to hysteria
Conscious deliberation   or quick solutions
Embracing the gift of the times   or withdrawal
Bringing about new order   or reacting with retaliation.

Life in this turning point
Requires renewal of vital energies
Deepening the inner healer,
Willingness to learn,
And making the moment by moment choices
That empower, open constrictions,
Bring in more hope
Like a ray of sunlight in the rubble.

Out of this chaos can grow deeper order:
Accept the vast gifts we truly have,
Acknowledge our sources of renewal,
Support each other in unprecedented ways,
Connect to the shaman within.

The transforming forces of nature
Allow seeds of change to grow
Slowly, deliberately
Making a gradual shift in direction.

The debris of destruction can become the altar
From which new life can grow.

Index